Applied
Improvisation

RELATED TITLES

Impro: Improvisation and the Theatre
Keith Johnstone
ISBN 978-0-7136-8701-9

Keith Johnstone: A Critical Biography
Theresa Robbins Dudeck
ISBN 978-1-4081-8327-4

Semiotics and Pragmatics of Stage Improvisation
Domenico Pietropaolo
ISBN 978-1-4742-2579-3

The Actor's Business Plan
Jane Drake Brody
ISBN 978-1-4725-7369-8

Applied Theatre: Facilitation
Sheila Preston
ISBN 978-1-4725-7693-4

*Applied Practice: Evidence and Impact
in Theatre, Music and Art*
edited by Matthew Reason and Nick Rowe
ISBN 978-1-4742-8383-0

Applied Improvisation

Leading, Collaborating, and Creating Beyond the Theatre

Edited by

Theresa Robbins Dudeck
and Caitlin McClure

methuen | drama

LONDON • NEW YORK • OXFORD • NEW DELHI • SYDNEY

METHUEN DRAMA
Bloomsbury Publishing Plc
50 Bedford Square, London, WC1B 3DP, UK

BLOOMSBURY, METHUEN DRAMA and the Methuen Drama logo are
trademarks of Bloomsbury Publishing Plc

First published in Great Britain 2018

A catalogue record for this book is available from the British Library.

A catalog record for this book is available from the Library of Congress.

ISBN: HB: 978-1-350-01435-0
PB: 978-1-350-01436-7
ePDF: 978-1-350-01439-8
eBook: 978-1-350-01438-1

Typeset by Newgen KnowledgeWorks Pvt. Ltd., Chennai, India

To find out more about our authors and books visit www.bloomsbury.com
and sign up for our newsletters.

To our teachers
And to our students, who are the best teachers of all

CONTENTS

FIGURES

FOREWORD

Phelim McDermott and Lee Simpson

It may seem strange that a foreword for a book about applied improvisation should be written by theatre makers. However, to study the applications of improvisation beyond performance, perhaps the base-camp for the expedition should be the place where it all started. It was in the theatres, comedy clubs, and experimental performance spaces of the 1960s and 1970s that the story of improvisation, as we now know it, began and developed. This is where it was first applied, a new kind of theatre, pitching performers and audiences into a thrilling new relationship.

As young actors we fell in love with improvisation and, as often happens in a love affair, our initial infatuation was intense. It made us feel more alive. Creating in the moment, saying "yes" to other people's ideas, sidestepping control, and connecting to our intuitive impulses in front of an audience was exhilarating. We were making people laugh, discovering success and failure onstage, creating comedy and drama from nothing but the air between us, and sometimes we told stories that moved people. But we soon discovered it wasn't just about the shows or the product, and the learning was not limited to the onstage crucible.

As we continued to improvise, our relationship with impro matured. It became a deeper love. We found ourselves in a Dojo (a practice arena) where we had to explore our strengths and vulnerabilities and engage in dialogue with our inner critics. Something much more profound and wide reaching was happening: a relationship was being forged to the chaotic part of nature that enhanced our experience of life. We were discovering that we had to confront and include our true selves in the process if we were to grow. We were engaged in a continual practice, which nurtured a set of beliefs and principles that would run through our careers and lives. Improvisation was the underground river that flowed beneath everything we did.

We have been "applying" improvisation to the making of theatre since the mid-1980s. During that time, we have made improvised shows, used impro to devise shows that end up scripted, and created shows that were hybrids of the two. When directing shows with preexisting scripts, we have used impro to ensure performances are played differently every night. We got puppeteers, opera singers, and "proper" actors in their eighties to improvise and the shows have played everywhere from comedy clubs to outdoors to the National Theatre.

At Improbable, the work has primarily been the creation of theatre shows; however, we also had to learn how to run a company. We admit there was often a mismatch between the improvisation we practiced onstage and how we organized our business—as if the two worlds did not share the same principles. We were not applying what we did with actors and shows to the running of our own company. We were in need of some applied improvisation!

It was about twelve years ago that we had a breakthrough when Phelim discovered Open Space Technology (OST), which, instinctively, we understood to be one enormous, self-organizing impro game. We began running forums for the theatre community (that we titled "Devoted and Disgruntled") to work on issues that people were frustrated about and wanted to take action on. OST quickly became an essential part of running Improbable, onstage and off. Offstage, it now informs our meetings; how we envision our future and how we make that vision happen; it supports how we deal with change; how we create fluidity around roles in the company and how we address conflicts. Onstage and in the rehearsal room, it has become an essential part of our theatre-making process and a guide for our teaching of improvisation. The boundaries between the different areas of our company have begun to blur. There's a long way to go, but our aim is to walk improvisational methods through all aspects of our company's life.

This is a book about Applied Improvisation, so perhaps we should unpack what "applied" means to us. One does not "apply" improvisation in the sense of adding something to what is already there. It is not like a coat of varnish or even, we would argue, a set of skills. It is more like a way of accessing and bringing awareness to processes that are happening anyway. Whether it is in a theatrical or in an applied context, improvisation, as a form, draws from the dreaming world and brings the imagination into embodied life. We must beware of the notion that people doing it in theatre or comedy aren't doing something in "real life." Dreams *are* its "real world" and this is one of its most valuable assets. Improvisation brings together, in a marriage, the imagistic world and consensus reality. It would be missing the point to lose (at least) half the value of impro when it becomes "Applied Improvisation." We must be awake to the tendency for it to become too goal or product oriented, stressing the technical skills over the more artistic and dreaming aspects of improvisation. When the improvisation gets applied, is the ineffable nature of impro diminished? This question is one that the best practitioners, such as those in this book, are courageously grappling with because not all deliverables are describable.

Of course, improvisation does have a set of skills and games that can be stated, taught, and learnt. Within these pages are many fine and diverse examples of non-theatre contexts where impro has been used to support change and increase creativity. Each demonstrates the value of impro and its impact. However, it's important we don't just pay attention to the measurable technical skills. This is not the whole story.

Between these stories lies a deeper set of skills that points toward what psychologist and process-work practitioner Amy Mindell calls "metaskills." These are the attitudes and sensitivities that inform how we use the technical skills. These metaskills would be such things as: an ability to be comfortable with uncertainty and "not knowing"; a willingness to say "Yes" not just to an offer but to the whole of reality as it truly is; a trust in the Tao and the wisdom of nature; an ability to see the bigger patterns in chaos; a desire to hold silence and sense what is beneath an atmosphere; the capacity to catch secondary signals and impulses within oneself and in the environment that are on the edge of awareness; a belief that everything happening around you is a valuable part of the process.

These stories are taking place in a wider context of an attitude to life that only improvisation fosters. It is this context that tells us how we practice those skills. The application of impro is not just technique but an invitation to explore the deeper understandings this work can bring to us as individuals and as a community.

Notice in these chapters where improvisation has been used to create new cultures within organizations and communities. How it creates intelligent climates where individuals own their own agency while being sensitive to ensemble responsibilities. Where new models of democratic collaboration promote true listening and self-organization. These improvisational cultures support emergent solutions and foster the kind of wisdom that our world is urgently demanding of us.

Life is full of uncertainty and each day our world gets more complicated and chaotic. The solution is not an attempt to tame the chaos. The answer is to find more robust and fluid ways of interacting with the chaos, which is merely a fact of life. The call is to become "wave riders," as Harrison Owen, originator of OST, describes those leaders who know how to trust the flow of nature and take advantage of its emergent energies. The call is to improvise because the practice of improvisation is one of allowing.

You don't apply improvisation, it simply applies.

Phelim McDermott and **Lee Simpson** met in 1986 after a Keith Johnstone workshop that Phelim had been to and Lee hadn't. They soon discovered that they were both interested in impro that was more theatrical and theatre that was more improvised and spent the next ten years making both these things. In 1996, alongside Julian Crouch and Nick Sweeting, they founded Improbable, a company that deepened and broadened that quest, taking improvisation into uncharted waters and, along the way, creating a bewildering diversity of work (e.g. *Animo, Lifegame, The Still, Theatre of Blood, Lost Without Words*, etc.). Lee is also one of the Comedy Store Players, and Phelim has directed shows at the Metropolitan Opera. Their latest venture is the International Institute of Improvisation, a way to celebrate, investigate, advocate, and connect all forms of improvisation from within and outside the arts; a way to tell the story of how the practice and philosophy of improvisation is what the world needs. Right now.

ACKNOWLEDGMENTS

Collaboration and benevolence are two of the most important characteristics of good improvisation, and this book would not have been possible without the wholehearted, committed collaboration we had with our contributors and without the benevolent support of our families and friends. Thank you for going on this adventure with us. In particular, we would like to thank the following for their thoughtful feedback, advice, and time: Tyson Hewitt, Doug Baldwin, Nell Schneider, Mary Lynne and Thomas Robbins, Sara Freeman, Kari and Daniel Knutson-Bradac, Jennifer Griffith, and Marianne Franck. Thank you also to Methuen Drama and Bloomsbury, especially to Mark Dudgeon and Susan Furber, for their consistent guidance and belief in this project.

Finally, to our loving and patient partners—Paul Rátz de Tagyos and Dale Dudeck—thank you for donning your capes, figuratively and literally, and leaping into the unknown with us.

Introduction

Theresa Robbins Dudeck and Caitlin McClure

This collection of Applied Improvisation (AI) stories and strategies draws back the curtain on an exciting, innovative, growing field of practice and research that is changing the way people lead, create, and collaborate. The authors in this anthology are professional AI facilitators working in all corners of the world. They come from disciplines as diverse as business, social science, theatre, education, law, and government. All have experienced the power of improvisation, have a driving need to share those experiences, and are united in the belief that improvisation can positively transform just about all human activity.

"Applied Improvisation" is the umbrella term widely used to denote the application of theatre improvisation (theories, tenets, games, techniques, and exercises) beyond conventional theatre spaces to foster the growth and/or development of flexible structures, new mind-sets, and a range of inter- and intrapersonal skills required in today's VUCA (volatile, uncertain, complex, ambiguous) world.[1] Top business schools everywhere are now offering AI courses for developing interactive teams, emotionally intelligent and expressive leaders, and innovative ideas. In science and health, the Alan Alda Center for Communicating Science based at Stony Brook University, New York, is helping scientists and physicians better communicate their ideas and messages to audiences and patients using improvisation. Even law schools and firms are adopting AI curricula to give new and seasoned lawyers the power of flexibility and spontaneous decision-making skills. And hundreds of organizations ranging from large Fortune 500 corporations to governmental agencies to nonprofits are increasingly hiring AI facilitators to train their management and workforce to do *offstage* what the best improvisers do *onstage*.[2]

So, what *do* the best improvisers do really well onstage? They work collaboratively and spontaneously in the moment, generate endless ideas quickly, remain flexible, find and solve problems, multitask, motivate others, practice active listening, take risks, graciously accept failure as part of the process, and engage authentically with and effectively deliver stories to audiences. Every night, professional improvisers fearlessly go onstage, without a script, and put into practice all the above for audiences worldwide. But as this book of case studies will reveal, anyone willing to practice the techniques and embrace the principles of improvisation can learn to adeptly function like an improviser in front of and in collaboration with their own "audiences."

Applied Improvisation: A Field of Its Own

Improvisation: the skill of using bodies, space, imagination, objects and all human resources to generate or to reformulate a coherent physical expression of an idea, a situation and a character (even, perhaps, a text); to do this spontaneously, in response to the immediate stimuli of one's environment, without preconceptions.

Anthony Frost and Ralph Yarrow (2016: xv)

Definitions of "improvisation" are largely based on the theories and practices of jazz music and theatre improvisation. We prefer Frost and Yarrow's definition above because it reinforces that improvisation is first and foremost a "skill" used to respond to one's environment, putting the focus "inside the box"[3] rather than outside. Improvisers are inspired by sources in the room (especially other people) as they give complete sensory attention to the moment unfolding.

In *Improvisation in Drama, Theatre and Performance*, Frost and Yarrow reveal the significance of improvisation used in theatre training and rehearsals throughout history and across cultures. Improvisation has been integral to the theatrical process—to develop truthful behavior in text-based performance, to liberate the actor's body and imagination, to generate material, to build an ensemble, to respond instinctively to the moment—for a long time, as evidenced by Stanislavsky's use of improvisation in rehearsals in Russia at the turn of the twentieth century. Even as far back as the sixteenth and seventeenth centuries, historians contend *commedia dell'arte troupes* improvised dialogue and action within preset scenarios. Improvisation as a performance in and of itself became extremely popular in the late 1950s and early 1960s thanks to the groundbreaking work of Keith Johnstone and his Theatre Machine in Europe and to Paul Sills and The Second City, the company he co-founded in Chicago in 1959. Many authors in this anthology trace their personal histories to these pioneers of improvisation.

One goal of this book is to establish AI as a field of study worthy of independent investigation. Currently, improvisation applied beyond conventional theatre practices and spaces is frequently categorized within the field of Applied Theatre; but just as Applied Theatre has come to mean theatre practice applied outside of conventional mainstream theatre (e.g. in education, community, and political spaces) to bring about positive change, AI, too, has taken on a new meaning, beyond the field of Applied Theatre.

While schools of business, law, science, and education are increasingly adding AI courses into their programming, surprisingly, the one discipline in academia that has not fully embraced AI is theatre, which seems to be the natural destination for training future AI facilitators. Improvisation classes are often offered in theatre programs and improvisational processes are utilized in acting classrooms and rehearsal spaces, but courses that specifically introduce theatre students—especially students not interested in acting careers—to AI training or to AI facilitation as a potential, viable career path are almost impossible to find.

Applied Theatre, theatre for/as social change, and community-based theatre courses often incorporate improvisation as part of their methodology, especially the games of Augusto Boal. The main objective of these courses is, generally, to train students to use theatre methods in/with nonprofit organizations and communities to bring about social, political, and restorative change. Within this anthology, at least half of the case studies apply improvisation to prompt similar change; however, Applied Theatre course work often involves creating a performance (sometimes scripted) that addresses the needs of a particular project. AI course work almost never involves creating a theatrical performance, in the traditional sense. The "performance" happens when students successfully function and respond like skilled improvisers, beyond the classroom, in collaborative environments. Furthermore, while AI work does happen in/with nonprofit organizations and communities, most AI work is happening in the private sector (with for-profit organizations), and it is this branch of the work that is not included for study in Applied Theatre courses.

This is understandable. Applied Theatre, a well-established field that contains numerous theatre approaches and practices, has so much to cover already; and the work, which often engages marginalized communities and tackles systemic problems, can have very different objectives than the work of AI facilitators working with, for example, corporate teams. So, if Applied Theatre courses are not introducing AI to their theatre students, and theatre students are already developing abilities relevant to professional careers in AI facilitation, what needs to be done? Just as schools of law offer courses in both Civil Rights Law and Business Law, and sociology departments prep students for careers as diverse as social work and urban planning, schools of theatre must offer both Applied Theatre and AI courses to better prepare theatre students, entering a very competitive market, for a range of careers.

Out of the 5,000-plus trainers, facilitators, consultants, executives, educators, scientists, artists, aid workers, therapists, and managers who have joined the Applied Improvisation Network (AIN), we conjecture that only a small percentage earned an undergraduate or graduate degree in theatre. We are optimistic that this percentage will increase once theatre departments begin adding AI courses to their curriculum. While the field has yet to attract theatre graduates, Paul Z. Jackson, president emeritus of AIN, told us, "Many AIN facilitators have been introduced to improvisation via theatre improvisation performances and workshops."[4] But even if the impro methods adopted by AI facilitators are rooted in *theatre* improvisation, as we said before, most theatre and theatre improvisation courses and workshops are not teaching students how to apply impro in non-theatre or nonperformance contexts. This brings up one final argument in support of assigning AI a field of its own. The majority of AI facilitators discovered independently, on their own, or through networking, how well impro cross-pollinates with disciplines beyond theatre; and while facilitators can and often do benefit from theatre theory and practice, most often they associate, substantiate, reinforce, and/or augment what they do (theoretically and practically) with leading studies in organizational behavior, strategic management, social science, critical pedagogy, group innovation, creativity, and so on. AI is interdisciplinary, multifaceted, robust, and ready to stand on its own; it is grounded in a theatre context yet deviates enough from Applied Theatre practice to warrant its own field of study. We hope this first collection of AI case studies will be instrumental in making that happen.

Improvisation Is for Everyone

Every day, moment to moment, we instinctively make decisions large and small, without a script. Yet even in life, our spontaneous decisions are formed within structures, schedules, and a set of personal and societal principles. The same is true for improvising onstage. If you've played basketball or a similar team sport, then you already have an understanding of what it takes to be a valued player on an improvisation team. "Anyone can improvise," wrote Charna Halpern, Del Close, and Kim Johnson (1994: 34) in *Truth in Comedy*, "but like any game, if the players don't learn and obey the rules, no one will play with them." One of the things you will notice as a recurrent motif in this book is that to benefit from improvisational practice, you do not need to come from theatre, or be a performer, or even an extrovert. You just have to be willing to adopt a set of improvisation tenets ("the rules"), as specifically defined in Appendix A, and then practice those tenets through a variety of exercises and games that can, in turn, be brought into other settings to teach those same tenets.

Our friend Patricia Ryan Madson (2005: 15), professor emerita at Stanford University, proposes: "A good improviser is someone who is awake, not entirely self-focused, and moved by a desire to do something useful and give something back and who acts upon this impulse." If this is true (and we believe it is), then it completely debunks the notion that good improvisers must have comedic ability or ingenuity. The best improvisers are being "obvious," that is, trusting their impulses and responding authentically to the moment. *Trying* to be funny, clever, or original "takes you far away from your true self, and makes your work mediocre," asserts Keith Johnstone (1979: 88), pioneer of impro. "*The truth is funny*. Honest discovery, observation, and reaction is better than contrived invention," wrote

Halpern et al. (1994: 15; emphasis in the original). Eliciting laughter from an audience feels good, so novice or fearful improvisers will mistakenly *try* to be funny or get a laugh at all costs, often at the expense of building truthful relationships, developing strong narratives, or engaging audiences on a deeper level. Good improvisers, as Madson suggests above, want their onstage performances to make a difference, to move audiences beyond superficial laughter, to be an experience everyone will remember for years to come. Likewise, good improvisers offstage authentically engage with others, trust their instincts, take risks, accept failure as a component of learning, and, most importantly, operate magnificently on "the edge of chaos."

Borrowing from complexity theory, for improvisers to operate on "the edge of chaos" means thriving in a zone that lies somewhere between order and freedom, between structure and surprise.[5] Keith Sawyer (2007: 56), an MIT graduate and leading scientific expert on creativity, who we were fortunate enough to interview for the last chapter of this book, views this balancing act as a "paradox": "The paradox of improvisation is that it can happen only when there are rules and the players share tacit understandings, but with too many rules or too much cohesion, the potential for innovation is lost." Organizations, too, operating on "the edge of chaos" are at their most "vibrant, surprising, and flexible" (Brown and Eisenhardt 1998: 12). Finding the right balance is not only necessary for improvisers in performance but also for organizations hoping to generate innovative, creative ideas and solutions, as many of our authors illustrate in their case studies.

The goal of AI training is not to create professional improvisers. Having a desire to perform for an audience is not a prerequisite to succeed in an AI course. However, to achieve better results, it is probably a good idea to follow a similar cycle of practice, application, and reflection adhered to by successful improvisation teams everywhere.[6] It is a repeatable cycle that involves: (1) *practice* offstage, in a safe, classroom environment, with every member of the team participating as both player and spectator, and providing constructive feedback, followed by (2) *application* of the practice on different stages, in front of various audiences, where the stakes are high, and many additional elements (e.g. lights, sound, audience responses) must be incorporated, followed by (3) *reflection* among group members post-performance (asking what worked, what didn't, and why?) which can influence the next practice. This cycle is required of those who want to adeptly apply improvisational methods to their organizations. The best improvisers are always "in training" and performances are simply an extension of that training. We applaud organizations that bring in that first AI course, but then the cycle must be followed if lasting change in the organization is desired.

A Brief Journey through AI History

Applying improvisation beyond the theatre to improve the lives of people as individuals, in communities, and in organizations is not new. Following is a very small sampling of the major AI movements and pioneers of the twentieth century. In 1921, Austrian psychiatrist Jacob L. Moreno, founder of psychodrama, created *Das Stegreiftheater* (Theatre of Spontaneity) which involved actors improvising daily newspaper articles in public (similar to the "Living Newspapers" produced by the Federal Theatre Project in the 1930s). It was a forum allowing for sociopolitical questions and personal issues of the actors to be examined and experienced (Frost and Yarrow 2007: 111). This early psychodramatic improvisational laboratory, so to speak, emerged from Moreno's belief that spontaneity is the most basic human trait and from the premise that "acting is healthier than speaking" (Innes 1993: 50).

Influenced by J. von Nuemann and O. Morgenstern's *Theory of Games and Economic Behaviour* (1944), two important studies arguing for "the importance of play and games in the development of the individual, in the growth of a child into maturity, and more broadly as a key to successful interaction and the formation of societies" were published: Johan Huizinga's *Homo Ludens: A Study of the Play Element in Culture* (1955) and Roger Caillois's *Man, Play, and Games* (1961) (Heddon and Milling 2006: 34). In Chicago in the 1920s, sociologist Neva L. Boyd was the first to apply games and play to group work and group experience as a means of social development at her Recreational Training School at Hull-House settlement house in Chicago.[7] From 1924 to 1927, Viola Spolin (Paul Sills's mother) trained under Boyd, and from 1938 to 1941, as teacher and drama supervisor for the Works Progress Administration Recreational Project, Spolin began developing her foundational theatre games (later used by Sills at Second City) to help immigrant and inner-city children unleash creative self-expression. The Theatre in Education (TIE) movement beginning in the mid-1960s saw theatre techniques, including improvisation, used as tools in the classroom. Notable postwar British TIE innovators such as Peter Slade, Brian Way, Dorothy Heathcote, and Richard Courtney applied and wrote about improvisatory methods encouraging creative play in childhood development.[8]

Augusto Boal, founder of Theatre of the Oppressed, working in his native Brazil in the 1950s and 1960s, developed a series of improvisational games and formats that would support individuals and groups seeking to understand and liberate themselves from oppressive social situations. Forum Theatre, one of Boal's most popular formats, is a structure that allows groups to explore solutions to problems improvisationally, on their feet. First, actors present a scenario of oppression and then spectators intervene as "spect-actors" trying out tactics with the goal of bringing the scenario to a more ideal conclusion.

AI in Organizational Development

Kurt Lewin (1890–1947), a leading psychologist of his generation known for field theory and the theory of group dynamics, provided the foundations of organizational development, which began to gain traction in the 1950s. According to the *Cambridge Business Dictionary*, "organizational development" (OD) today is defined as "the process of making a large company or organization more effective, for example, by giving employees the skills they need to develop and to deal with new situations or markets." In 1971, OD was defined as "an educational strategy employing experienced-based behavior in order to achieve a self-renewing organization," and the goals were:

> Creating an open, problem-solving climate; supplementing the authority of status with that of competence; building trust; reducing inappropriate competition and fostering collaboration; developing reward systems which recognize both organizational and individual goals; locating decision-making and problem-solving responsibilities close to the information sources; increasing the sense of "ownership" of the organization and its objectives; and increasing self-control and self-direction for organizational members. (Kegan 1971: 456)

In our research, we have yet to find evidence of improvisational theatre processes specifically applied to OD programs in the 1960s through the late 1980s to meet these goals. However, we'd like to point out how most of the goals outlined above are analogous to the goals of AI. Consequently, we are somewhat surprised that early workers in OD, a field that is rooted in behavioral science, did not see the connection to improvisation as had others mentioned earlier working in disciplines of psychology and sociology.

By the 1990s, we know that organizations were welcoming improvisation into their training. Several of our authors, in fact, began their AI work at this time.[9] Still, as Dusya Vera and Mary Crossan (2005: 203) discovered, while conducting research on improvisation training for innovative performance in teams, "limited theoretical work is available on what it takes to develop this skill. Also, there is a lack of empirical evidence supporting the success of any improvisational training effort." In 2007, Keith Sawyer wrote that we are now in a "culture of collaborative organization … based on flexibility, connection, [and] conversation" in which "improvised innovation is standard business practice" (156). So why was there and why is there still a dearth of theoretical and empirical research on improvisation integrated into OD strategies? Why is OD so late to the AI party? Over the past decade, a handful of distinguished authors have published significant monographs that point to the relevance of improvisation practice to spontaneous decision-making, to marketing and sales, to communication, to structuring of organizations, and to collaborative creation and innovation.[10] But the amount of published research widely available does not proportionately represent the growth and diversity of AI practice happening around the globe. We hope that this book will inspire other AI facilitators to begin immediately documenting, writing about, and publishing their own stories and strategies.

Considerations for Educators and Facilitators

Coming from both theatre and business, and having worked in academic, nonprofit, and for-profit sectors, we have strategically shaped this first anthology of AI case studies with several audiences in mind. First, this book offers college and university theatre educators, interested in introducing AI into their curricula, a range of work that will enable students to see improvisation in a new light and, hopefully, serve as a point of departure for students to generate their own AI ideas and projects for their communities, groups, and organizations on campus and beyond. This book can serve undergraduate and graduate theatre courses in Applied Theatre, the business of theatre, arts administration, as well as topic courses taught by theatre faculty skilled in improvisation. Good theatre emerges from collaborative creation. AI courses will train theatre students to use their collaborative processes in multiple settings and in various roles, increasing their marketability in a competitive industry.

Faculty from across disciplines at academic institutions that encourage interdisciplinary initiatives will also benefit from this anthology. For leadership and education courses, for example, several of the case studies offer AI tools for developing emotionally intelligent, expressive, and authentic future leaders and educators. For business courses, case studies focused on collaborative creativity, risk-taking, and emergent innovation will be especially useful. Additionally, this book augments the work of people already working in AI, offering a range of improvisational methods used and/or created by leading AI facilitators.

In Appendix A, you will find a list of "Key Improvisation Tenets and Terms." This list gives facilitators a handy guide to tenets and terms frequently used in improvisation and throughout this book. The inclusion of this section also allowed our authors to focus on their unique cases instead of redefining these terms. Two other terms, "impro" and "improv," are also used throughout, depending on each author's preference. Both are synonymous and are abbreviations for "improvisation." The preferred use of one or the other typically depends on how "improvisation" is spelled, pronounced, or syllabified in languages other than English.[11]

To validate our anecdotal understanding of how widely each term is used, in 2016, we conducted an informal, online survey with "Improvisational Theatre: A Group for Players Worldwide," a closed Facebook group that currently has over 12,000 members. We simply asked members for the preferred abbreviation of the word "improvisation" in their country—"impro" or "improv." Players from thirty-five different countries answered our inquiry, giving us the following results: twenty-four countries (mostly those with official languages other than English) use "impro"; six primarily use "improv"; and five use both "impro" and "improv" depending on preference, regional dialects, and/or what part of the country they lived in. We feel it is important to advise facilitators to be sensitive to and inclusive of improvisers everywhere. By simply asking a group of participants, "Do you prefer 'impro' or 'improv'?" you are building a reciprocal environment and could possibly ignite a stimulating conversation.

Chapters one through twelve each include a workbook component outlining one to three of the exercises used by the author in their case study to give facilitators and students a model for their own application. The case studies offer a context for the exercises but most exercises can be adapted to meet the specific needs or goals of any group. Appendix B lists the exercises and provides additional guidelines for customization. We also highly recommend to anyone serious about studying, teaching, or performing improvisation to read the two most formative books on improvisation: Viola Spolin's *Improvisation for the Theater* (1963) and Keith Johnstone's *Impro: Improvisation and the Theatre* (1979).

Everyone who contributed to this anthology will readily tell you that improvisation has positively transformed their lives—making them more present, benevolent, curious, brave, and willing to laugh out loud and often! They will also say that teaching and facilitating AI is a privilege that requires years of hard work, continual education, self-assessment, and an ability to work improvisationally, that is, to model what you are teaching. If you are fearful of going off-script or veering away from your predetermined lesson plans to respond to the evolving needs of the group, then it might be a good idea to enroll in an impro class (or two!) before endeavoring to facilitate an AI course or workshop on your own.

Overview

The case studies that follow offer significant, detailed examples of professional AI work generated by leading facilitators in the field. We are delighted that our authors were willing to reveal their AI secrets to give readers more than a surface understanding of what they do. By no means is this collection exhaustive. AI facilitation includes many forms not detailed in this book; however, the range of work represented here is indicative of our field's diversity and influence.

Part One, "Bringing Brands to Life," opens with Gary Hirsch and Amy Veltman's story of On Your Feet's ten-year collaboration with Burgerville—a popular restaurant chain in the Pacific Northwest—which reveals how AI, over time, has the power to transform a company's culture. Faris Khalid then shares his experience conducting market research in Pakistan and proposes that AI can be more effective than standard focus group discussions, especially with target audiences living in countries where cultural norms may inhibit authentic responses.

Part Two, "Resilience and Connection," begins with Cathy Salit's AI work with oncology nurses over a two-year period at The Johns Hopkins Hospital in Baltimore, Maryland, designed to create a culture of resiliency. Lacy Alana and Jim Ansaldo give us a detailed look at the AI curriculum they've developed to support youth on the autism spectrum and their teachers. Brad Fortier's case study explores how theatre games and the ethos of improvised theatre help build a sense of community for refugees brought together by chance, providence, or happenstance. To end this section, Mary Tyszkiewicz takes us on a journey to the Philippines, 100 days after Super-Typhoon Haiyan, where disaster survivors not only validate her rapid rescue theory but show us that the human desire to help others is more powerful than our fears.

How Caitlin McClure brought AI to Tiffany & Co., one of the world's top luxury retailers, launches us into Part Three, "Leadership Development." McClure's case study explores how specific improvisation activities were selected and modified to fit the ambitious objectives of Tiffany's core management programs. Teresa Norton then gives us an inside look at her work with clients in Greater China over the past two decades, using improvisation and role-play techniques to encourage more emotionally intelligent, dynamic, and effective leaders. In the final chapter of this section, Julie Huffaker and Karen Dawson introduce us to the AI tools they use to help their clients unleash collaborative intelligence and bring about lasting behavioral change in organizational leadership, teams, and culture.

The final section of this anthology, "Higher Education," provides a space for case studies by practitioners and scholars who conduct their interdisciplinary work in academic institutions and beyond the academy. Barbara Tint, who works in and teaches conflict resolution, discovered the healing potential of improvisation and, in her chapter, shares how she integrates improvisational principles and methods into her training with conflict resolution professionals, mediators, and lawyers. Annalisa Dias illuminates how the principles of improvisation and, in particular, the games of Augusto Boal can develop skills in dialogue facilitation and empower students to instigate change toward social justice. Jonathan Rossing and Krista Hoffmann-Longtin give us a detailed look at the AI program they designed to help scientists and doctors better communicate and connect with their audiences, patients, and students. Finally, bringing this anthology to a close, Theresa Robbins Dudeck facilitates a thought-provoking conversation on emergence between two people well known within the AI community: Keith Sawyer, a prominent scientific expert on creativity, learning, and collaboration; and Neil Mullarkey, a popular British writer, comedian, and co-founder of The Comedy Store Players.

In the foreword, Phelim McDermott and Lee Simpson liken their relationship with improvisation to a love affair that deepens over time and the impro process to an underground river that flows beneath everything they do. Mullarkey, in his conversation with Sawyer, used the word "joy" three times to express what the foundational principle of Yes, And means to him. Among our community of players, teachers, and facilitators, we often hear things like improvisation has been life changing, a joyous method of discovering self and others, or a process that has evoked feelings beyond description. When we came across this quotation by American free jazz bassist, poet, and composer William Parker, we knew we had found a description of improvisation that comes very close to capturing our collective sentiment:

> Improvisation is joy! Improvisation is a spirit, it is a living thing, and it is a being that alters our reality, a natural force like the wind, ocean, and rain. Improvisation is a bird in flight, it is also gravity. Improvisation is a language that embellishes our movements as we make it through life. Improvisation is a ritual that helps us to seek the higher self. A kinetic flow that allows us to reach for limitless landscapes of possibility using the known and unknown. (Caines and Heble 2015: 450)

If you are willing to walk the edge of chaos in a classroom free of hierarchies, where process and problem-posing are more important than problem-finding, where empathy, respect, and authenticity are crucial, and where learning and creation emerge from the collective efforts and experiences of all participants, then you are ready for improvisation. Applied Improvisation is changing the way we lead, create, and collaborate. It also brings joy into this uncertain, crazy world. We hope you find as much joy in this anthology as we experienced putting it all together.

Notes

1   Originally an acronym used by the Army War College in the 1990s, "VUCA" was appropriated by the business community to signal a world of continuous change requiring new survival strategies that bring people together to co-imagine and co-create possible futures and solutions.
2   We use the term "facilitator" because its various definitions align with the range of AI facilitation work. A facilitator can be someone who facilitates a process, makes a process easier, and/or helps organizations and groups anticipate, find, or solve problems and/or navigate change. Good teachers are often called "facilitators of learning" when they create environments where students can co-create and co-construct knowledge. AI professionals also use other titles such as trainer, coach, instructor, and teacher.
3   Drew Boyd and Jacob Goldenberg outline "inside the box" thinking for innovation in the workplace in their book *Inside the Box: A Proven System of Creativity for Breakthrough Results* (2014).
4   Email message to authors on June 26, 2017.
5   See also Huffaker and Dawson's description of "collaborative leadership culture" in Chapter 9; and Mullarkey and Sawyer's discussion on "bounded instability" and "minimal structure, maximum autonomy" in Chapter 13.
6   Kolb's (1984) experiential learning cycle is widely used in higher education and applies a similar structure of practice, application, and reflection. In Chapter 7, McClure applies Kolb's theories to her facilitation.
7   Boyd's *Handbook of Recreational Games* was published in 1945 and is still in publication to this day.
8   See Slade (1954); Way (1967); and Courtney (1968).
9   In 1993, Jim Ansaldo used impro games to develop cognitive flexibility and communication skills for a theatre class of students with moderate cognitive disabilities. In 1997, Gary Hirsch was invited by forward-thinking associate dean Scott Dawson to bring impro into his MBA classes at Portland State University (Julie Huffaker was in one of these classes!). From 1996 to 1999, Cathy Salit's newly founded company, Performance of a Lifetime, had groups of people from various professions participate in a program that applied impro and theatre for interactive growth. In the late 1990s, Caitlin McClure was hired by Fratelli Balogne, a business theatre company in San Francisco, to assist with an AI ideation workshop for UPS, although "AI" was not the term used at that time.

10 We recommend the following: Halpern and Lubar (2003); Gladwell (2005); Sawyer (2007); Pink (2012); Koppett (2013); Leonard and Yorton (2015); Salit (2016); Alda (2017); and Kulhan and Crisafulli (2017) (listed chronologically).

11 Mistakenly, "impro" is often interpreted to mean British-style improvisation, due in large part to the influence of Keith Johnstone's work and his book *Impro: Improvisation in the Theatre*. Johnstone, who is British, used "impro" because in "standard British pronunciation, the first and fourth syllables of 'improvisation' are given more stress, and the 'o' in 'pro' has a partially open 'ə' sound as in 'the' (ˌɪm-prə-vī-ˈzā-shən) which is closer to the ō in 'imprō'" (Dudeck 2013: 4).

PART ONE

Bringing Brands to Life

1

A Burger, Fries, and a Side of Improv

Gary Hirsch and Amy Veltman

Gary Hirsch is the co-founder of On Your Feet, pioneering Applied Improvisation since 1998. He is also a visual artist and the creator of Botjoy, a global visual art experiment that uses over 30,000 hand-painted robots to explore collaboration, inspiration, and how art can help people.

Amy Veltman is a partner in On Your Feet. She is an award-winning actor and writer who has been studying improv for over fifteen years in New York, Los Angeles, and Portland. She began her career as a professional screenwriter and then worked as a marketing executive before joining On Your Feet in 2010.

It's a set of skills to reinforce. It is the biggest rut-busting approach I've ever seen before, but to be effective, you've got to keep at it.

JEFF HARVEY, PRESIDENT AND CEO OF BURGERVILLE

The Transformational Milkshake

Gary Hirsch was first introduced to Burgerville in 1990 when his mom decided to relocate her teenage son, her business, and her entire life from Ohio to the Pacific Northwest by throwing a dart at a map and moving wherever it landed. On the last leg of their 2,500-mile drive west, Gary and his mom crossed the Idaho border into Oregon. They were hot, tired, and driving each other crazy, when they stopped at what they thought was a typical fast food joint to grab lunch and a much-needed break from each other. Gary quickly realized, though, that this place was far from typical. The restaurant was packed, there were shakes made with fresh, local strawberries, and the delicious burgers were topped with Oregon cheddar. Suddenly, his mom no longer seemed annoying; she was a pioneer. He wasn't leaving a life behind; he was starting a new one. As he finished his first meal at Burgerville, everything began to look better.

In 1998, eight years after his mom threw her dart, Gary found himself starting On Your Feet, a consulting firm that uses improvisation as a training tool for business organizations such as Starbucks and Nike, a field that would come to be known as Applied Improvisation. He was also teaching this approach at the local university's business school. Little did he know that that first milkshake would eventually lead to a ten-year working relationship between Burgerville and On Your Feet, full of experiments and discoveries that would have a lasting impact on both of their organizations. Amy Veltman leapt into the work with Burgerville when she joined On Your Feet in 2010, and her hybrid background in improv, marketing, and screenwriting helped On Your Feet to recognize and articulate the powerful story created by these two renegade organizations.

The duration of their partnership with Burgerville has allowed On Your Feet to both validate and expand much of what they've always believed about improv practices' immense potential to transform a company's culture over time. This is that story.

The First Experiment: Leadership Models Risk-Taking

In December of 2006, On Your Feet was eight years into their work, and surprising themselves daily with new ways of applying improvisation to their clients' business issues. The budding consultancy was developing training and programs to enhance collaboration, presentations, creativity, and communication, asking questions like, "Is there anything that doesn't have a connection with improv?" Then someone would yell out a random profession like, "Lion taming!" and the whole office would riff on how you could be a better lion tamer by being a better improviser (e.g. focus, work with the unexpected, and don't get eaten!). These were giddy and experimental times.

It was into this fun-fest that the phone rang at On Your Feet one morning, and Gary was greeted by the deep, jovial voice of Jeff Harvey, CEO of Burgerville. Since their founding in 1961, they've sought to make food that's fresh, local, and sustainable, long before those became fashionable marketing buzzwords. Instead of a mission statement that focuses on growth and productivity, the Burgerville mission, "Serve with Love," illustrates the company's deeper commitment to their customers, employees, supply chain partners, and communities. There's a business case for this regional chain to build connections with their guests, too. Sourcing food responsibly and compensating workers ethically costs money. Strong relationships with customers are a big piece of how Burgerville stays competitive despite prices that are a bit higher than the global chain competition. The fantastic flavor of their food is the other piece!

Jeff explained that, on an upcoming afternoon, they were going to close all their locations early and gather all 1,600 of their staff in one place to celebrate a history-making year. As part of this celebration, they wanted to reinforce their culture, demonstrating their commitment to developing their people. For this unique event, Jeff wanted to create "something that would be totally uncommon for employees to engage with senior leadership."[1] As a longtime fan of improv, he had a hunch that exposure to this high-wire art form could provide what he was looking for, so someone recommended that he give On Your Feet a call.

Jeff is a former electrical engineer, active guitar maker, and a philosopher king whose beliefs are deeply aligned with the practices and tools of improvisation. Even during that first call, he talked about the importance of collaborative partnerships and showing up with an attitude of possibility and curiosity. Building on each other's ideas, Jeff and Gary eventually hatched what would be their first experiment together: On Your Feet would give

the Burgerville leadership team a crash course in improv performance. Then, with the help of a few On Your Feet team members, these senior leaders would perform an improv show for their
employee base. In this way, they could publicly model the risk-
taking and collaboration behaviors that Jeff was hoping to build
more of in the organization.

As a cornerstone of the two rehearsals we held with fifteen of
the organization's top leaders, On Your Feet facilitators gave them
a primer on the practices that allow improvisers to co-create something spontaneously without the benefit of a director or a script:

1. **See everything as an offer:** Seeing the world as full of "offers"
   means looking at everything as something you can use. The
   On Your Feet team introduced the Burgerville leadership to
   two possible dynamics for engaging with offers: accepting
   ("yes, and") and blocking ("yes, but" or "no"). The accepting
   mode is generative and collaborative, helping them problem-
   solve productively, while blocking shuts down collaboration
   and the flow between people.

2. **Notice more:** Improvisers create new ideas by being extremely
   "tuned in" to their environment. The simple practice of
   "noticing more" allows any group to extend the resources
   that they have to work with any problem.

3. **Be willing to be changed:** To create meaningful work together,
   the collaborating parties need to be willing to be changed by
   the opinions, constraints, or offers of the other.

4. **Be "Fit and Well":** Gary was first exposed to the memorable phrase "Fit and Well," by impro guru Keith Johnstone
   in 2002, at the Loose Moose International Improvisation
   Summer School.[2] It refers to the attitude you bring to anything you do and is easier to understand when you hear its
   opposite, "Sick and Feeble." When faced with uncertainty,
   improvisers make a conscious choice to say to themselves, "I
   don't know what's going to happen, but I know it's going to
   be great." This is the essence of "Fit and Well." In our experience, choosing to adopt this attitude has a remarkable power
   to impact any interaction for the better.

We were curious to see what behavior Burgerville leaders would
model when faced with the ambiguity of improvising together. With

no director, no script, and an audience of employees, would they hold back because they might "look bad"? Would they practice and rehearse like crazy in an attempt to "get it right"? Or would they embrace the uncertainty and dive in? Jeff wanted his leadership team to face these questions together head-on.

Sure enough, the rehearsal process had its hiccups. Jeff recalls that when it came to accepting offers, for one of his senior leaders, it was a "file not found," no matter how many times peers and the On Your Feet facilitators gently brought it to his attention. Another leader just did not enjoy the process. Even so, Jeff had the group, himself included, persist. He had a hunch that something valuable would emerge from this experiment.

On the day of the performances, the leadership team showed up jittery, but mostly eager to perform. The hundreds of employees had no idea that they were about to have their leaders "serving" them. Because the venue could hold only one-third of the employees at a time, the plan was to deliver three separate, unique performances, one after the other, for separate groups of employees. This space constraint ended up providing an unforeseen and wonderful "offer" for the leader-performers. To create a sense of safety, On Your Feet facilitators performed alongside the leadership team on stage during the first performance, taking part in "freeze tag" scenes for example, and leaping in during a lull. For each of the two subsequent performances, On Your Feet's improvisers were able to step back further and further as the Burgerville performers were increasingly able to step forward and make each other shine without the safety net of our seasoned performers.

In the end, the performances were funny; they were strange. There were awkward moments and moments of brilliance. For all of it, Gary remembers the crowd going wild at the sight of their leaders improvising on the stage. The shows were such a hit that, for the second and third performances, we had to turn back folks who wanted to see the leaders perform again. Each leader tried something new, different, and allowed themselves to be vulnerable in front of their colleagues, demonstrating that it's okay to "go for it," even if it doesn't always end up perfectly. Together they created scenes and stories that employees would be talking about for years to come.

Jeff still remembers how beneficial it was for him and his leadership team to share the experience of struggling together with the new skills and mind-set of improv—and then to succeed together on the stage. Jeff credits Beth Brewer, now the company's chief innovation and learning officer, with recognizing the deeper potential of this single experience. It was Beth who noticed the strong analog between the way the team interacted while preparing for this performance and as a team at work, the "applied" part of the experience.

Jeff looks back on Burgerville at the moment of this first experiment as having a culture deeply resistant to change. He knew that, as CEO, he would have to send a signal—a loud one—that it was okay to do something with an unknown outcome and a real risk of failure. Only his modeling of that behavior would give the organization permission to behave similarly. This experiment was the first step in creating a company culture for Burgerville that would be agile and innovative enough to thrive during changing times ahead. As for On Your Feet, even at this early stage in our relationship, Burgerville seemed like an exciting partner for our own giddy experimentation.

The Second and Third Experiments: Building Great Teams

In 2010, Burgerville reached out to On Your Feet for our second experiment together. They asked us to help the crew of their traveling food truck, The Nomad, to quickly build relationships with customers as they road-tripped from site to site in the Pacific Northwest. During pre-interviews with the Nomad crew to find out more about their needs, Amy remembers the team expressed an additional need for tools to work better with each other in the tight, steamy quarters of a food truck on long road trips in the height of summer. To help this mostly young crew create an instant relationship with guests and build stronger relationships with each other—even under stress—we designed a two-day deep-dive into the practices we had shared with the leadership team four years earlier. To make sure the practices stuck, Burgerville wisely built into our contract a follow-up where we visited the Nomad crew on site while the truck was parked in front of the Portland Children's Museum. Our job was to side-coach the crew in real time to notice, create, and accept more offers in their real environment: "What's the offer when you have few customers and things are slow?" "What's the offer specific to serving to kids?" "What's the offer when someone doesn't want to play a game with you?"

At the time, we saw this work with the Nomad team as a finite engagement to help a specific group achieve two relationship-based outcomes. In fact, this second experiment would have an impact that would only be realized years down the line.

When the Nomad's peak season cooled, many of its crew members headed back into the fixed Burgerville locations. Beth noticed a difference in those who had been through the Nomad improv training when she visited them in stores. They seemed to be better listeners and bigger risk-takers, and they readily created connections with fellow team members and customers. They built on the ideas of others and were confident in their actions. Beth observed, in the dispersed Nomad crew, behaviors she wanted for all Burgerville employees.

Two years later, as Beth thought about optimizing Burgerville's hiring process for a new location, she wondered how she could screen for people who had a strong capacity for the behaviors she'd seen among the Nomad crew. After all, she knew that Burgerville could train almost anyone to grill well, but to help Burgerville with their mission of contributing to their communities, they wanted to find service-oriented people with the capacity to relate well to others. It was then that Beth got in touch with On Your Feet again to create our third experiment.

Though we had not yet applied improv to the hiring process, we understood at once that Burgerville wasn't scouting for talented stage performers. Instead, they wanted to evaluate in real time a candidate's ability to work collaboratively, think on their feet, have a positive attitude in the face of the unknown, and step outside their comfort zone to make connections with people. In other words, Burgerville was looking for people who had an improviser's mind-set.

As we began our session design, we started by asking ourselves what the ultimate improv partner might look like. How do they allow for flow and possibility to flourish? We landed on a single evaluation question, which both the On Your Feet facilitators and a Burgerville observer would answer after a session with the potential candidates: "Who would you want to be on stage with?" If you ask an experienced improviser this question, they can give you an immediate (often instinctive) evaluation. Improvisers want to work with fellow performers who are easy to interact with, who accept far more offers than they block, and are comfortable in their own skins. They want to be on stage with someone who's focused on making their fellow players look good by giving them "gifts" that make it easier to develop the scene. Most importantly, they want to be on stage with someone who can give the story what it needs rather than putting effort into controlling the story and hogging the limelight.

The design of the event itself was simple. Candidates were put through two rounds of traditional one-on-one interviews with Burgerville employees in a local hotel ballroom for an evaluation of the standard qualifications such as work history, education, and availability. For candidates who made it through the standard interviews, much to their surprise (and sometimes dismay), round two was a thirty-minute callback to participate in an Improv 101 class in a meeting room across the hall. We (truthfully) assured candidates that we were not looking for them to be funny or evaluating how well they improvised; we just wanted them to have a good time and try something new. The game of Presents (Johnstone 1979: 100–101) was our way of introducing the idea of offers. We continued with exercises such as I Am a Tree (Workbook 7.1) to give people opportunities to step forward, interact with each other, and build on others' offers.

This hiring experiment yielded some surprising results. One candidate's improv audition unearthed behaviors that didn't show up during his standard interview, where he had seemed like an ideal candidate. Without watching him improvise with others, we, too, would have hired this friendly guy on the spot. However, when the improv began, on multiple occasions when he got on stage with women, his comments became alarmingly personal for a professional setting. He was not an improviser we would want to be on stage with, and we recommended that Burgerville not hire him.

As this methodology for evaluating candidates was new, and he had come across so strongly in the other parts of the process, Burgerville hired him anyway. Within a week, Beth recalled, they had a significant HR issue on their hands. Even we were surprised to learn that a thirty-minute improv diagnostic had so effectively ferreted out a red flag on a candidate.

Another candidate came across as remarkably shy during the basic interviews. However, she showed up as an improviser. She wasn't loud or showy, but she was present with her scene partners and pushed herself to keep stepping forward. Largely on our recommendation, she was hired. Now, Beth tells us, she is training to become a manager. Along with going through a Burgerville internship program, Beth credits improv tools with helping this young woman blossom.

Ever since this hiring experiment in 2012, for all new restaurant hiring events, Burgerville has used the question "Who would you want to be on stage with?" to identify both unlikely leaders and hidden risks, building a more collaborative culture of employees chosen for their ability to relate with others.[3]

The Fourth Experiment: Building a Wider Community

In 2013 Portland, Oregon's transportation authority, the Port of Portland, asked Burgerville to open a location at Portland International Airport (popularly known by its IATA code PDX). Jeff's immediate reaction was "No thanks." While the airport might have been viewed as a coveted high-revenue concession for a quick service restaurant, the opportunity didn't look like it would forward Burgerville's commitment to building community, at least not at first glance. Jeff was thinking of the airport as a place that people pass through, not a place where people convene and connect. What changed his mind was a conversation with Bill Wyatt, the Port of Portland's executive director, who focused on the port's role in the region's economy, how it moves agricultural products to market, stimulates business, and creates jobs. As the meeting progressed, it became clear that the Port of Portland saw Burgerville as an innovation partner to forward their own mission. Perhaps by supporting the port, Burgerville would be advancing its mission, too. However, the challenge remained: How to create a sense of fresh, local, sustainable community at this location?

Beth and Jeff wanted to talk to the actual people who used and worked within the airport. However, they knew they didn't want to make this interaction a focus group where suggestions were put on the table for people's reactions. They wanted the community conversation to begin without any preexisting assumptions about what this audience needed. "How could you consciously work with an audience to birth the iPod for Burgerville?" Jeff remembers asking. "The only thing we could see that would get us into that 'Don't know what you don't know' domain was improv." Again, Burgerville reached out to On Your Feet as they entered this unchartered territory.

Together, we designed the next experiment that took place on a rainy November evening in an airport conference room. Burgerville had gathered representatives of the entire PDX community—travelers, vendors, security, and administrators. Using improv, we uncovered what would serve this disparate group in a restaurant.

We started the session with an exercise we call Picture Library, where numerous images are thrown on the floor and participants are asked to pick up the image that represents the feeling of being part of the airport community. As participants described why they'd chosen their images, Burgerville learned tons about PDX. As everyone might imagine, an airport is a world of unpredictability, but it is also a world of camaraderie where people work with friends who remain a comforting constant.

To gather further details about what would serve this group, we used an exercise we call Incorporations, but this exercise has been given many other titles. This popular exercise encourages participants to self-organize into clusters of affiliation. For example, to teach the dynamic of the exercise, we might tell participants, "Find others who have something in common with your shoes!" Soon, a brown shoe group, a black shoe group, a flats cluster, and a sneaker contingent form standing around the room. People must choose one cluster or another, but you can switch clusters at any time. A facilitator hears from each group about their choice. Once the dynamic is clear, we dive into more relevant questions and hear from each cluster that forms: "What's the best part of being part of the airport community?" "What is most difficult?" "What is the most challenging pain point of travel?"

We built onto the pain points that emerged from Incorporations using an improv storytelling technique called Verbal Chase (Johnstone 1979: 128–30) to elicit ideas about what could be done to alleviate the inconveniences of travel without overthinking the question. One pain point stood out. Beth recalled that this session validated ideas they had been hearing: "People over and over and over said, 'I don't want to stand in another line,' 'I don't want to be a number,' 'I don't want to be just in a queue and processed through.'" This insight led to the most transformative innovation for the PDX Burgerville: The abolishment of the counter.

At the PDX location, open since 2014, the crew stands out front greeting customers (Figure 1.1). Not only are they able to take orders without a line or the barrier of a counter, they are also freed to improvise how they serve customers. Stories abound of PDX Burgerville employees running forgotten phones and food to people at their gates, going on a hunt for peppermint tea to soothe someone's travel tummy, and helping to distract kids cranky from their journeys. The Port of Portland told Beth that Burgerville's extreme focus on customer needs has raised the bar on service throughout the airport, contributing to yet another year when PDX was awarded best domestic airport by *Travel & Leisure* magazine.

This was just the beginning of what these community ideation sessions would accomplish for Burgerville and the communities they serve. One memorable session focused on a small remodel of an existing store in Battle Ground, Washington, about twenty miles north of PDX over the Columbia River. Jeff recalled that Battle Ground itself was a community divided along religious and political

FIGURE 1.1 *Burgerville's PDX location, December 2014, seven months after opening.*

lines, compounded by a split between the aspirations of newer and longtime residents. Adding to the heaviness was the community's heartbreak over recent teen suicides. The environment was fraught.

On the day of the ideation session, about twenty-five people from disparate groups in the community showed up to a venue where the Nomad was giving away Tillamook Cheeseburgers. Then, On Your Feet introduced them to improv. "It turned out kind of magical," remembers Shelley Darcy, a director at On Your Feet, who played an integral role in most of our work with Burgerville. "People who lived there for two months and people who lived there for 50 years were all in the same boat together." And then, this broken community played. They were vulnerable together. Silly together. Beginners together. And Shelley noted something else that people often say about this work, "The playing field was completely leveled."

The community had been trying to spark a healing conversation for a while, but without success—until the ideation session. Subsequently, people from the city of Battle Ground came back to Jeff astonished, saying things like, "'I just saw something extraordinary happen. How did that happen?'" Shelley thinks she understands. Burgerville convened a discussion between a group of people who otherwise never would have come together. "Through that, and through the improv work, really difficult conversations started to happen in a way that didn't feel tense or heightened. I think just the people interacting with each other was a huge step."

By this time, On Your Feet's collaboration with Burgerville had lasted about eight years. Because of the sustained and varied ways Burgerville was enabling us to apply improv practices to their business challenges, both our organizations were stretching beyond even what we knew was possible, touching people beyond the employees we were hired to train, affecting communities beyond the objectives we had set out to achieve.

The Fifth Experiment: Scaling Improv

In 2014 Burgerville was continuing to innovate their business and was about to launch a new point of sale (POS) system when Beth called On Your Feet with a challenge. Much to our relief, Beth explained that she had no interest in On Your Feet teaching Burgerville employees the mechanics of their new POS system.

Crews would catch on quickly to the intuitive computers; and if crews would no longer be spending their focus and energy battling with the old ordering system, they could spend it making deeper connections with the guests. But they needed training: "Teach them how to start to relate to the guest, how to make an offer, how to accept an offer, how to listen for the clues about what kind of experience they wanted," proposed Beth, revealing her own mastery of the language of improv.

It wasn't a challenge for us to design a training that could help crew members relate differently to their guests. The difficulty was in delivering this training to 1,600 employees across forty-two locations throughout the Pacific Northwest in a way that was economically feasible for Burgerville. As an outside consultancy, we know that eventually we need to train ourselves out of the job. The learning needs to pass from our expertise into the bones of the organization. After ten years, it was time. With that in mind, the Burgerville Improv Ninjas were born.

We trained six high-potential Burgerville employees from around the company to train managers in all Burgerville locations. These managers, in turn, would train their crews in both the improv skills to build relationships with customers and the straightforward mechanics of the new POS system. This was also a stealth change management operation, because, as Beth explained to us, it was critical to have manager buy-in when a new system or policy came from on high. If crews figure out that managers don't like or understand a new policy or process from HQ, adoption is slow and messy. Beth attributes the quick adoption of the new POS system largely to the Ninjas' work training managers. And quick adoption translated into fewer mistakes when ringing up orders. Most surprising to Beth, however, was her discovery that the Ninjas were now looking at everything through an improv lens. One of the Ninjas from the Newberg, Oregon, restaurant, for example, emailed Beth about her store's approach to a new menu launch. The new menus got rid of the popular option of "baskets," Burgerville's former terminology for adding a drink and a side to a sandwich. After the new menu debut, guests kept asking where the baskets went. This Improv Ninja described her crew's reaction. "They shifted from 'Now I've got to defend why we don't have baskets,' to 'Oh, it's an offer! They're actually telling me a ton of information!' " Armed with that information, that a guest was looking for the old basket option, the crew could accept the offer by helping the customer add a drink and a side to their meal. In other words, crews were behaving like improvisers.

For us at On Your Feet, hearing about this Ninja's email was as much of a signal as we could hope for that we had made a significant contribution to a profound cultural shift at Burgerville. What started a decade ago with top leaders performing improv as a way to model behavior they hoped would cascade down has moved all the way to the other end of the spectrum: Improv thinking and behavior is now bubbling up from the ranks to the leadership—and the leadership at Burgerville has both the wisdom and humility to accept that offer.

Looking back on our partnership with Burgerville that spanned ten years, five big experiments, and a ton of discovery, we asked Jeff to tell us what he thought the benefit was to their organization. Before our partnership, Jeff explained, "You would not get anything to go anywhere unless it was what we did yesterday." He credits the improv work for infusing a spirit of experimentation and a willingness to take risks throughout Burgerville's culture that has allowed them to adapt to an ever-changing business climate.

Now that they are armed with their own set of Improv Ninjas, Jeff shared with us their thoughts for the role that improv will continue to play in their organization. We liked what he said so much, we included it at the start of this story and here: "It's a set of skills to reinforce," Jeff observed. "It is the biggest rut-busting approach I've ever seen before, but to be effective, you've got to keep at it." We feel the same way about our own practice of improv, always trying to stay fresh, to stay present enough to ask ourselves, "What's the offer here?" even in the most trying circumstances. At On Your Feet we often make the analogy of going to the gym. Just like nobody will ever be "done" getting in shape, improv is a practice that needs constant renewal.

Jeff sees the importance of improv thinking beyond the restaurant business: "I'm going to say that we as a people, as a world, are right in the middle of an unknown that we have never seen before. We are in the middle of a fundamental question, which is 'What do we want to become together?'" When Jeff thinks about this new world, he laments the idea of people navigating its challenges without "the benefit of doing any improv work or training. So, we can either enter this new world by choosing sides and working against each other, or learn how to accept each other's offers and work together."

Jeff sussed out our covert agenda when we work with clients. Yes, we want to help their businesses, but we are also massive believers in the power of applying improv theatre practices to change lives. Indeed, our lives have all been altered by its practices and their ability to strengthen relationships, to help us find the good in people and situations, and to engage with the world more fully. The beginning of this improvisational adventure with Burgerville began in the 1990s when Gary's mother threw a dart at a map. It continues because of leaders who have a deep belief in the power of community, relationship, conversation, and experimentation. For Gary, Amy, Shelley, and everyone at On Your Feet, it has been incredibly gratifying to work with such an open and committed organization that sees the potential of improv not only for their business but also for a higher purpose.

Notes

1 Unless otherwise noted, direct quotations by Beth Brewer and Jeff Harvey as well as most of the follow-up information on how Burgerville has grown from their collaboration with On Your Feet comes from an interview session Gary facilitated with both Beth and Jeff on August 1, 2016.
2 See also Johnstone's (1999) "You're Interesting" technique.
3 Now that we have seen the effectiveness of improv as a diagnostic for hiring teams and customer service providers, we hope this methodology will be more widely adopted. There's an economic argument to be made for this approach: A meta-analysis by the Center for American Progress found that the typical cost of turnover for positions earning less than $30,000 annually is 16 percent of an employee's annual salary. Using that figure and a wage of $12 an hour, an improv workshop built into a hiring event that costs up to $8,000 would essentially pay for itself if it prevented only two bad hires or ensured two good ones (Boushey and Glynn 2012).

WORKBOOK

1.1 Swedish Story

Why is it called "Swedish Story"? We've asked real Swedes, and we still have no idea. This exercise is a fun and potent experience, introducing participants to the concept of accepting offers, so central to improv and to life.

At the end of this exercise, participants will have ...

- experienced giving and accepting offers,
- accomplished what initially may have seemed impossible,
- reframed interruptions as gifts, and
- practiced responding to curveballs with agility.

Running the Exercise

1. Ask the participants to form pairs.
2. Ask for a simple title for a story that has never been told before (e.g. "The Red Boat"). Tell the group that one of the facilitators will tell the story of "The Red Boat," and as they do so, another facilitator will periodically interrupt the storyteller, interjecting words that have nothing to do with the story (e.g. the word-giver avoids offering words like "water," "oars," "fish," and instead gives disassociated words, such as "pudding," "dinosaur," and "Sean Connery").
3. The storyteller must instantly incorporate the random words into their story. The word-giver waits until each word is incorporated before calling out a new word.
4. Demonstrate for three to four interruptions.
5. Tell the group it is now their turn. Ask each pair of participants to determine who will be the storyteller and who will be the word-giver.

6. Begin the exercise. At around two minutes, ask participants to find a good stopping point for their story.
7. Switch roles and repeat Step 6.

Debrief

- Which role did you find more difficult? How did that surprise you?
- When you were the word-giver, how did it feel when your partner incorporated your word into the story? (That's the feeling of having your offer accepted. It's good!)
- Whose story was it?
- What in your work or life mirrors this experience of having random, unrelated offers fly in while you are headed toward a goal? (Meetings? Projects?)
- What would happen if you viewed those random, unrelated changes or interruptions as "offers"? What would it feel like to accept them?

Suggestion

This can be done seated, but participants have more energy when standing.

Connections: The authors learned this exercise from Randy Dixon of *Unexpected Productions* in Seattle. Also, because the word-giver is essentially giving "blind offers" to the storyteller, you might want to warm-up with Johnstone's (1999) Justify the Gesture, a fun, benevolent exercise that teaches blind offers using abstract physical gestures.

1.2 Flying Idea Cards

This exercise makes it easy for a group of up to forty-five people to Yes, And what's happening in the room and generate multiple ideas. Extroverts have a satisfying outlet supporting the group's energy, and introverts can express themselves quietly at their own pace.

At the end of this exercise, participants will have ...

- generated multiple ideas organically, without a large-group debate or discussion;
- safely put forth risky, foolish, blue-sky, or uncharacteristic ideas—expanding the range of options for the group;
- understood what's on their colleagues' minds and where their energy lies;
- practiced generating ideas and suggestions without judgment or censorship; and
- experienced the joy of throwing things at facilitators!

Running the Exercise

1. Have enough index cards to allot six to ten per participant and pens for everyone.
2. Pre-populate the room with clearly numbered flip chart sheets on the wall, each clearly marked with a specific topic. For customer service, for example, you might have a flip chart that says, "Ways to start a conversation with a customer," or "Actions to put the customer first." For innovating in your sector, you may have a category that says, "What else should we be doing to help us stay relevant in our changing landscape?"
3. Introduce this exercise to express ideas as they arise, not waiting for a break in the action. Whenever an idea strikes, each participant should immediately write it down on an

index card, including the number of the flip chart it pertains to, then throw the card at one of the facilitators, doing their best to hit them.

4. During breaks, collect the cards and place them on their designated flip chart.

5. At least two or three times during the day, give participants a dedicated five minutes to generate ideas and throw them at facilitators, thus amply populating the flip charts.

6. Toward the end of the day, participants do a "gallery walk," viewing all the ideas generated.

7. After the gallery walk, ask participants to vote for their top two ideas on each flip chart, using either a sticky dot or a pen dot.

8. Invite volunteers to be topic leaders and "champion" each idea that emerges. As part of the day's close, invite each topic leader to share plans for follow-up.

Debrief

- What surprised you about the exercise?
- As you looked at your colleagues' Flying Idea Cards, what themes emerged? Where does the group have the most energy?
- How was the exercise different from the way you typically come up with ideas?
- Is there anything about that process you would like to replicate?
- How did this help you coalesce ideas?

Connections: This exercise was created by Gary Hirsch of On Your Feet.

2

Candy in Karachi: Sweetening Market Research through Play

Faris Khalid

Faris Khalid is a Pakistan-based Applied Improvisation (AI) practitioner, designing and conducting soft skill development workshops for the corporate sector. He also conducts AI sessions at Karachi Grammar School and Cedar College. Although no longer an improv performer himself, he does host shows for the Karachi-based short-form comedy troupe Improvistan, and has acted in three Pakistani feature films.

Growing up in Dubai (UAE), my entertainment diet comprised of American and UK TV shows and films. I was a fan of the show *Whose Line Is It Anyway?* but it looked like TV magic and I had no idea how it worked. I moved to Pakistan in 1996, but got my first taste of improv in 2002, when I was introduced to Saad Haroon (who later became one of Pakistan's first internationally acclaimed comedians, even voted the second "Funniest Person in the World" in a competition at the Laugh Factory in Los Angeles in 2014). Saad had recently returned from the United States where he had done some improv and wanted to start a troupe in Karachi. Since no one else had any experience in improv, the sign-up criterion was just the willingness to commit to meeting twice a week and "figuring this improv thing out." After a few weeks, we were seven people strong (three women and four men).

We called our short-form comedy troupe Black Fish, which is a literal translation of Karachi's old name, Kolachi ("kola" meaning "black" and "chi" meaning "fish"). Besides being the only English-language improv comedy troupe, we were the *only* improv troupe! To our great surprise, we went on to become Pakistan's most commercially successful theatre troupe, putting on weekly live shows and even representing Pakistan in the British Council's Contacting the World theatre festival in 2004. Pakistanis were as wowed by our improv magic as I had been of *Whose Line*. What also set us apart was our group's diverse composition, especially given Pakistan's conservative cultural views on interactions between members of the opposite sex. I was working in marketing at the time and the idea of developing training modules using improv for people in the corporate world sounded interesting, but none of us in the troupe knew how to implement this idea.

In 2007, I moved back to Dubai to pursue an opportunity with an advertising agency, marking the dissolution of Black Fish. I continued to research and read about (applied) improv online and eventually started offering free improv workouts with the hope of forming a troupe. I called the workouts "HaHaHabibi" ("Habibi" is a commonly used term of endearment in Arabic). Like the city of Dubai itself, our group was a potpourri of different nationalities, ethnicities, backgrounds, and professions. It was the perfect recipe for a truly dynamic, multicultural improv outfit. United Colors of Benetton would have been a proud sponsor.

Once we had formed a core group, it became obvious that the members were not particularly keen to get up on stage and perform for an audience. Rather, they started telling me how the improv sessions were helping them in their personal and professional lives. My initial disappointment at not performing quickly became an opportunity to refine my skills as a Learning and Development (L&D) facilitator. Since the workshops were no longer being used to train potential performers, the format of the sessions changed. I went back to more basic activities and short-form games. The important addition to the sessions was a debrief at the end of the activities in which the participants were encouraged to reflect on those activities and understand how the experience helped them build their soft skills and brainstorming techniques. HaHaHabibi turned into my Applied Improvisation (AI) lab and helped me develop my skills as an AI facilitator.

By this time, I had been in marketing for ten years and was seeing more similarities between improv and advertising/marketing, especially in terms of clear and effective communication. In advertising, we were taught to design a campaign and its message using a document called a "creative brief." This essentially categorized various components of the campaign in terms of audience profile, desired response, insights, and brand values. In improv, we are trained to develop and carry on a scene by ensuring we share information with our scene partner(s) and audience. The common denominator is empathy—understanding your audience and ensuring that they and the other players in the scene follow your idea while you follow theirs, so you can collectively weave a story or paint a picture. This is teamwork at its best.

I continued to build my understanding of AI through various improv sites on the internet and Facebook, studying emotional intelligence, and working with the incredibly valuable book *Business Improv* (Gee and Gee 2011), which was a gift from a friend at HaHaHabibi. I began to realize that if we deconstruct improv and its methods, it becomes obvious that we are applying these principles in our everyday lives, regardless of our profession. We work collectively toward a shared goal/vision, and along the way—to ensure things run smoothly—we empathize, communicate clearly, share responsibilities, and adapt to new situations and circumstances. Life is improv. And improv is life.

In 2014, I was again living in Karachi and set up a small L&D company called DeveloPlay Consulting. My experience of making numerous cold calls and presentations to potential clients taught me how to rephrase my pitch to help clients understand how theatre/improv activities would help their HR requirements. Besides not understanding the concept or applicability of improv, most potential clients only knew of trainings to be classroom-like lectures that provided the participants with hackneyed acronyms, mind maps, and formulae for improving productivity in the workplace. Corporate workshops are expected to reflect their work cultures—extremely serious and not fun. I attribute this, in part, to our Mughal Dynasty and the bureaucratic systems left behind by the British colonists. The concept of Yes, And had to be rephrased to collective thinking/ brainstorming. "Being Spontaneous" had to be called adapting to change. And "Scene Work" was introduced as engaging observation and listening skills, working in groups, supporting team members, and enhancing collective productivity. Fortunately, there are a lot of clients who understand the value of soft skills, and after a year, I had managed to successfully conduct various improv-based work-shops for different organizations.

Online, I discovered people using improv for all sorts of non-performance applications including spirituality and understand-ing human psychology! Why not use improv games for market research? If improv encourages you to free associate to tap into your creative conscience, wouldn't that level of spontaneity reveal inner thoughts we would otherwise filter if asked in an interview? The potential was exciting. I casually discussed this idea with a Karachi-based research consultant named Mehwish Rafi. Not only was she similarly intrigued by these possibilities, but she also had an immediate need to do some market research.

The Client

A chocolate-covered wafer candy, created by a leading global con-fectionary company, had strong trade level marketing in terms of product availability and shelf display, but their advertising presence was low-key in the Pakistan market. Their primary competitor, also an international brand, however, was very visible on TV, outdoor, print, and radio. Converting this first company's famous "Have a break … " line into a campaign was a simple and smart idea to help connect with its target audience. Mehwish was tasked with conducting market research to evaluate and assess what the brand's tagline meant to its local customers, if anything at all. The research was two-pronged: first, to test how much the tagline resonated with the new generation, and second, to understand what they associ-ated with "taking a break."

As Mehwish knew, the most important technique when con-ducting any kind of direct consumer research is being able to cre-ate a comfortable climate for the participants to freely share their opinions. In my experience in marketing, the focus groups I saw often seemed a little creepy, with the respondents and facilitator in one room divided by a one-way glass from the client and other research team members in another room. In my opinion, this tends to skew their responses instead of encouraging respondents to speak openly. Now I'm not saying *all* focus groups are conducted in this manner, but I knew that since improv games are fun and the structures allow participants to relax, laugh, and speak freely, we might collect a higher quality and quantity of information and insights than any traditional focus group format.

Mehwish had never attended an improv workshop. Her primary interest was mining a rich set of information, not how well the games themselves worked for this purpose. This is noteworthy for those AI practitioners out there who are finding their footing; remember to describe your work in terms of benefits to the client, not just the methodology, and it really helps if the people you can pitch to are genuinely interested and receptive to new ideas.

Mehwish was on board, but would her advertising agency go along with this idea? As far as I know, I am the only AI practitioner in Pakistan, which should tell you how far-fetched the idea of an AI-based focus group would sound to the client. Luckily, I could promote my experience in marketing, and Mehwish had a proven track record with the client on a few projects. AI practitioners may find it helpful to partner with another expert outside your field that can help sell what you do. After all, improv teaches us to appreciate the value of collaboration!

Project Details and Scope of Work

Mehwish and her team designed the research to take place in Karachi and Lahore, the two leading metros in Pakistan where we would find the brand's target audience. They recruited the respondents through word of mouth, asking for volunteers to participate in a social experiment designed to understand how people their age think and feel about life in general, and specifically the stresses and triggers they are experiencing. At the end of each session we would reveal to the respondents that they had participated in a focus group and offer to strike their responses from the findings if they requested us to do so.

The brand was reaching out to youth in their late teens and early twenties, from middle to upper middle class backgrounds. The assumption was that they all consumed chocolate bars at least once a week. To get a sample size of approximately fifty respondents, we ran five ninety-minute sessions with ten to twelve respondents each. This was also conducive to improv activities since you want equal participation from all respondents.

We started in Lahore, where the brand's Pakistan operation is headquartered, so the brand team could sit in on the first two sessions and observe the quality of responses. The research team and myself were put up in a chic, boutique hotel where we also ran the sessions. The unassuming venue didn't feel "corporate" or stuffy.

The participants sat in the middle of the room. I was up front with a white board. In the back was a representative from the candy maker along with Mehwish and her team of research assistants. I thanked the participants for volunteering in our social experiment and introduced those in the back as members of my team who will observe the session and note down their responses.

As a facilitator, I was well aware of how important it was to get the participants to like me, or maybe even just not dislike me. The more at ease, the more willing they are to share. This was doubly challenging because not only would most people hesitate when told that they will be included in improv or theatre activities, in Pakistan, this would be magnified by being in a group of strangers that included members of the opposite sex. On top of that, they had a panel of five observers. I am really grateful to have honed my emceeing skills with Black Fish, which helped me quickly focus the attention of the group on me and away from the observers. I also assured the group that they would work in interactive games and not perform for the observers. We began with an icebreaker.

Activity One: Introductions

There are multiple variations of this form of introduction (Workbook 2.1). We decided to have participants introduce themselves by adding a verb/adjective that started with the same letter as their first names. This round tends to be quite amusing, especially when participants find themselves challenged to find a suitable alliteration. I also asked them what profession or line of work they planned to pursue. Finally, I asked them what superpowers they would want to possess. This question isn't as arbitrary as it sounds because we wanted to scratch the surface of our session objective, to identify a need for a "break." If, for example, the participants said they wish they were endowed with the ability to see into the future, it could hint at their need to "know where my life is going." The icebreaker worked and got the participants to speak in front of the group and share a laugh. It was time to take things up a notch in terms of delving deeper into their perception of a "break."

Activity Two: Word Association

I have always used word association games as a mental warm-up activity for my workshops because it establishes a judgment-free environment and encourages creative thinking. These games can be likened to a verbal version of a Rorschach Test. I asked the participants to associate words that related to the (still undisclosed) brand and its values, like, "taking a break," "stress," and "relief." It takes a couple of rounds to get the participants comfortable and, more importantly, confident with sounding off the first thing that comes to mind when they hear a certain word.[1]

It was interesting, but not surprising, for us to hear these groups of young men and women express stress points that stemmed from academic dilemmas, career choices, and family pressures like the liberty to hang out with friends without having to be answerable to their parents. The most common concept associated with "break" was a vacation to the beach or trekking in the mountains. The common thread was finding a place that is peaceful, serene, and away from city life. At the end of a few rounds, I sensed a deeper level of comfort in the group. The participants were sufficiently warmed up and ready for a more interactive group activity that would delve further into sharing their ideas for the ideal "break."

Activity Three: Emotional Endowment

This activity is known as Emotional Endowment (Workbook 2.2). In pairs, the participants were given situations and relationships and observed as they tried to make each other feel a certain way. The situation could be where one person wants to sell a car to their partner. The first is given a piece of paper saying "confused" and must try to evoke the feeling of confusion in their partner. The game appears easier than it is. For example, giving your partner contradictory information may not result in them feeling confused. Successfully evoking a specific emotion in the other requires careful thought in terms of how to communicate and to empathize with the other person, as well as deep listening skills. We challenged our participants to evoke feelings of relaxation in each other, to best collect data regarding having a "break."

Afterward, I took the opportunity to help the participants reflect on their experience, just as I would have with HaHaHabibi. I walked the participants through why they might have not been successful in making their scene partners feel a certain way. The most common reason is that they started the role-play with a preconceived notion about how their partner would respond, and stayed so focused on their own idea that they did not truly listen to what their partner was offering. The activity works best when the players take their time and are more receptive to what the other is saying instead of trying to make a mad dash for the finish line.

At this point in the session, I had managed to mine a considerable amount of information from the participants about some of their interests and needs, in an oblique fashion. The way the session had been layered thus far was getting the participants to open up and share their individual thoughts on what causes stress and the ideal break from it all. In the final activity, I ask the questions directly.

Activity Four: The Dating Game

Conventional focus groups are designed and run like group interviews. The format is to pose open-ended questions to the participants and get them to elaborate on their preferences, perceptions, and feelings about whatever is being tested. But when asking people to elaborate on their thoughts about something, you could potentially be faced with discussions dragging on for too long, being dominated by a few people while isolating the others, as well as veering off topic. To keep the discussion on track and to get the information we needed, we played The Dating Game, but changed the title to The Friendship Game, keeping in mind social and cultural sensitivities. Being a Muslim country, the concept of dating is not openly encouraged in Pakistan, and asking participants to assume the roles of single people looking to find a mate on a game show posed the possibility of making them uncomfortable and reluctant to share. We nominated a member of our research team, Umair, to play the role of the Bachelor, and by changing his role to be "The New Guy in Town" looking to make friends, we were still able to use this useful format to lead into a targeted discussion while remaining fun at the same time.

Umair sat in the front of the room opposite a panel of potential friends consisting of two male and two female participants. He then proceeded to ask each participant a series of questions to check his compatibility with each one. We made sure the questions were general (e.g. type of music or films they preferred) as well as related to the topics of stress and breaks (e.g. their immediate life choices that worried them and their ideal getaway). He asked things like, "What makes you happy? If you were an inanimate object, what would you be? I need a friend who can bail me out of trouble, so if I need money, would you loan me a small amount?" The participants seemed to enjoy it as much as the observers did. I stood by as an external facilitator who, from time to time, interjected and asked participants to elaborate on certain points when I thought they could share more information that could be useful to meeting our objective

The Response

Participant Reactions

By the end of the last activity, the research team, the client, and myself felt very satisfied with the level of enthusiasm, participation, and the quality of the responses. The participants also revealed how much they enjoyed themselves. They got to play these unusual games as well as express themselves about their dreams, aspirations, and things that stress them out. In Pakistan, it is unusual for young people (or anyone!) to be asked to speak openly about things that bother them or truly make them happy. In my opinion, this is because it could be considered a challenge to the status quo. Like other countries with traditional (some might say archaic) social systems such as China, Japan, and the Middle East, the younger generation in the subcontinent is expected to accept norms established by older generations without question, as a means of preserving the culture and set of values. I am continually heartened to find opportunities like this in which to offer people the chance to express themselves within this larger context.

Finally, it was time to reveal that we were mining for insights for our client, not just doing a social science project. The first time we did so, I was concerned about how the group would react, but because we had established a rapport with the participants, not only did they not mind when we informed them about the true nature of the project, most of them stayed an additional half hour to further express their thoughts. This, to me, was the strongest validation for this kind of methodology—we not only collected candid information from the target market when they were unaware but we also created a climate where they willingly volunteered ideas on how the brand could revisit its positioning and launch marketing plans that resonated. The research team put together a "goody bag" for each participant as a token of appreciation. It was a packet of—yes, you guessed it—the brand's chocolate bars.

Client Feedback

Between breaks and after the sessions in Karachi and Lahore, I took the time to chat with the client to get their thoughts and feedback on the way the sessions were being conducted, especially their thoughts on AI as a methodology for mining insights. I was thrilled to hear them tell me that they were very pleased since this unique methodology made connecting with the young target audience fun and approachable and yielded the results they were looking for. Mehwish described AI as "an effective methodology that facilitated flow of information from respondents to the observers." I'll take that as a compliment!

Conclusion

I consider the project to be a resounding success and a milestone in my portfolio. A marketing firm was willing to risk a previously untested methodology with a prominent multinational brand, and the result was a rich collection of candid information and validation that AI was significantly more effective than traditional focus group processes.

My new venture is to try to reach a wider audience by creating opportunities for play and improv in the education sector. By running soft skill development sessions as well as improv theatre classes at schools in Karachi, I am seeing students, their parents, and academic professionals start to appreciate AI and its importance in their personal development and emotional intelligence.

I have experienced how powerful AI can be for personal growth, education, communications skills, and now market research. Improv and its various applications have yet to make a lasting mark in a country such as Pakistan, but the opportunities I have had so far remind me that it is possible.

Note

1 Learning to loosen the grip of one's internal censor usually takes a lot of practice. Improvisers regularly practice free-association games because as soon as we become conscious of our responses, we tend to filter our thoughts even more, killing spontaneity. This is especially challenging in Pakistan where any hint of adult themes must remain censored. In our focus groups, we created a playful environment that allowed the participants to speak more freely than they would with strangers, but not so intimate that adult-themed topics might be shared.

WORKBOOK

2.1 Introduce Yourself!

This exercise can be run in infinite ways. The key is to give everyone the chance to speak in front of the group, to say their name, and playfully share something about themselves.

At the end of this exercise, participants will have ...

- learned the names and some characteristics of their fellow participants, and
- expressed themselves freely, with little pressure or judgment.

Running the Exercise

Ask the participants to stand in a circle and introduce themselves one at a time by sharing a few pieces of information, such as:

1. Alliteration Name—a descriptive word or phrase starting with the same letter as their first name (e.g. Friendly Faris)
2. Life Ambition—desires and objectives they want to pursue
3. Desired Superpowers—for instance, if they could fly or be invisible

Modify these questions to best meet the objective of the session.

Suggestions

The silly/playful nature of these questions helps participants relax and can set the tone of the rest of the session. The more freely you share and accept others' offers, the greater the level of comfort in the room. If shy respondents wish to skip their turn, offer them the chance to introduce themselves once they are more comfortable.

Connections: There are many variations of introduction games used by AI facilitators. For example, see Upside-Down Introductions (Workbook 3.1) and Name and Motion (Workbook 5.1). We also encourage you to find others that work for you and/or create your own!

2.2 Emotional Endowment

The format of this exercise develops skills in active listening, methods of persuasion, and emotional intelligence. It provides an opportunity to discern one's own emotional state from another's and to utilize empathy in evoking change in another.

At the end of this exercise, participants will have ...

- become aware of their own ability to impact the emotional state of others;
- experienced the extent to which they are open, or filter, another person's emotions; and
- practiced evoking a specific feeling in another person, without explicitly directing them to do so.

Running the Exercise

1. Ask the participants to form pairs.
2. Assign a simple fictitious situation (relationship, location, circumstance) such as a customer shopping at a butcher's, or two friends organizing a birthday party.
3. One person in each pair is given a piece of paper on which a word expressing an emotion or mood is printed. That participant tries to make the other "feel" that emotion or mood during their conversation, without acting out that emotion themselves or explicitly stating the emotion. All pairs work simultaneously.

4. After two minutes, switch roles and repeat with a new situation and a new emotion.

5. After both scenes have been played, ask participants to reveal their emotion to their partners.

Debrief

• How successful were you in evoking the emotion in your partner?

• What did you have to do to succeed?

• Where did you run into challenges?

• What approach did your partner take to evoke this emotion in you?

• When you had to evoke emotion, what did you do when your initial approach did not have the intended impact?

• How challenging was it to evoke one emotion in your partner, while feeling another?

Suggestions

While appearing simple, it can be challenging to try to evoke an emotion in another without feeling it oneself. You might also coach participants to "endow" their partners with the emotional quality they are attempting to evoke, that is, act as if their partner is already expressing that emotion. Encourage participants to enjoy the experience and not rush even if they feel they are out of their comfort zone. Make explicit that the characters they are playing like each other, to avoid having the scenes devolve into conflict. As needed, side-coach the participants to slow down and try new approaches.

Connections: The author adapted this exercise from a short-form game called Emotional Waiter. For another fun endowment exercise, try Johnstone's (1999) Party Endowments and change the qualities he suggests to the emotions or moods you want your participants to evoke.

PART TWO

Resilience and Connection

3

Oncology Nurses Creating a Culture of Resiliency with Improvisation

Cathy Salit

Cathy Salit is a social entrepreneur, musical comedy improviser, executive coach, and CEO of the training and consulting firm Performance of a Lifetime. She started her career as an innovator and upstart at 12, when she dropped out of eighth grade and started an alternative school in an abandoned storefront in New York City. She's a weekly columnist for Inc.com, and her work and thought leadership have been featured in *Harvard Business Review, Fast Company, The Wall Street Journal, Forbes, Wired,* and Daniel Pink's *To Sell Is Human.* Cathy is the author of *Performance Breakthrough: A Radical Approach to Success at Work* (2016).

This is a second career for me. I've been a nurse for two years, and I've come to see that I was becoming a protocol, a machine, and the door was closing on my humanity. I didn't know if I could continue to do this work. The arts,

improvisation and performing are the best way to reconnect us with our humanity, and I feel like a human being again.
ONCOLOGY NURSE, THE JOHNS HOPKINS HOSPITAL

It should come as no surprise to anyone that oncology nursing takes an emotional toll on its practitioners. The stress of dealing with gravely ill patients, many of whom don't survive, is easy to imagine. National statistics bear this out, showing that oncology nurses experience higher "burnout" rates than any other specialty—including emergency nurses—and lower job satisfaction than nurses in general.

Sharon Krumm, PhD, has been the director of Oncology Nursing at the Sidney Kimmel Comprehensive Cancer Center at the Johns Hopkins Hospital since 1988, and for her, the statistics told only part of the story. The Kimmel Center is one of the country's pre-eminent cancer treatment facilities, with a well-earned reputation for being on the cutting edge of cancer care. As a teaching hospital and research center, its cancer patients often arrive having tried everything else, with cases far more complex than the norm. Physicians and nurses there are called upon to make Herculean efforts to save their patients, many of whom still die.

Dr. Krumm was keenly aware of the extraordinary stress her nurses were under, well beyond the fact that burnout was leading to high turnover and vacant positions. In 2006, she began conducting focus groups and surveys and found that her nurses needed more support in a wide range of areas, including:

- handling the emotional impact of patients dying;
- greater community and collegiality among staff;
- an improved mental and physical environment—more quiet space, time to eat meals, less clutter, more control of schedules; and
- acknowledgment after successfully managing difficult patient situations.

These findings helped Dr. Krumm see that—beyond the structural and environmental issues that had to be addressed—something more personal and developmental was needed. Oncology nursing requires enormous emotional energy, compassion, and commit-ment, and she wanted to give her nursing teams more skills, sup-port, and mastery for managing all the emotional, personal, and social challenges of their jobs. To Dr. Krumm, this meant helping the nurses to develop greater resiliency, which she defined as "a dynamic process in which healthy skills and abilities enable indi-viduals to thrive, maintain, and restore personal and professional well-being."[1]

Dr. Krumm went to work, spearheading a Bereavement and Resiliency initiative, funded by a Maryland Health Services Cost Review Commission grant. She started small, offering meditation and yoga classes, and providing a quiet physical space for the nurses to take breaks and regroup. It was a good start, but she also wanted to provide an "intervention" that was interactive and dynamic to help nurses address their emotional needs and give them additional tools to handle the demands and stress that they faced every day (and night).

One day in early 2008, Dr. Krumm attended a presentation at a meeting of the Center for Innovation in Quality Patient Care at Hopkins. Karen Davis, at that time the director of nursing for medi-cine, was reporting on a recent training program for nurse leaders from both the emergency medicine and general medicine depart-ments. The training had been designed to improve the strained rela-tionships between the two departments, who interfaced regularly during "hand-offs"—transfers of patients from emergency to gen-eral medicine. The program had been a big success, leading not only to greater efficiency and effectiveness of the hand-offs but also to significant improvements in the working relationships between the two departments' personnel.

While those results were impressive, they weren't all that piqued Dr. Krumm's interest. The program Dr. Davis described was highly unorthodox—it involved play, theatre, and improvisation, and she told stories of nurses who had long been frustrated and angry at each other now playing and laughing together. And in describing all this, Dr. Davis was excited and joyful—which was pretty much unheard of in a data-driven academic setting.

I'll have what she's having, Dr. Krumm thought. (She's a big *When Harry Met Sally* fan.) What Dr. Davis had been "having" was my company, Performance of a Lifetime (POAL). And that's where our story begins.

A Bit of Background

I'm an improviser, performer, and the CEO of Performance of a Lifetime, a consulting and training firm that helps leaders, teams, and organizations perform and improvise their way to growth, learning, and development. My company's methodological roots stretch back to the 1980s, when I began working with people who become my lifelong mentors: the developmental psychologist Lois Holzman; the philosopher, psychotherapist, and playwright Fred Newman; and the educator, psychologist, and community organizer Lenora Fulani. Influenced by the work of the early-twentieth-century Soviet psychologist Lev Vygotsky, they were making practical-theoretical discoveries in bringing together theatre, improvisation, and therapeutics in efforts for social change, education, and personal growth, a pursuit that has come to be called "performative psychology."

Founded in the late 1990s, POAL employs an approach we call The Becoming Principle®. Drawing on the discoveries of performative psychology, the basic idea is this: We humans are all performers, and we collectively create our lives through performing—by simultaneously being *who we are* and *who we're not*—that is, *who we are becoming*. As babies, this comes naturally to us. As children, we're supported (for the most part) in performing, playing, imagining, and improvising; and it's these kinds of activities that account for the rapid learning and development we all experienced when we were young.

Unfortunately, for most of us, "growing up" means moving on from that kind of developmental learning. We're told (explicitly and implicitly) that it's time to learn the rules, behave properly, know what we're doing and how to do it, and figure out (and then be) who we are. Play is relegated to structured contexts (sports, video and board games, party games); performing and improvising are reserved for the professionals. For most adults, "who we're not" is stifled.

Luckily, our ability to perform, play, and improvise—as a fundamental catalyst for growing into who we're becoming—never goes away. At any time, it can be reignited, and POAL provides teams, organizations, and leaders around the world the support and direction to do so. We teach them that they are, in fact, natural performers, and immerse them in the language of performance and improvisation (much as I will be explicitly using performance language throughout this chapter). We help them grow, learn, and develop by both creating new performances and helping them to *see* performance—that they can both be in a scene and see it unfold; they can write, perform, and direct it simultaneously. They can make creative choices that impact the scene, the characters, and the relationship—all at the same time. As Shakespeare said, "All the world's a stage," and what makes that world go round is our amazing, creative, and unique ability to perform.

A New Kind of Play, for All of Us

Dr. Krumm reached out to us shortly after she heard Dr. Davis speak. Over the spring and summer of 2008, my colleague Maureen Kelly (a brilliant designer, improviser, educator, and social therapist) and I had a series of conversations with her and her assistant director, Suzanne Cowperthwaite, to learn as much as we could about the "play" that was being performed daily in the oncology department. It was our version of a needs analysis—we were the observers (audience) for the everyday occurrences (scenes) taking place in various units (stages). By the fall of 2008, together with Dr. Krumm and her team, we had roughed out a program design.

We were excited and nervous about getting under way. Excited, because our observations and conversations had shown us the enormous stress and pressure that the nurses were under, and we were hopeful that the program could have a meaningful impact on them and this pressing healthcare concern. Nervous, because to have that kind of impact, we had to raise our own game. POAL had been working with businesses and nonprofits for about ten years by then, and the principles I articulated above were always the foundations of our programs. But in improv terms, our work up to this point had been "short-form." We provided a design, customized a set of exercises to address the client's needs, and created a supportive environment in which they could improvise, play together, and explore new performances. Then, after our day or two together, we all moved on.

This was going to be different. It was "long-form." We were going to be able to explore and integrate an Applied Improvisational (AI) approach into the day-to-day activity of nursing at Hopkins over a sustained period. There would be multiple touch points that would inform each other and build over time. And like any long-form performance, it would be unpredictable, with each new moment emerging out of what had just been created. It felt risky, challenging, and exciting, and had the potential to make a significant difference for the oncology nurses and to go deeper than anything we (and they) had ever done before.

Part 1: Performance Workshops

We kicked off our Performance of Resiliency program in September 2008. The first "scene" was a mandatory half-day performance workshop, attended by about twenty nurses at a time. Over a four-month period, we delivered fifteen of the workshops to different groups of nurses, offering an intensive immersion into performance and improvisation. Each session was introduced by Dr. Krumm or Suzanne Cowperthwaite, who provided an overview of the Hopkins Bereavement and Resiliency initiative. Then, either Maureen or I would give an opening talk in which we set the stage for an unusual four hours.

We introduced the nurses to our approach, and shared that our focus was twofold—we wanted to both build their resiliency and support them in collectively creating a new "play" for oncology nursing—a resilient, supportive, improvisational ensemble performance of their daily work.

Then we began performing and improvising together. They passed an imaginary ball of energy around a circle, stood in pairs mirroring each other's movements, explored different ways of walking (from fast to slow to "normal" to slow again), and improvised different ways of speaking (using gibberish, using English with pauses, making extended eye contact, and adding silence). We introduced them to the improv principle of Yes, And and other tenets improvisers adhere to onstage to collaborate, focus, and create connections.

While the nurses had been informed that the Performance of Resiliency program was going to be "different"—a theatre- and improvisation-based creative and emotional outlet/space and a chance to open up and talk about their experiences together—they were still initially taken aback. Workshops or meetings at Hopkins were typically about policy, process, and new or changed requirements. So, at first, they were shy, skeptical, nervous, and confused.

But as Applied Improvisers around the world can attest, when workshop participants begin to realize that they're not being judged or tested or "taught," and that they're really going to play, an invisible but palpable burden begins to lift. *We're actually allowed to laugh and play around here? And we're getting paid to do it?* Our (collective) answer? *Yes! Not only are you* allowed *to play, but you need* to play—*if you want to grow, learn new things, and create some new tools for resiliency.*

Upside-Down Introductions

One of our (and their) favorite exercises was Upside-Down Introductions (Workbook 3.1). In pairs, the nurses told each other about themselves, including why and how they became a nurse. Then, each introduced their partner to the full group—but did so in the first person, playing the role of their partner. Of course, the nurses told their partners' stories differently than their partners would have, and often added insight, color, and nuance that the actual person might not have. This was a surprisingly touching exercise. Hearing someone else share your story "as you" gives you (and others) a chance to observe how others see and hear you and how they are impacted by you. The upside-down introductions gave the nurses a direct experience of "being who you are and who you're not," and it opened doors for them to express their pride and passion about nursing in a new, improvisational, and collective way. And through this simple exercise, we saw a caring, open, and collaborative ensemble very quickly coming into existence.

Performing Your Life in One Minute

A centerpiece of each workshop was our signature exercise, the One-Minute Performance of a Lifetime, from which we take our name. One at a time, with no advance preparation, we welcomed the nurses onto the stage for sixty seconds to "perform their lives." The subject matter could be anything: from their entire life, to just the essence of their life, to a single representative moment; it could be important or mundane; about being a nurse or not. The only requirement was that it had to be explicitly a *performance*, not an explanation. We also directed the audience in how to perform the role of audience—as supportive and attentive, with enthusiastic applause.

The nurses' performances were richly varied: some were slices of everyday life, like rushing to leave for work while getting kids ready; some were expressions of challenges at the hospital, like a young nurse's struggle to find a vein for an IV, or a veteran nurse's simple portrayal of caring for a pediatric patient, gently lifting the arm of a toddler and whispering to him tenderly that she needed to give him more medicine. Others went further afield—saying goodbye to a grandmother on the eve of emigrating from the Philippines, or a son trying to communicate with his father who had Alzheimer's. One nurse, who had shyly insisted that she wasn't a performer/hated performing/would never perform, told the group she wrote poetry (which nobody knew) and then performed one of her poems.

Following each performance, Maureen and I gave the performer a theatrical direction to improvise and perform beyond what they had done so far. These short "sequels" were inspired by what we saw, and often included another POAL improviser as a co-performer. They weren't designed to resolve the conflict of the scene; instead they revisited, extended, or heightened whatever we wanted to see more of. A few directions we offered were: perform the scene again as a rock-and-roll song with others providing vocal backup; do it again in your native tongue; try it as a silent modern dance; or play your grandmother this time.

By the end of the performances, the group (including Maureen and me) had traversed the emotional spectrum. Together, we had co-created a supportive environment and structure in which the nurses performed as they never had before. They worked as a performance ensemble—exploring, taking risks together, and giving one another their honest enthusiasm and appreciation.

We led the group in reflecting on their experience—an important aspect of the workshop that helped broaden and deepen their understanding of what they had just been through. Nurses spoke about how they had worked together for years, but today learned more about each other than ever before. They expressed their appreciation for getting to know nurses from other units, and some spoke about the "old days" when there was more camaraderie across the department.

Some talked about how good it was to express their emotions and connect differently with people they work with, side-by-side, usually under tremendous pressure. In one workshop, for example, a nurse shared her one-minute performance about her father and uncle both being treated on her unit, portraying the stress of trying to be a nurse, daughter, and niece all at the same time. In the sequel, we created a "nurse chorus" who sang, "How can we be there for you, now and always?" Afterward, several nurses reflected on how she always seemed so strong, "a pillar of strength," and that they had no idea she had been struggling.

Some nurses spoke about their strong commitment—both at work and at home—to always being the "helper," and their inability to ask for help from others. They said their "nurse identity" provided a strong sense of self-worth but was also a source of stress. Others talked openly about how, after a patient died, the need to "turn the bed" did not provide time for grieving, or that grieving at work was simply not possible: "If I let myself go I may not be able to pull myself back together. It's better to buck up and move on."

While many of the nurses expressed appreciation for the intimacy of the session, others expressed strong discomfort. When the one-minute performances portrayed personal or emotional events, some nurses said that what their colleagues had shared was "too much" or was inappropriate in the work environment. These discussions began to show us how high a value many nurses placed on the performance of "being strong" and "keeping it together," and the resiliency-diminishing cost—physical, emotional, spiritual—of these choices. Several nurses insisted that compartmentalization and emotional detachment were in fact practical strategies for resilience. From our years of working in healthcare, we knew that this was a very common outlook, one that couldn't be ignored. Moreover, we were attempting to create a different culture that could include more voices, so we certainly didn't want to shut any down. We would later see some shifts in these attitudes as the nurses observed their colleagues' growth, but at this early stage, we wanted to make sure everyone was heard.

Post-workshop Follow-Up

At the end of each of the fifteen sessions, we gave the nurses "resiliency performance homework"—exercises to help them improvise, perform, and play in their day-to-day lives, as well as to experiment with some specific new performance choices. Homework included:

- Walk down the hall very slowly, at least three times a week.
- When a problem comes up, write a poem about it instead of trying to solve it.
- Invite a colleague you don't know to have coffee together.
- When something goes badly with a coworker, a loved one, or a friend, say, "Let's play that scene over again," and then perform it in a different way.

Dr. Krumm also circulated an evaluation to the participants, and on the standard questions about the effectiveness of the instruction, format, and content, the nurses gave 95 percent positive scores. We were especially interested in the comments the nurses provided when asked what they liked most and least about the work. Surprisingly, the same workshop elements—performing, exploring emotions, being pushed out of their comfort zones, and playing games—showed up in equal numbers in both the "most liked" and "least liked" columns. In several instances, nurses listed these activities as what they liked both most *and* least. I had to smile at that result—anyone who's ever gotten onstage to perform recognizes that abject dread and profound exhilaration can and do really exist side by side!

Part 2: Performance Coaching Groups

Performance coaching groups offered ongoing support in developing greater resiliency. They were designed to provide the nurses with a space—a "stage"—for reflecting on their work and lives, and to receive (and learn how to give) ongoing support. Participation was voluntary, and nurses could attend as many sessions as they wanted. For two hours, once a month for six months, groups ranging from six to fifteen nurses from different units gathered with Maureen or me. Sessions were loosely structured, allowing us to improvise based on the nurses' needs, and—perhaps most importantly—create the conditions in which we and the nurses could build the group into an ensemble.

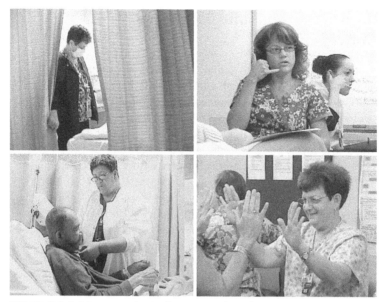

FIGURE 3.1 *Nurses in the Performance of Resiliency program.*

A typical coaching group session began with warm-up games to help the nurses to transition from the intensity of work on their unit to a creative environment (Figure 3.1). One exercise that always had a big impact was I Made a Mistake! (Workbook 3.2), in which participants learn one another's "superhero" names, attempt to fluidly and correctly identify others' names, and when they make a mistake, they bow, proclaim "I made a mistake!," and receive an enthusiastic round of applause.

When we debriefed the activity, the nurses talked about the ways in which they and their units related to mistakes. Some described efforts that had been made to provide a space to talk about and not hide mistakes. Others spoke about a culture of fear—where there was no way one could admit a mistake, big or small. They described "beating themselves up" (and their colleagues) in response to life-threatening mistakes but also for the little stuff—being nasty to a colleague, getting frustrated with a patient, or not doing something perfectly—and the toll this was taking on their resiliency.

Improvisational and Emergent Conversations

Following the warm-up games, we asked the nurses what they wanted to talk about, get help with, or simply share—the topics were entirely up to them. We explained that we would create the conversation together, and do exercises or improvise scenes as the need or opportunity arose. At first, most nurses were surprised by how open-ended this was. They had expected the performance coaching to be more like a class, and found the loose structure very challenging.

We meant it to be. We were asking nurses to be both who they were *and* who they weren't. *Who they were* was professional caregivers—highly skilled and empathetic. *Who they weren't* (yet) was people who felt comfortable not knowing what to do and asking for help. Performing and improvising both the form and the content of the coaching group sessions would develop their skill and comfort with listening, being open, building their relationships, creating trust, and asking for, giving, and accepting help. In this way, it would be part of their becoming more resilient. It was an improv workout for us as facilitators as well! We had to vigorously practice what we were preaching: Yes, And everything the nurses said and did; relate to their (and our) mistakes as gifts; and be willing to "go into the cave" of subject matter that was often unexpected, uncomfortable, or emotionally demanding.

With the freedom (and responsibility) to co-create the coaching groups, nurses began to bring many different issues and challenges they wanted help with, and Maureen and I functioned both as coaches and improvisational/theatrical directors. We asked the nurses to talk about their experiences when they did the "performance homework" we had assigned in their initial workshop. Some had tried new performances and made valuable discoveries, others had tried and "failed," still others had lost their nerve. Whatever the outcome, these were offers, and we directed the nurses to respond like improvisers, to explore and build on (Yes, And) whatever their colleagues shared, in order to create greater intimacy and support, learn more about one another, and not rush to problem-solving. We worked with the group as we would with a performing ensemble, and treated their conversations as an improvised play-in-the-making.

In an early group session, nurses from both the outpatient and inpatient units were talking about their week. Within a few minutes, it became clear that neither unit knew what the other one did, or had even been on the other half's floor. They lamented that they felt isolated and didn't have a feel for the bigger picture of oncology nursing. So, I made what seemed to be the obvious directorial choice (though they initially thought I was nuts). I suggested we do some "research" by taking a tour of their units, a field trip in which they'd perform as tour guides for each other in their departments.

I assigned characters and roles to each of the nurses. The newest nurses on their unit led the tour, with the direction to speak up with confidence and authority. I gave others the role of "the friendly one," whose objective was to say hello to as many patients and coworkers as possible along our way; and the "curiosity captain," whose role was to ask questions and help the group learn more as they toured. On one stop of the tour, the thirty-year veteran nurse who handled all phone inquiries from chemotherapy outpatients showed us the closet-like office where she managed what she calls "central command." The nurses had no idea how many patients called every day or that one person handled all the calls. For the veteran nurse, this was the first time her colleagues had ever acknowledged, let alone expressed appreciation for, her work. When the tour was done, the session ended with the nurses spontaneously giving each other a standing ovation, hugs, and thanks for their hard work.

Now What?

In March of 2009, the official program was nearing its end, and we could clearly see how the process had impacted the nurses' resiliency, development, and growth, both individually and as a community. A core group of nurses had attended the coaching sessions regularly, eagerly bringing in challenges and new performances they wanted to work on. They were now using the language of performance and improvisation—Yes, And, accepting and building on offers, asking for help, "take two" scenes—and developing close relationships across units. These nurses told us they felt stronger, more empowered, and happier at work and in life.

But at the same time, participation in the coaching groups had been relatively low. Only about a third of the nurses who had attended a performance workshop came to one or more group sessions, and only about 15 percent (a core group of about thirty) attended all sessions that were offered.

We met with Dr. Krumm to discuss possible next steps, if any. Should we continue Performance of Resiliency in some way? If we did, what could we do about the low participation? We didn't want to make it mandatory or pressure people to come—the last thing these nurses needed was more pressure! We realized—in keeping with the improvisational nature of the program—that if we wanted to build on the offers coming from the nurses, we needed to ask them what they wanted to do. We started by inviting our core group of actively participating nurses, along with Dr. Krumm, to a meeting to talk about the resiliency program. Did they want to continue? What were their thoughts on the low participation? Did they want to do anything about it, or should we wrap it up at this point and support them in continuing, on their own, with the organic relationships that had evolved? Here are some of the responses:

- "Nurses are constantly in problem-solving and helper mode, and we need a place to stop to see and feel what's happening, to not 'have to have it all together,' to share our various emotions. Doing a different kind of performance was both very challenging and helpful."

- "I feel more aware of the unit's performance, and not just my little scene. I work to be more aware of how I talk to colleagues, and see things from the other person's perspective, so I'm not as speedy and reactive in tense situations."

- "Each unit has a different culture and it was helpful to hear how other units handled things, and really nice to know that you were not the only unit struggling with a particular thing. It helped to build a sense of solidarity, a connection, across all of Oncology Nursing."

- "These performance coaching groups are very important to me. I don't know if I would have made it through my first year without the support I got here."

Stress relief, emotional support, enhanced community, better teamwork—those had been Dr. Krumm's goals from the start, and we were touched and gratified to hear those goals were met. The nurses also told us that the program was stimulating conversation beyond the coaching groups, across the entire department, about what it means to be an oncology nurse, the level of openness that was acceptable, and the kind of emotional support that was needed.

The nurses also shared several reasons for the low participation in coaching groups. For many nurses, they said, it was just too difficult to get off the unit to attend group sessions, and they spoke candidly about the lack of support from some of the managers. "If you're looking for more emotional support but you feel judged by your unit and your manager for that, it's really hard," one commented. They also said there were some who felt that the program was "too weird," that it was for the "touchy-feely types." One nurse was philosophical: "It seems that we nurses are at a crossroads. What does it mean to be a nurse? What can we do with our creativity, our emotions?"

Improvisational Grassroots Democracy

At the end of the meeting we asked the core group: What do you want to do? And how can we help? They said they wanted the program to continue, to see more of their colleagues participate, and to try to get more managerial support going forward—and they wanted us to teach them how to do all of that. They wanted to put a big question on the table for all the nurses to discuss together: Could they create a culture together that would enhance resiliency by helping one another to—in the words of one nurse—"bring their whole self to nursing"? And could they handle their disagreements about this in a way that still grew and developed the community?

This core group of nurses dubbed themselves the Resiliency Leadership Group (RLG) and decided to host a series of voluntary meetings in which they could share with their colleagues the experiences they had had in the program, explore both the development and the disagreements the resiliency program had produced, and invite their colleagues to participate in coaching groups going forward. They helped us to create a video that included interviews with nurses who had participated in and benefitted from the program, as well as with nurses who did not benefit from the program, did not understand it, or were ambivalent about it.[2]

We worked with the RLG to prepare them to facilitate the series of meetings, which we also co-designed. Showtime arrived, and four nurses from the RLG led the first meeting. They welcomed their colleagues, some who had only been to one of the early performance workshops, others who had also attended one or two coaching groups, and a handful who had not participated in the program at all. The RLG facilitators told a few personal stories about how the program had helped them to develop greater resiliency, and then played the video. Next, they opened a discussion, asking colleagues to respond to what they had just seen and heard, and to share whatever experiences they'd had in the program.

One nurse said, "I found the improv games and acting very hard. I'm pretty shy. But I'm here today because [a nurse in the RLG] is just different. She speaks up more, she challenges how we're doing things, she has more confidence and she seems happier. I'd like to grow like that."

A nurse manager said, "Look, I didn't want to attend the first workshop and I don't want to be here right now. I take offense at being told that I need to be more resilient. I think I'm doing a damned good job, and so is my unit."

Others talked about how much fun they'd had in the performance workshop, and laughed as they remembered the improv games and performances. They said they weren't sure why they hadn't come to a coaching group — maybe because it had been hard to get off the floor, or that they simply hadn't made it a priority.

The RLG facilitated twenty meetings in all, and after the final one was done, they were thrilled. Many nurses who had previously chosen not to participate in the coaching groups now expressed a clearer understanding of what the program was and how it could be helpful. We shared this with Dr. Krumm, who decided to continue the program for a few more months.

The RLG took responsibility to increase participation in the performance coaching groups, and personally invited the nurses who expressed interest in attending to come to a session with them. In the four months following the RLG meetings, nine coaching group sessions took place, with seventy-five nurses participating (thirty-five for the first time). The RLG was excited and proud that they had grown in their ability to provide support to other nurses, and had taken the risk to develop and perform in ways that were beyond what they had ever done before. The nurses who either continued or attended for the first time expressed gratitude for being given a chance to come back and talk about their challenges. Most importantly, the RLG members were now clearly taking on the role of leaders, providing help and coaching to their colleagues by modeling their own growth, and by helping others to perform in new ways that helped them grow.

Conclusions

We wrapped up our work with the Hopkins oncology nurses in the fall of 2010. As a kind of coda to the program, the RLG gave a presentation at Performing the World, an international conference of performance activists that takes place in New York City every two years. Their session, attended by over 125 people, was a semi-improvised performance designed to share their growth and development through performing and improvising in new ways. The opening moment will be etched in my mind forever. Fifteen nurses in scrubs struck poses on a bare stage, frozen in place. On a cue that was apparent only to them, they began to move; first walking around and not seeing each other at all, going about their work. Then slowly they began to look up at each other and nod, and smile. They began passing balls and dolls and stethoscopes and charts to one another, giving an occasional hug, or touch. It was both ordinary and extraordinary; a sort of avant-garde dance; and it was beautiful (Figure 3.2).

Ultimately, our impact at Johns Hopkins was modest, but I believe significant. A mix of AI, performative psychology, and the Becoming Principle helped many of the 250 oncology nurses tap into their ability to perform, transform, play, and grow. The program brought out a voice among the nurses that hadn't been audible

FIGURE 3.2 *Performance by Resiliency Leadership Group nurses.*

or organized. The leadership group—and the 75 other nurses who joined in again at the invitation of their colleagues—broke from their scripts and constrained roles and performed as *who they were not yet* by creating an intimate, developing community of support and resiliency.

And so, many of the original objectives of the program were met: there was now more teamwork, collegiality, and community among staff—nurses have been able to initiate and deepen relationships both within their unit and across their departments. They gained improved communication and support skills and developed a shared language for handling the emotional impact of patients dying. There was more consistent acknowledgment and appreciation after successfully managing difficult patient situations.

Years later, I still marvel at all of this. The oncology nurses discovered that they could change the play they perform every day. It was a creative and improvisational bringing together of art and science in how they care for each other as they care for their patients.

Notes

1   Personal communication, email.
2   To view this video, please visit the Performance of a Lifetime website: http:// performanceofalifetime.com/clients.

WORKBOOK

3.1 Upside-Down Introductions

This exercise, for four to twenty-five participants, works well for the start of a workshop, and replaces typical spoken introductions. Participants spend six to ten minutes getting to know one another, and then introduce their partner to the group. The twist is that the "introducer" plays the role of their partner, performing the introduction in the first person. This is an unscripted and improvised introduction that allows participants to gain greater intimacy and connection.

At the end of this exercise, participants will have ...

- learned about each other in a creative and intimate way—if used with a preexisting team, they will mine richer information than previously known and if used with a new group, they will quickly start to know each other better;

- heard and seen how someone else perceives them—what touches or impacts their partner—and as a result learn more about themselves; and

- experienced an immediate, and easy to accomplish, step toward performing a "character."

Running the Exercise

1. Ask the participants to form pairs, ideally with someone they don't know well or at all.

2. Give them three to four minutes for one person in each pair to tell their partners about themselves. On a flip chart or slide, list one or two questions (e.g. a childhood relationship and why it was important, or two things about them that might seem contradictory). These guiding questions can also be thematically linked to the workshop.

3. Switch roles and continue for another three to four minutes.

4. Reconvene the full group after both partners have shared. Each participant introduces themselves to the full group *as if they were their partner*, in the first person. Encourage them to feel free to use their partner's physical gestures, way of speaking, and so on. For the first few participants, reinforce the idea of introducing the other person by *impersonating* them (i.e. using their partner's name, speaking in the first person).

Debrief

- What was it like to introduce yourself as your partner?
- How did it feel to see and hear your partner perform as you? What surprised you?
- How did you experience this differently than the more traditional "going around the circle" introductions?

Connections: This exercise is a POAL original. For other introduction exercises, see Introduce Yourself! (Workbook 2.1) and Name and Motion (Workbook 5.1).

3.2 I Made a Mistake!

This exercise is a good warm-up with some powerful takeaways. Participants learn names while proclaiming ownership of their "mistakes" and receiving resounding support for making a mistake.

At the end of this exercise, participants will have …

- experienced a radically different approach to responding to mistakes—their own and those of others,
- learned many names of their fellow participants,
- experienced the camaraderie created when "mistakes" are turned into opportunities to play, and
- heightened awareness of how their own reaction to making a mistake can impact how others feel.

Running the Exercise

1. Ask participants to form groups of five to ten and then get into a circle with their group.

2. Ask the participants in each group to state their names one at a time. If they know each other, ask them to say a nickname or middle name, or made-up superhero name (e.g. Chair Woman or Desk Dodger).

3. Give participants ninety seconds to memorize all the names in their circle.

4. One person starts by pointing at someone across the circle, saying the chosen name of that person. Demonstrate this. The person pointed at must then point to someone else and state the chosen name of that person, and so on. The pointing and naming should come in a perfect rhythm, one person speaking after another.

5. If the person pointing cannot remember the name of the person they are pointing to, gets it wrong in any way, or if they pause at all, they have made a "mistake." The mistake-maker must then raise their hands in the air and yell, "I made a mistake!" with joy, take a big bow (see Failure Bow in Workbook 4.1), while the rest of the group applauds wildly. Demonstrate this. Then the mistake-maker leaves to join another circle.

6. When a participant moves to a new circle, they introduce themselves by name, "Hi, I'm Desk Dodger," and no one can point to them until three others have been named. If they are pointed at before three have been named, the pointer has made a mistake (see Step 5).

Debrief

- How did you do? Raise your hand if you made a mistake.
- How did you feel about making mistakes?
- How did your feelings about mistakes change as the exercise continued?

- Is this how you typically address mistakes? Why not?
- How did it feel to be applauded for mistakes?
- What impact does celebrating mistakes have on risk-taking, creativity, leadership?
- What makes it hard to embrace or look at mistakes?
- What is a leader's responsibility in handling mistakes?

Connections: The author learned this exercise at an early Applied Improvisation Network conference. Use this in the middle of a full-day or multi-day workshop to energize the participants and reinforce both participant names and improv tenets.

3.3 Performing Curiosity

This exercise introduces a structured approach to accepting and building upon others' offers that the participant may disagree with, or find difficult to support. Attending to one's partner and listening without judgment are integral to developing the skill of Yes, And.

At the end of this exercise, participants will have …

- practiced responding in a connected and appreciative way to otherwise unwelcome offers,
- experienced being responded to with curiosity and not argument, and
- exercised directorial or coaching skills in helping others listen and express openness and curiosity.

Running the Exercise

1. Ask the group to brainstorm topics that would generally be considered controversial and would likely elicit differing points of view. Capture on a flip chart.
2. Ask participants to form triads.

3. Each participant takes a role (then will switch): Questioner, Talker, and Coach.

4. Within each triad:

   a. Ask the Questioners to pick one topic out of the generated list, and share their point of view (briefly) on that topic with their triad (e.g. "I oppose gun control").

   b. Then tell the Talkers that for this exercise, they are assigned to perform as if they have the *opposite* point of view from the Questioner (regardless of their personal opinion).

5. Explain the interaction:

   a. The Talker will make a short statement (no more than three sentences) to the Questioner, expressing the point of view established above.

   b. Then the Questioner will respond by asking a "curious" question, that is, a question that satisfies the following three criteria:

   (i) Open-ended—cannot be answered with Yes or No or any single word. Questions that begin with *what, when, where, why,* or *how* are most effective here.

   (ii) Connected to and builds upon what the Talker said.

   (iii) Not a leading statement disguised as a question.

   c. The Talker will then answer the question, and the Questioner will respond with another question. They will continue in this manner.

   d. The third person is the Coach. The Coach's job is to alert the Questioner anytime their questions do not meet the criteria.

6. Instruct the Coach to stop the Questioner any time their questions do not meet these criteria, and work with the triad to come up with an alternative.

7. After four to five minutes, ask the triads to rotate roles, choose a new topic, and run again. Rotate through three rounds.

Debrief

- How was this experience?
- What was hard about it?
- What words start open-ended questions?
- What triggers us to ask closed or leading questions?
- How do you see the difference between inquiry and curiosity?
- Could there be a downside to curiosity, and if so, what?

Suggestions

It can be helpful to demonstrate a Coach's intervention: For example, if a Talker said, "My grandfather used to take me out to the desert to shoot at cans," and a Questioner responded with, "Do you know how many people die of gun violence every year?" ask the group to consider why this question does not meet the Question criteria. (It is close-ended and not built on what the Talker said. It is also leading and argumentative, conveying the Questioner's point of view, instead of engaging with curiosity and a willingness to learn.) Help the Coaches be stringent in guiding the use of the "Curiosity" criteria.

The verb "perform" in the title "Performing Curiosity" is deliberately chosen, even if it may connote something artificial. This exercise offers a way to move forward when you don't "feel" curious. Whether it's genuinely felt or not, a curious question can generate a productive discussion that would not be possible otherwise, and which is completely authentic.

Connections: This exercise is a POAL original. To facilitate additional responsive listening practice, see chapter 5, "Reaching Out and Making Connections," in Halpern and Lubar (2003) and try the Active Listening exercise in Bowles and Nadon (2013).

4

The Connect Improv Curriculum: Supporting Youth on the Autism Spectrum and Their Educators

Lacy Alana and Jim Ansaldo

Lacy Alana is a licensed clinical social worker and improviser who eclectically combines her clinical expertise with her passion for creative expression. Accordingly, she has created several innovative and experiential therapeutic and arts programs for at-risk youth and youth with autism, and training programs for educators and clinicians who work with youth.

Jim Ansaldo conducts research, supports school change efforts, and facilitates educator professional learning around Applied Improvisation, culturally responsive practice, curriculum design, instructional consultation, and online learning at the Center on Education and Lifelong Learning at the Indiana Institute on Disability and Community at Indiana University. Jim has performed and taught improv comedy and musical improv for twenty-five years.

For several years, Lacy Alana and Jim Ansaldo have used Applied Improvisation (AI) to support youth on the autism spectrum and educators. Lacy has directed Building Connections, a weekly improv class series for autistic youth in Austin, Texas. Lacy and Jim have codirected Camp Yes And, a summer camp offered through Indiana University. The Connect Improv Curriculum (CIC) forms the core of both programs, and evidence suggests that the curriculum has brought significant benefits to youth on the spectrum and educators alike.

Building Connections

Prior to starting Building Connections, Lacy worked at an adolescent boys' neurobehavioral unit in a residential treatment center that often served as a "last resort" for patients who had exhausted other, less restrictive interventions. The patients were complex and often presented with multiple mental health, developmental, and social system challenges. Many were regarded as challenging patients who were oppositional, aggressive, and disconnected from others. Moreover, they felt they had been failed chronically by a broken mental health system and often resisted treatment. After about a year, Lacy began integrating improv exercises and games into more traditional group and family therapy sessions as an experiment, and she found this approach to be highly successful. Youth who previously refused treatment began to demonstrate a willingness to participate and to make progress.

One particular youth, Joshua, comes to mind who exemplifies this transformation.[1] He was 17 and had been in and out of psychiatric hospitals since early adolescence. He was diagnosed with autism, along with a mood disorder and several learning disorders. At home, his behaviors were described as "out of control." He struggled to communicate with others, and he often became aggressive. In treatment, he vacillated between being despondent and highly resistant. He largely refused to participate in individual, family, or group therapy, and was oppositional and guarded in those few times that he did participate. When improv initially was introduced in group therapy, Joshua didn't join in. Over the next few weeks, he slowly increased his involvement: first standing near group members who were engaged in an improv game, then standing in the circle with peers, later gesturing silently and half-heartedly, and ultimately participating fully with body and voice. Improv seemed to unlock something for him. He began to laugh with peers. He wanted to teach improv games to his family during therapy sessions. According to his parents, he became more expressive, engaged, and connected than he had been in years.

Joshua was not alone. As Lacy continued to add improv into the curriculum with autistic youth, she noticed a marked improvement in many of her students' communication and social interaction, flexibility and spontaneity, and ability to integrate sensory information. It was exciting to discover an intervention that consistently showed strong benefits. Improv supported a framework of enhancing and expanding strengths that these youths already possessed, rather than focusing on remediating deficiencies. With this success as a guidepost, Lacy and a group of Austin improvisers discussed the possibility of creating improv classes specifically for autistic youth. In 2013, Building Connections was established at Austin's Hideout Theatre.

Initially, two simultaneous six-week trial classes were offered—one for ages 10–13, and the other for ages 14–18. Class structure, exercises, and intervention models were designed by Lacy with the overall objective of giving youth a safe place to have fun, express themselves, and improve communication and social skills (Figure 4.1). Building Connections met with quick success, and program offerings expanded to full semesters, prompting Lacy to develop the full CIC. The curriculum offers practitioners of AI a framework for understanding autism, evidence around the utility of improv as a key teaching and learning strategy, and full instructions for facilitating a thirteen-week improv class. In 2014, an opportunity to use the CIC outside of Building Connections came when Lacy and Jim met, and the two began to design Camp Yes And.

Camp Yes And

Jim has been a performing improviser since the late 1980s and has facilitated educator professional learning since 2000. In 2014, he attended Lacy's presentation at the Applied Improvisation Network

World Conference. Jim spoke with Lacy about bringing her work to Indiana, but given the distance, a weekly class wouldn't be practical. They treated the distance as an offer and instead developed a summer improv camp for teens on the spectrum.

As the collaboration continued, Jim also saw the need to design a learning component aimed at the learning professionals that work with these teens. Parent feedback from Building Connections often contained phrases like, "I didn't know she could do that!" Jim reasoned that if improv unearths skills in autistic youth that their own parents haven't seen, it is possible that educators chronically underestimate and under-challenge these young people in school. Moreover, research suggests that many educators lack confidence in their ability to support students on the spectrum (Cassady 2011), and professional learning that provides practice, feedback, and coaching supports educators to transfer new skills from the workshop to the classroom (Joyce and Showers 2002). Camp Yes And is designed intentionally to provide educators with this critical support as they learn improv skills and apply them in an authentic context, working directly with autistic teens.

Camp Yes And has been structured as a five-day summer camp for teens on the autism spectrum and educators, including general and special education teachers, speech-language pathologists, social workers, arts educators, and others. During each morning of camp, Lacy and Jim work alone with educators to practice improv techniques and discuss their application to supporting the academic and social success of youth on the spectrum. Each afternoon, the entire group works together to facilitate an improv camp for these teens (Figure 4.2). Each day, roughly two of the CIC modules are used to guide camp activities.

A Framework for Understanding Autism

Both the CIC and this chapter employ varying terms to describe youth in Building Connections and Camp Yes And, including "autistic" and "on the spectrum." The term "neurodivergent" comes closest to describing the CIC's framework for understanding autism. "In its broadest sense, the concept of neurodiversity regards atypical neurological development as a normal human difference."[3] Ultimately, Lacy and Jim regard autism as a set of perceptual and expressive differences, rather than a disability. Building Connections and Camp Yes And seek to use improv as a way to connect with people who move through the world in a unique way—not as a "fix" or "cure" for those who are different. Every student (adult, child, neurotypical, or neurodiverse) brings unique strengths and challenges into the classroom. Experienced educators assess students' prior knowledge and skill, build on their strengths, support their struggles, and help them find success and fun through progressive learning and skill development. There is a saying used in the autism community: "When you have met one person with autism, you have met exactly that: *one* person with autism." This saying underscores the belief that each person, though she may share a diagnostic label with another, is unique and can't be lumped together under one generalized set of characteristics. That said, a common core of significant challenges exists for people on the autism spectrum. Broadly speaking, these challenges include difficulties with communication and social interaction, flexibility and spontaneity, and processing sensory information. Each of these three common challenges is discussed below.

Improv as a Key Teaching and Learning Strategy

The CIC was designed from the theory that improv creates a safe, supportive, and authentic context for strengthening the skills needed to address the challenges listed above. Research affirms the idea that drama and dramatic play are valuable tools for supporting youth on the autism spectrum to improve their communication and social skills (Caplan 2006; D'Amico et al. 2015; Kempe and Tissot 2012; Schuler 2003). In addition, people on the spectrum themselves have recommended improv as a valuable outlet to reduce anxiety and increase spontaneity (Caplan 2006).

The CIC focuses on teaching improv in a highly supportive environment that encourages self-expression, connection with others, and self-confidence. Due to the fundamental emphasis in improv on collaboration with others, CIC exercises and games lend themselves well to providing autistic youth with experiential practice

FIGURE 4.1 *Participants in the Building Connections program.*

and do not need significant adaptation for this population. Rather, the focus on becoming successful improvisers is an authentic and nonthreatening way to redirect challenging behavior and social miscues that also occur "in real life." Additionally, improv offers an excellent framework for educators to meet students where they are, connect with them, and support their growth. If anything, the biggest shift needed for improvisation to succeed with youth on the spectrum rests with educators, who often come to realize that they hold the key to creating the optimal learning conditions that promote autistic students' success or failure.

Optimal Learning Conditions

The conditions for optimal learning occur when educational systems provide learners with both appropriate challenge and frequent, ongoing opportunities for success (D'Amico et al. 2015). In other words, effective educators apply the "Goldilocks Principle" by facilitating learning activities that are "not too easy and not too difficult." This practice usually calls for educators to increase the challenge of a learning task incrementally. Logically, then, there

FIGURE 4.2 *Participants in the Camp Yes And program.*

is a risk of failure in any authentic learning task, and educators' approach to risk management is critical in supporting student engagement, motivation, and learning.

Improv games like Whoosh Bang Pow (Workbook 4.1) support learners to push their limits, and failure actually is a sign that the game is being played correctly. Pairing the game with the Failure Bow (Workbook 4.1) creates group safety and support by encouraging the celebration of risk-taking and letting go of mistakes and reframing them as opportunities. Early introduction of these games provides learners (and teachers!) with a tool to defuse stress and anxiety throughout the entire class period. In both Building Connections and Camp Yes And, it's not unusual to see youth and adults taking failure bows to acknowledge anything from messing up a game to spilling popcorn at snack time. These techniques are particularly important for supporting youth on the spectrum, who often experience significant anxiety around "getting it right." In fact, difficulty with communication and social interaction may be related to the desire to avoid failure and frustration as much as anything else.

Strengthening Communication and Social Skills

Autistic people often struggle with interpreting and responding to the unwritten rules of communication and social interaction in societies and cultures. Roy, for example, a teen from Camp Yes And, had trouble moderating his volume, stood more closely to others than was comfortable, and spoke excessively on topics of interest to him without seeming to notice whether his conversation partners were engaged in the discussion. Following the guidelines and strategies in the CIC, adults at camp valued and celebrated his enthusiasm, eagerness to connect, and bold communication strategies—all of which are great strengths in improv. At the same time, they also side-coached him and pointed out when these qualities impeded his capacity to co-create with others on stage and compromised his ability to fully connect and communicate with others outside of improv.

As mentioned earlier, rather than having to address social communication directly, a focus on "doing good improv" has impact on behaviors on stage and off. The CIC provides students with numerous opportunities to practice understanding and responding to social cues through improv games and exercises. In Roy's case, games that focused on "offers" being made by fellow players were particularly helpful. The Cycle of Deep Yes, And (Workbook 4.2) helped him to see how accepting and supporting others' ideas—with others returning the favor—resulted in stronger and more fun improv. The cycle also delivers a concrete road map for successful communication and social interaction offstage. Additional games offered practice around initiating social interaction in a variety of contexts and a framework for understanding how and why to stay on topic. This focus was particularly helpful for Roy. After the camp's final showcase, his parent remarked, "I could tell from the showcase that he had learned to control his conversation and let others speak."

Increasing Flexibility and Spontaneity

Connected to the communication skill of "staying on topic" is the reality that many neurodivergent youth have a limited range of specialized interests, are dependent on routines, and struggle responding to unfamiliar situations. Improv creates the opportunity to Yes, And youth interests and rewards flexibility and spontaneity. Linda, another teen in Camp Yes And, was very reserved and slow to engage with the group. Despite encouragement, she chose to initially watch rather than participate. Through the camp application form, instructors knew that hippos were her main interest, so they set up a scene at a zoo near a hippo tank. Linda was the first to volunteer to be in the scene. Instructors said "yes" to her interest to engage her in participating with the group.

The "and" happened as instructors facilitated games and exercises that purposefully brought new ideas and topics into the mix. For example, New Choice (Workbook 4.3) challenges players to remake verbal and physical offers in a variety of ways. Players are encouraged to combine new ideas with preferred interests, ultimately resulting in stronger improv and increased areas of interest. The phrase "new choice" also becomes helpful code throughout classes and camps. When problem behavior occurs, instructors often say "new choice" to signal the need for redirection. Miguel, also in Camp Yes And, demonstrated an early habit for playing characters that used alcohol or drugs. After a couple of those scenes, Lacy said, "New choice! We know you can play that kind of character, but you know about lots of other things. Let's see something new."

The focus is on doing good improv, not a personal criticism. Many youth on the spectrum are encouraged to explore diverse interests, but the redirection often comes with a message of irritation from those who may be tired of hearing about a particular topic. New Choice is a perfect example of a way that instructors can help students understand that improv requires the exploration of a variety of interests in order to co-create with other players and utilize audience suggestions effectively. Over time, the words "new choice" may become sufficient to prompt students to self-redirect. As needed, instructors may offer more specific redirection or explanation within the improv, as above, or in private conversation after a game has concluded. In either case, a playful association with the game of New Choice seems to remove undue stress from behavioral redirection.

Integrating Sensory Information

The challenges of processing sensory information for people on the autism spectrum take different forms. Some individuals may be extremely sensitive to sensory input, such as bright light or loud noise. Others may be notably insensitive and speak in an overly loud voice. Also, sensory seeking behaviors, such as humming or waving arms, may become more prevalent in stressful environments, and an individual may have limited awareness of their body movements, and may encroach on others' personal space. Roy, described earlier, fell into this last category. Games that focused on "offers" were helpful in illuminating the "hidden rules" of social interaction. Viola Spolin's (1963) basic Mirror exercises and the traditional game "Who Started the Motion" supported Roy's development of greater body awareness.

Another helpful strategy employed in Building Connections and Camp Yes And is to identify "who has the focus" in any given moment. When someone is speaking, or is on stage playing a game, adult educators remind the group of who has the focus: "Joe has the focus now, because he has asked us to listen and everyone is looking at him. Let's watch him to see what offers he makes." This strategy supports students in identifying extraneous sensory input and filtering it out.

To support individuals who are sensitive to sensory input, overhead lighting is kept relatively low. In addition, classrooms always have a designated "chill out" area, where students may take a break from activities and still be able to see what's happening. Often, students can be brought back into participation by asking them to provide suggestions for, or input about the game being played on stage.

Conclusion and Future Directions

The CIC is a valuable tool to support people on the spectrum to strengthen communication and social skills, increase flexibility and spontaneity, and integrate sensory information. It also equips educators with practical and flexible tools that can be implemented in a variety of educational settings to support the development of critical skills for teens.

While adolescence is a particularly critical time for intervention, the curriculum provides an instructional foundation relevant to any age population. Building Connections has expanded to serve multiple age groups (9–13, 13–18, and 18+), and Camp Yes And is building the capacity for similar expansion. In addition, tools are being developed to measure the impact of the CIC, and a train-the-trainer model is being created to support those interested in implementing the CIC and replicating the Camp Yes And model.

Teen registration for Camp Yes And has filled within twenty-four hours each year, and many teens are left on the waiting list. In the coming years, it will be critical to expand capacity and bring this work to more people and licensing the curriculum for use in a variety of settings.

The power of the work is expressed best in the words of participants. For teens on the spectrum, improv is empowering: "This camp's just opened me up like an eggshell—just cracking open my true self." For educators, it is freeing: "It has changed me as an educator because it has expanded my sense of not only what I should be bringing to the table, but it also has expanded my inner sense of myself ... I felt like I rediscovered my sense of play. And I realize now that's an element that's been missing." For Lacy and Jim, it is a joy, a privilege, and a calling.

Note

1   All names have been made up.

WORKBOOK

4.1 Whoosh Bang Pow and Failure Bow

This is a full group activity, which invites and encourages risk-taking and letting go of mistakes.

At the end of this exercise, participants will have …

- learned soft focus, listening, and staying in the moment;
- experienced positive outcomes of "failure": a mistake can be made without shame or any need to hide it;
- managed risks by making small mistakes in a supportive environment; and
- learned a tool to defuse stress and anxiety.

Running the Exercise

1. Ask participants to stand in a circle.
2. Demonstrate "passing Whoosh" by facing the person to your right, saying "Whoosh," and moving your hands in a way that indicates energy passing to them. Ask that person to pass it to their neighbor and repeat until the Whoosh has made it completely around the circle. Then "pass" the Whoosh to the left in the same way.
3. Once the group seems comfortable, introduce Bang. Ask someone on one side of you to pass a Whoosh to you. Once they do this, cross your arms in an "X" across your chest, and say "Bang." Explain to the group that this means that the Whoosh changes directions. The person who had attempted to pass you the Whoosh then turns back around and passes the Whoosh in the opposite direction.
4. Inevitably, the Whoosh will get stuck, as some participants will Bang on either side of another participant. Use this as a

natural point to introduce Pow. Instruct students that whoever "has the Whoosh" can also choose to pass the energy to someone *across* the circle by making eye contact with that person, clapping their hands together and then immediately pointing at the person while saying "Pow." Instruct the person receiving the Pow that they can then choose to Whoosh in either direction.

5. Mid-exercise Debrief

   a. Once the group has played for a bit, stop and discuss. Is the group playing with risk? Or are they going slowly to ensure they don't make mistakes? How can we increase the fun in this game? (Increase speed, commitment, and willingness to make mistakes.)

   b. Engage the group in a conversation about the benefits of mistakes. What are the good things about making mistakes? (We learn from them, we can find unexpected gifts, etc.)

   c. Teach the group the Failure Bow (see Workbook 3.2). Let them know that at any time, anyone can put their hands in the air, take a bow, and say, "I failed!" When they bow, the entire group will celebrate wildly for them. Demonstrate this, giving everyone an opportunity to practice in pairs or in the group. Ask the group to state a real-life "failure" (as big or as small as they'd like: I failed a quiz, I spilled milk, I forgot to put on deodorant). The group celebrates each failure bow.

6. Play Whoosh Bang Pow again, inviting them to take Failure Bows anytime they feel they've made a mistake.

Debrief

- How did willingness to make mistakes change the game?
- How did celebrating your own mistakes (either in the game or a real-life mistake) make you feel?

- How did it feel to witness your colleagues celebrating their failure?
- Anything from this that resonates out in the world for you?

Suggestions

- If a participant excessively uses Bang, this may signal that the participant likes to "block" their peers.
- At times, if the Bangs are so excessive that it slows the exercise down significantly, it may be necessary to create a "Whoosh must make it around circle before Banging it" rule.
- Celebrating failure can be a difficult concept for some to grasp—especially for those who struggle with rigidity. However, most participants are thrilled to be celebrated in their mistakes, and teaching the Failure Bow provides a framework for diffusing worries about making a mistake.
- If a participant won't identify a real-life mistake to use, just ask: "Is it okay if we just celebrate and applaud *you*?"
- "Failure" can feel like a loaded word. However, saying "I failed!" with enthusiasm creates an opportunity for reframing: "I failed and made a mistake, *and* I learned from it, *and* I am still okay and awesome!"
- Review how making a mistake—even to the point of utterly failing—doesn't make us failures. Alternatively, a "lighter" word, such as "oops" or "uh-oh," may be used. It is impactful, however, to give participants an opportunity to reclaim the powerful and loaded language of "failure."

Connections: Whoosh Bang Pow is another version of Zip Zap Zop and Zip Zap Boing. All versions of this exercise can teach students the concepts of accepting and building on offers (Yes, And), redirecting offers (Yes, But), and blocking offers (No). For example, a "Whoosh" is a Yes, And because it accepts the offer and keeps the energy moving quickly in the same direction; whereas a "Pow" accepts then redirects the offer across the circle, which tends to slow the momentum a bit. Finally, a "Bang" is a block because it does not accept the "Whoosh" at all.

4.2 The Cycle of Deep Yes, And!

This exercise uses pairs to demonstrate the power of Yes, And in co-creating scenes.

At the end of this exercise, participants will have ...

- experienced how to Yes, And in scene work;
- understood how and why Yes, And is such a powerful concept; and
- understood the larger framework of Yes, And so it may be internalized and used in scene work and in life.

Running the Exercise

1. Ask participants to sit as an audience, except two who are told to plan a party by making offers that provide details about the party (e.g. "We should have balloons at the party"). Label them Player A and Player B.
2. **Round One:** Player B is told secretly to respond by beginning every sentence with "No, we should ..."
3. For each of the following four rounds assign two new players. Continue to secretly give Player B their prompts.
   a. **Round Two:** Player B starts every sentence with "Yes, or ..."
   b. **Round Three:** Player B starts every sentence with "Yes, but ..."
   c. **Round Four:** Player B starts every sentence with "Yes, and ..."
   d. **Round Five:** Player B starts every sentence with just "Yes!"

Debrief 1

- Which party do you want to attend? Why?
- What did you notice about each of the parties? Which parties were planned? Generally, participants will make the

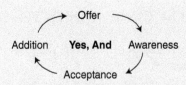

FIGURE 4.3 *Cycle of Deep Yes, And.*

following assessments, but they sometimes require structured support as this exercise is processed:

- **No, We Should** Party: No plans are made, ends in an
  argument/disagreement
- **Yes, Or** Party: No plans are made. Many options generated, but no forward movement
- **Yes, But** Party: Ends in argument, very much like "No,
  we should ..."
- **Yes, And** Party: Results in an actual plan (even if wacky),
  and ideas are connected. (Ask: Why did this party actually get planned? How did that happen?)
- **Yes!** Party: Sometimes results in a plan, but Player A
  does all the work and receives no support. Sometimes
  goes nowhere because Player A feels extensive pressure to create everything independently and runs out of
  steam. (Ask: Even though we are saying "Yes!" here, why
  is this not enough? Even though we are not saying "No,"
  why is this unhelpful?)
- How does this relate to improv?
  - We are making things up together. We need to be able to
    build on each other's ideas, say "yes" to each other, and
    make each other look good. Because we are creating things
    together on the spot, we need to be able to join our ideas
    with other people's ideas to make something together.

Debrief 2

Now that the group understands the basics of Yes, And, explore
what it means to truly Yes, And each other. Draw the Cycle of
Deep Yes, And on a board (Figure 4.3). Start first with Yes, And

then Offer, Awareness, Acceptance, and Addition, in order. After each new word, draw the connecting arrow(s) and describe in the following ways:

- Offer: An offer in improvisation is anything a player says or does (see Appendix A).

- Awareness: The first step of accepting an offer is having awareness that an offer has been made. If we aren't paying attention, we will miss all offers.

- Acceptance: The next step in Yes, And-ing is to accept the offer. This doesn't mean that you *always* must say "yes" to every offer. But, you must accept *the reality* offered by the other player. For example, note the differences between Player A saying, "Here is a glass of milk," and Player B saying, "No, thank you, I'd prefer coffee today," vs. "That isn't milk." The second response doesn't accept the spirit of Player A's offer and creates difficulty in moving forward with the scene.

- Addition: The next phase of Yes, And-ing is to add on to the offer the other person made. In the scenario above, this could be saying, "Ah, thank you, I love milk," or "No, thank you. No milk today, Jonathan."

Discuss how each of these steps is important. What happens if we skip being aware? What happens in life sometimes in the "space" between becoming aware and acceptance? What happens if we are aware of someone else's offer/idea, but we negate it with our own offer/idea? What is the feeling when an offer/idea is not accepted (blocked)? How does the story/situation change and build when an offer is built upon?

Connections: This exercise is rooted in Keith Johnstone's offer/ block/accept exercises found in both *Impro* (1979) and *Impro for Storytellers* (1999).

4.3 New Choice

This exercise rewards flexibility and spontaneity by challenging players to remake verbal and physical offers in a variety of ways.

At the end of this exercise, participants will have ...

- developed more flexibility, spontaneity, and risk-taking;
- less attachment to their own predetermined story lines and agendas; and
- greater openness to experiencing new outcomes and turns in the road.

Running the Exercise

1. Ask two participants to start a scene. At any point, you can ring a bell and say, "New choice!" indicating the player should "take back" what they just said or did and make a new offer. Continue to call for new choices until you are satisfied. When you stop ringing the bell, the scene continues as though the most recent offer were the only one made. For example:

    a. Player A: Hello grandma! (Ding! "New choice!")

    b. Player A: 'Sup grandma! (Ding! "New choice!")

    c. Player A: Hi Grandma, it is me, your most favorite grandchild. I am here to pet your canary. (No ding.)

    d. Player B: Well, great to see you. Here is the bird.

2. Remember, physical offers can also be "dinged."

Debrief

- What did it feel like to keep getting interrupted by the "ding"?
- What was your reaction when you had to "give up" your first offer? How did that change if you got "dinged" on your second and third offers as well?

- What did you observe in your partner when they got "dinged?"
- How was it easy/hard to come up with new choices?

Suggestions

This exercise can be challenging for some. If participants get stuck, side-coach with "New emotion!" or "New gesture!" or "New topic!" or offer another adjustment (verbal or physical) you would like participants to explore.

The group may also stand in a circle and play New Choice together. For example, everyone is told, "Greet your mom." When you say, "New choice!" everyone greets again in a different way.

Connections: Also called Quick Change on the TV show *Whose Line Is It Anyway?* and Ding Game (Fotis and O'Hara 2016).

5

Creating a Spontaneous Village: Community from Play

Brad Fortier

Brad Fortier has been studying, teaching, performing, directing, and writing about improvised theatre for over twenty years. He currently works as the training and development coordinator for the Oregon Health Authority's Office of Equity and Inclusion applying interactive and experiential methods from his improv toolkit. Brad is the author of *Long-Form Improvisation: Collaboration, Comedy, and Communion* (2010) and *A Culture of Play: Essays on the Origins, Applications, and Effects of Improvised Theatre* (2013).

In 2014, tens of thousands of unaccompanied children crossed the Mexican border into the United States fleeing danger from violence and exploitation by the military and drug cartels in countries like Honduras, El Salvador, and Guatemala creating a shelter crisis (Chishti and Hipsman 2014).

Most of the shelters receiving these children have a high churn rate, or turnover, in their populations. The average stay in the shelter described here was three weeks. That's about how long it takes to be processed by the U.S. Citizenship and Immigration Services (USCIS), and the justice system attached to that. In that time, the children are either deported back to their origin, placed in more long-term housing and school while their trial awaits, or connected to family who are already living in the United States. Roughly half of the time, the children are sent back to their country of origin and back into the danger they had fled.

Currently, there are over sixty million refugees on the planet. When splintered and itinerant people who have no relation to one another end up together for a few weeks of time at a camp or facility, the dearth of familiarity and trust has a heavy cost on a person's ability to be mentally and physically healthy. The uncertainty and anonymity of refugee life can have the effect of creating a competitive atmosphere in situations with limited resources. This can lead to a sense of powerlessness and despair that can be toxic to creating any sense of community or safety.

I met Dr. T (see Chapter 6) at the 2012 Applied Improvisation Network conference, held that year in San Francisco. We became fast friends and collaborators. At the time, she was part of the Field Innovation Team (FIT), a nongovernmental organization that emerged from a project at the Federal Emergency Management Agency. FIT had been invited to design and pilot a multifaceted education and recreation plan for the international school of St. PJ's children's home, a best-practices facility in San Antonio, Texas.[1] They were seeking arts-based education solutions to help manage this crisis. FIT was looking to include drawing, science, design, and theatre in the plan. Because of my background in pedagogy, improv, and anthropology, I offered to draft an Applied Improvisation (AI) curriculum that would meet FIT's theatre requirements and address the circumstances of the children who were sheltered at St. PJ's. Dr. T told me to go for it.

I proposed a multiphase strategy for organizing a theatre games-based curriculum that concentrates on rapidly satisfying the four key needs of refugees, as identified in seminal anthropology literature: familiarity, trust, routine, and community (Peteet 1995; Voutira and Harrel-Bond 1995; Sommers 2001; Lubkemann 2002). Clarifying those areas of concern helped me identify which activities and games would be most effective, as well as when in the process to deliver them. These needs tend to occur in sequence. One need must be established in order to build on and achieve the next.

I created a structure for the forty-minute lesson that was simple and flexible, with specific games chosen depending on the age/demographics of the participants and whether, or not, they were participating for the first time or over repeated sessions. The following is the basic structure for a lesson plan:

1. Begin with a name game.
2. Move to a game that would encourage the sharing of sociometric information (personal likes and similarities mainly).
3. Play a fun energetic game that would let participants practice a key skill.
4. End with a slightly more complex game that draws on elements of previous games.

The reasons for this lesson structure center on the assumptions of refugees' challenges: (1) They are strangers to one another for the most part, and, as mentioned earlier, there is a great deal of turnover in the population, meaning people arriving and departing the shelter regularly. Hence, doing a name game regularly is fun and removes any awkwardness associated with learning new names. (2) Learning about people's preferences begins to create a sense of mutuality and familiarity (more of an "us" than a "you-and-me"). This has the potential for heading off tension and assumptions, ideally creating connection among the participants who share interests. One and two have also allowed the group to sample success working together. (3) Play and laughter move cognition away from an amygdala-centered place (fight or flight) to the neocortex, where higher social functions are processed (Mithen 1996). They also create subtle social grouping due to the shared artifacts of humor that are discovered during play (Fine and DeSoucey 2005). If we want people to be creative and in a solutions-focused mind-set, these are essential ingredients for making that happen.

On August 18, 2014, I arrived in San Antonio with the other FIT members to pilot our drawing, science, design, and theatre programs. My goal was twofold, first to see how well the curriculum worked to address the challenges listed above, and second to enable the recreation staff of St. PJ's to lead the program themselves. During our thirteen days in San Antonio, we interacted mainly with St. PJ's recreation staff and, occasionally, the teaching staff of the shelter.

We were informed prior to our arrival that the children would be expected to attend all four programs in rotation and that they would be divided up by gender and age group. After twenty-two years of instruction experience, my expectations were as follows:

- Having worked in schools and businesses with non-self-selectors (those who are required to attend versus those who choose to enroll in an improv program), I know that non-self-selectors fall somewhere between 50–50 percent and 70–30 percent in terms of interest and willingness to participate, with 70 percent in the later proportion being "interested and participating."

- Girls tend to be socialized to be more supportive and collaborative.

- Boys tend to be socialized to be more bold and independent.

- Girls 5–12 would be shy and warm up quickly once they became competent in the first activity (60 percent participate fully, 40 percent participate reluctantly).

- Boys 5–12 would be the boldest and take more time for instruction because they may get tangential with elements of the games (70–80 percent participate fully, 20–30 percent participate reluctantly or not at all).

- Girls 13–17 would be cautious and temper their enjoyment based on how an alpha or beta of the group responded (60 percent participate fully, 40 percent participate reluctantly or not at all).

- Boys 13–17 would be skeptical but curious because "men" do not do things related to the theatre or looking foolish and would also likely look to an alpha or beta for approval (50 percent participate fully, 50 percent participate reluctantly or not at all).

The Kids

Over the course of two weeks, we did a total of twelve, forty-minute sessions, with sixteen kids in each session, using a variety of lesson plans. In addition to the improv games, occasional coaching notes were thrown in to help "tune up" the interaction (make or maintain eye-contact, listen, be helpful, make your partner look good, etc.). Side-coaching is a key component in improv and can be used to lessen an individual's social inhibitions by requesting a change to more connective and supportive behaviors. It is also a strategy for reducing anxiety because it not only focuses an individual's attention on the immediate environment but shows the facilitator working supportively alongside players as they solve problems together.[2] For the theatre curriculum, coaching and explanation had to be minimal and concise because the recreation staff translated our instructions and side-coaching from English into Spanish, the common language spoken by 90 percent of the children coming through the shelter.[3]

My assumptions and expectations regarding the character composition of each group were largely validated. This was not necessarily a good thing. The recreation director, who everyone called Miss Jewel, was not a fan of kids not wanting to participate in activities or of my practice of letting those who felt nervous simply observe for a while. The reason I allow non-self-selectors to observe is because they rarely stay out of the activity for long. When they begin to see other participants having fun and after they gain a deeper understanding of how to play, they tend to become curious. Everyone wants to be a part of something fun. Learning new things is always fraught with some level of stress or discomfort, but once a few people are joyfully engaging in an activity, reticent observers will likely want to participate in the action. These participants also tend to be learners who are more comfortable seeing something done first before taking the risk.

This pattern of reticence and observation before participation may also relate to the psychological concept of *emotional contagion*, meaning that people can absorb the mood of the company they are with. A person sees joy in another person, and they may begin to feel that vicariously, as a result. This did happen to some degree in the teen boy group, which was the most resistant and uncertain that day. One of the older boys, Julio,[4] was unwilling to look foolish while playing I Am a Tree (Workbook 7.2), a game that requires one to take fanciful poses. He took to the sidelines along with a couple of others. Within two rounds of watching others playing, Julio's interest grew, and he began making suggestions. I have seen this time and again from folks who feel vulnerable and uncomfortable because of how exposed an activity initially makes them feel. His comments and suggestions from the periphery prompted one of his cohort to challenge him to get in the game if he was so interested. By the final two rounds, Julio came into the circle to play as intently as the others. To me, that was a great sign that the tools were working as planned.

After we worked with a group of older girls the same day, one staff person, Mr. Elizondo, confided in us that he was surprised by how the games had influenced the power dynamic among the girls in one session. When Juana, the alpha girl, began complaining and trying to command attention, other girls, including her closest friends, asked her to stop it and join in the fun. She did, and according to later accounts, it widened the circle of friends among the girls.

My sense is that individuals who are more comfortable in forums of unranked, open, equitable communication are likely to be attracted to, or validated by, improvisation games. These are the pioneers of a community who tend to explore new places making them safe for their more reticent community members. The fact that other children gave Julio and Juana the directive to join was also very promising in terms of seeing group self-regulation emerging, indicating that community was being built and that this approach was succeeding.

The FIT Team

After running the curriculum a few times, Miss Jewel was beginning to see its value but was quite concerned that her recreation staff would not be able to replicate it, because none of them had any improv training. She tasked us with creating three different lessons that other FIT volunteers would then run without any supervision or input. The stakes were high here—if the FIT volunteers could lead the program well, she would let us teach it to her staff. If Miss Jewel was not convinced, the curriculum would most likely get dropped.

I worked with the FIT volunteers for only two hours before they led the program themselves. Luckily, I had been leading morning improv workouts with them since our arrival (I offered and they gladly accepted), and they had been able to observe some of the earlier sessions with the kids.

Not being allowed to facilitate or interrupt in any way was initially quite uncomfortable, but gave me the freedom to float from space to space to see how the lessons were progressing. As I passed from room to room to patio, the looks on children's faces changed from confusion to curiosity to enjoyment. Some of the adult staff of the shelter began to join in the games and laugh with the children.

There was one instance where one of the younger boys, Armando, asked if a game could be changed a bit to see what would happen. The FIT volunteer looked my way and said, "He wants to change the game," and I replied, "Try it!" The change was made, and it immediately led to peals of laughter from the kids and adults. In my own experience, it can be a good thing to allow folks the ability to explore and change things. It creates a sense of agency and owner-ship of the experience, which heightens the bonding experience in both directions. It was quite moving to see this idea grow beyond myself.

I still had not settled on a name for my curriculum. Then, on one of the van rides from the hotel to the shelter, the other FIT members had a lively discussion about project names and I suggested calling mine "Spontaneous Village." People liked it, and it stuck.

St. PJ's Staff

We had passed the second test. Miss Jewel, now less skeptical, wanted confirmation that her recreation staff could continue with the work and lessons that the FIT team had created in cooperation with St. PJs. One thing that I've learned from working in the AI field is that there is always tension between how much time is required for a program to have lasting impact and how much time a client or organization is willing to give. We were allowed only one hour for training her staff. The staff themselves were extremely helpful and vested in doing the best for the kids, but watching the last program day made me doubt if the entire curriculum would be able to con-tinue to this degree.

The After-Action

Before we left San Antonio, Miss Jewel met with the FIT team along with several teachers and recreation staff. About the improv sessions, Miss Jewel confided:

> When the types of improv exercises were demonstrated, I was definitely skeptical and outright said I didn't think this would work with our teens. I became even more skeptical when the first time the improv team met with groups of kids in a rotation schedule, I watched as kids sat out or refused to participate. In my line of work, that is not a good sign. But surprisingly, as the week went on, I began to see the improv games showing up in random places throughout the day. It kind of became the inside jokes between the teens in the everyday chatter. It even helped bridge connections between staff and kids. I could go on and on, but I will say for sure that improv does bring and connect people together, even teenagers! It ended up being the underdog program.[5]

During that same meeting, Rosalba, one of the staff members who oversaw dorm life for the teen girls, shared a story. One evening, as she entered the dorms to get the girls to bed, she noticed a couple of girls snapping their fingers at each other, specifically Spanish-speaking girls snapping at a Quechua-speaking girl. Rosalba, who had not seen them play Snap Pass (Workbook 6.2), interpreted this as antagonism and teasing and intervened saying that snapping like that was not nice. She was surprised at what happened next. The girls corrected her by showing her the game that they had learned that day. They were including the Quechua-speaking girl into their game by snapping at her. The girls then continued playing, and Rosalba joined in briefly before getting them to bed. Rosalba said she was touched by the fact that these girls were finding another way to connect that went beyond language. This was an incredible sign of success.

Staff members also shared comments with me about how reliable and effective playing games together was for quickly building rapport with the kids. More effective, in fact, than any approach they had previously tried. Simply incorporating name games and snapping and clapping games had changed the feeling and tone of their work for the better.

When it came time for some critique, my suspicions were confirmed about the recreation and housing staff feeling too uncertain about running a full lesson of improv in our absence. The name games and sociometric games were likely to stay in circulation, though. They were the simplest to remember and run, and they were something that took about five minutes and could bookend the days or help get focus back. Considering how reticent the recreation staff and Miss Jewel had felt a week prior, this seemed like a significant victory.

There were also the more personal thank you messages that came directly from students. Julio, the boy who was resistant at the start, was able to participate several times in Spontaneous Village, either with me or one of the other FIT volunteers. During the last session, he asked to sit out again, politely, after asking me what colors I liked. I had picked up enough Spanish to understand his question and answer him. He went to the side and was working on weaving

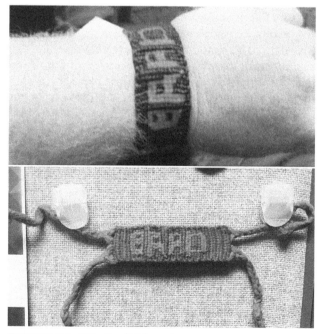

FIGURE 5.1 *"Mr. Brad's"* bracelet.

something pretty intently. After the last session of the day let out, Julio ran back up to me calling out "Mr. Brad!" He held up a green bracelet with the letters B-R-A-D woven into it in red (Figure 5.1). He clapped me on the back. We shook hands smiling at each other, and he ran off to catch up to his dorm group. I stood there with the bracelet across my palm and a knot in my throat.

People who play together are always more likely to stay together. This I believe. This I have seen. This I know.

Conclusion

From informal interviews with staff and teachers, there was a fair amount of anecdotal evidence for community emerging much quicker as a result of introducing some of the tools of improvised theatre. These outcomes had validated something that I had long considered with applied work. If you want to change someone's (or an organization's) perspective or understanding, a singular workshop can be a jolt. If you want to change habits, transform culture, or build community, one needs to embrace a more regular practice (of improvisation, meditation, yoga, or even basketball).

It is unfortunate that the public's perception of improvised theatre is one of trite theatre games that are best played by professional comedians or the office clown. AI has the capacity to improve many human-centered processes and projects that require communication, collaboration, and creativity. Additionally, it has the capacity to enhance the mental and emotional health of individuals and communities. It is an effective approach for generating positive growth in human groups. Improvisation is our natural state as beings, and direct, in-person, social connection makes us more whole. With the challenges we face as a species, strengthening our collaborative skills is extremely prudent.

Notes

1   Best Practices Facilities are usually identified that way because the level of care they offer goes well beyond the minimum of shelter and food and can include education, recreation, counseling, and spiritual life. These were all part of the St. PJ's approach while the children awaited trial.

2 See also Spolin's (1963) tips on side-coaching.
3 There were several Mayan languages from Guatemala and Honduras that made up the other 10 percent of languages spoken.
4 All participant names are made up.
5 From private Facebook message to author on January 10, 2016.

WORKBOOK

5.1 Name and Motion

This is a full group exercise that aids the memorization of names by coupling them with a unique physical motion.

At the end of this exercise, participants will have ...

- taken a risk in moving their body in a unique way in front of the group;
- applied the concept of Yes, And by listening, accepting, and repeating the names and accompanying motions of the other participants; and
- increased their connection to others in the circle.

Running the Exercise

1. Ask participants to stand in a circle.
2. One at a time, each participant says their name and adds a movement to go with it (e.g. stretching their arms out wide).
3. In response, the entire group repeats the name and movement. Do this until everyone in the circle has a unique motion to accompany their name.
4. Quickly repeat steps two and three (but using the same names and motions) to help with memorization.
5. Now play the game in "call and response" form: You do your own name/gesture, then someone else's name/gesture. It is now *that* person's turn to do their own name/gesture, then another participant's, and so on. Continue until each participant's name/gesture has been repeated at least twice.

Debrief

- Which motions were fun to do? What about this activity challenged you?
- Ask which names need to be practiced more, providing open exchange time for people to make corrections on their own terms.

Suggestions

- Encourage participants to notice and repeat motions of another body. This helps them become present, free from individual worry, and engaged with others.
- Be encouraging by affirming participant's choices (Great! Wow! Flexible!), especially those who look puzzled or skeptical of their choices at the beginning.
- As participants gain competence, up the challenge by picking up the pace: "We're getting good. Let's speed it up!"
- For a bigger challenge, shift to using just the motions and omit the names.

Connections: This exercise is adapted from various exercises that ask students to connect with others through vocal (sound) and physical expression (motion). For further ideas, especially for groups that need additional work on connecting with and really seeing others, we recommend Spolin's (1963) "Orientation" games, particularly Who Started the Motion and her basic Mirror Exercise.

5.2 Night Watch

This is a full group exercise that requires a response to the actions of a night watchperson. Everyone except for this person is a "living statue" and together they pose or freeze into tableaux, without getting caught moving by the watchperson. The exercise helps participants to notice that even small gestures can have a big impact on how we connect.

At the end of this exercise, participants will have ...

- rapidly developed connection with the group;
- experienced the rhythm between individual movement and group movement;
- used eye contact and body language rather than spoken word to communicate intention; and
- utilized collaboration to surmount tension and challenges.

Running the Exercise

1. Explain that participants will pretend to be single-person or group statues in a museum at night.
2. Ask a participant to volunteer as the first watchperson.
3. The watchperson will walk around slowly and pause occasionally like a guard. All others will be statues in the museum, moving quickly to make new scenes whenever the watchperson is not looking.
4. The statues must freeze before the watchperson catches them moving.
5. If the watchperson spots someone moving, they may choose to continue in their job, or ask the person caught moving to be the new watchperson. If the new person accepts the job, the first watchperson now joins the group as statues. And the exercise continues.

Debrief

- How did the way you play the game change over time?
- How did you connect with others to make pictures without speaking?
- If you were the watchperson, how did it feel?
- These questions help participants notice their strategies in connecting and communication, as well as allow them to hear others' strategies.

Suggestions

- Remind participants to work collaboratively in making the tableaux.
- Encourage participants to take risks.
- Encourage the watchperson to occasionally let people continue being statues even if they have been seen moving. Participants can often turn this into a game of "I got you!" which could be fun for those who feel secure in life but if someone has had trauma, a succession of these could be very triggering. This also deepens the exercise allowing the group more time to connect.
- Encourage statues to explore different physical levels (e.g. standing, sitting, kneeling, lying).

Connections: The author adapted this exercise from Chishti and Hipsan (2014). This seems to be an adaptation of the traditional game Red Light/Green Light (see Spolin 1963).

5.3 Sound and Motion

This is a full group activity that encourages participants to pay close attention to one another, accepting and communicating subtle changes.

At the end of this exercise, participants will have ...

- expanded their observation of others to include the whole body and vocal inflection;
- moved their body and used their voice in unique ways;
- discovered excitement and fun through incorporating mistakes; and
- bonded with other participants.

Running the Exercise

1. Ask participants to stand in a circle.
2. Face the player on your right and make a simple vocal sound, along with a simple body motion.
3. The receiver then faces the person to their right and passes the sound and motion, imitating what they received as closely as possible.
4. All subsequent participants repeat what the person immediately before them does. This includes anything that may arise that is in addition to the original sound and motion (a giggle, an eye-roll, a groan, etc.).
5. Continue until energy falls or participants are laughing too hard to continue.

Debrief

- How does noticing and incorporating feel? (This lays the groundwork for discussing collaboration as more productive than competition.)
- What discoveries were made from beginning to end? (This helps participants recognize that innovation happens when we pay close attention and value novel ideas and/or mistakes.)
- How did "mistakes" (e.g. additional gestures or sounds that were not part of the original sound and motion) change things?
- How does this change the way you think about mistakes?

Suggestions

- Encourage participants to exactly copy the person before them from head to toe.
- Give praise when participants incorporate subtle nuances.

- Let each participant start a sound and motion and let it go around once. Encourage a slight raise in energy of sound and motion with each subsequent player.

Connections: Also known as Energy Pass (Fotis and O'Hara 2016), this imitation game is similar to many exercises that ask participants to increase their awareness of others in the group. For additional awareness exercises, we recommend Boal's (1992) A Round of Rhythm and Movement and "The Space Series" of games.

6

Practicing for the Unimaginable: The Heroic Improv Cycle

Mary Tyszkiewicz

Mary Tyszkiewicz ("Dr. T") has devoted her career to research-
ing how to innovate for social good in the Washington, DC,
area. She is a small-group innovation expert and impact evaluator. Her Heroic Improv programs help small groups experience
innovation through theatre improvisation activities to respond
to life-threatening emergencies. She received her PhD in public
administration from Syracuse University.

I describe myself as a small-group innovation expert and impact
evaluator. Essentially, my work is to illuminate how small groups
innovate. Through various social science research methodologies, I discovered that groups of sixteen or fewer people that
care and connect with each other find creative solutions to high-
stakes crises—accidents, disasters, and terrorist emergencies. If
you had told me ten years ago I'd be using the tools and techniques of improvised theatre to improve disaster preparedness,

I would have laughed! For most of my career, I had been preparing analysis for top decision-makers in different government areas such as the Federal Emergency Management Agency (FEMA), the US Congress, the US Department of Defense, and the US Department of Homeland Security. It was serious, detailed work. But after September 11, 2001, my career goals suddenly shifted.

On 9/11, I was working on Capitol Hill as a defense analyst for the Congressional Research Service, which is part of the Library of Congress. When we learned that the first plane had hit the World Trade Center, the lead researcher on international terrorism grabbed his briefcase and left. That was my first clue that I should be concerned about our society's disaster preparedness. The rest of my colleagues and I dutifully went outside as we were instructed, crowding around the Capitol area, awaiting instructions on that otherwise perfect fall day, with blue skies and crisp autumn smells. Unfortunately, there were no further instructions. The multiple Washington, DC, area police jurisdictions seemed unable to coordinate their response to this terrorist crisis. Each police force blocked the areas around their government building, clogging the streets. They were protecting the buildings and not the people. Even emergency vehicles could not move. The local train system shut down, so people were left to trudge down the sidewalks. Meanwhile, members of Congress forgot their terrorism event training. They had been briefed and trained to follow a clear plan for a terrorist crisis at the Capitol, yet they did not follow those plans. Anyone in Washington, DC, that day can tell you of the chaos and confusion that reigned.

Because of an afterwork reception, I had worn heels to work that day rather than flats. I stood near the Capitol looking around at my unprepared, unprotected, fellow citizens wondering where I should go and how to get there. I also remember thinking, "Hey, my grandmothers could have organized a better response than our nation's capital did!" I'm only exaggerating a little—one grandmother was a church lady and the other a citizen activist and these women knew how to get things done. I decided right then and there that, first, I would always have spare walking shoes at work and, second, I would use my policy analysis skills to help all of us better prepare for disaster. It was obvious to me that our society had a problem. I wanted to be part of the solution.

Toward a Solution: Discovering the Heroic Improv Cycle

In my quest to prepare citizens for disaster since 9/11, I found a natural cycle that described how small groups solve emerging problems instantly. (A "small" group is defined as sixteen or fewer people; as a group grows beyond sixteen, the dynamics shift from small-group interactions to large-group behaviors, which are less conducive for instant problem-solving.) This cycle is driven by the desire to help and the ability to work together. I uncovered this natural heroic process through participant observations, case studies, media accounts, and from my own experiences. I call this process the "Heroic Improv Cycle" since small-group abilities are used heroically to solve life-threatening problems. And I discovered that the five small-group abilities—Alert, Ready, Connect, Focus, Move—in this cycle could be practiced using my Heroic Improv exercises, which are based on theatre improvisation methods.

Emergency managers know that disasters are inherently chaotic, so they want their plans and teams tested in situations that mimic the chaos of real disasters. Traditional disaster preparedness training, however, does not adequately prepare people for real-life disasters or for the real emotions they might experience. So, actual disasters end up becoming the testing grounds for most emergency management personnel. Only then do they discover whether or not their training works and whether they are suitable for the job. I embarked on a quest to discover a way for people to feel like they are in a high-stakes crisis but within a safe training environment where no one gets hurt.

One of my main objectives was to make the training enjoyable, so ordinary citizens, emergency responders, and government officials would use it frequently. In my preparatory research, I found that government officials routinely skipped disaster training, because they thought it was routinized, boring, and not worth their time. In the early 2000s, for example, officials would be given a paper "playbook," which outlined roles and responsibilities for particular disasters from tornados to terrorist bombings.[1] The training would be like a first rehearsal table read of a theatrical script, where officials sit around a conference table and go through the playbook page by page. Some official playbooks were as thick as a Bible, so this type of "training" must have felt agonizingly slow. Moreover, current training either provides book-based "knowledge" *or* teaches hands-on "skills" but does not strengthen one's "ability" to put "knowledge" and "skills" together in high-stakes situations. Just think of any first-aid training you have had and you will know what I mean. A person's "knowledge" of heart attack symptoms and the "skills" of CPR do not test that person's "ability" to move into action when there is a heart attack victim in front of them. Disaster preparedness training has to go beyond table reads and drills—the practicing of skills—in order to develop this ability.

In 2007, my mother began performing with the Oak Lawn Community Theatre in Illinois. I was impressed by how a community of mostly amateurs could create a complex musical theatre performance in just two months, and I thought, "Wow! Community disaster preparedness could be similar to community theatre, except that the stakes are higher!" With clear leadership and focus, a group of willing people with a variety of abilities can conquer complex problems together.

After that flash of insight, I enrolled in a series of improv classes. As a policy analyst, I am not trained as a quick thinker. Fast analysis in my world takes about six months from start to finish. These fast-paced improv classes took me way beyond my comfort zone as I responded quickly with others to emerging situations created with theatre improvisation exercises. I learned that good theatre improvisation is experienced in small groups with people that, over time, learn to deeply trust each other and become a team. These team members respond immediately to the action unfolding on the stage. Each member helps their team using improvisation principles like give and take, accepting/building on offers, and keeping the focus on what the team is creating together.

When my improv team was about to step onstage for our first unscripted performance in front of hundreds of people, I was nervous yet confident. Our team had practiced over eight weeks to build trust with each other. I knew my teammates would have my back. After that powerful, exciting performance, I realized that theatre improvisation was the ideal way to bring knowledge and skills together to develop abilities for disaster preparedness. The beginning of an improv scene feels exactly like a disaster. In both situations, people don't know where they are, whom they are with, or what comes next.

Solving Unimaginable Crises Together

I think we get it wrong when we feel powerless to help in high-stakes crises. When lives are on the line, it is the heroic action of a small group that makes a difference. Here are a few "ripped from the headlines" stories I collected in 2016 that describe the natural impulse of ordinary, caring people to take heroic action to save lives:

- When people at an Orlando nightclub saw victims of the mass shooting, a six-person group quickly created a human stretcher using their hands and arms, in order to evacuate a wounded person to medical help.

- When flash floodwaters trapped a woman in her car in Ellicott City, Maryland, a group of six passersby formed a human chain to pull her out of the car as water dangerously rose to submerge the car.

- When the Baton Rouge area was flooded, many boat-owning residents formed an informal rescue service known as the "Cajun Navy" to help neighbors leave their flooded homes.

These amazing stories, underreported by the media, illustrate how people from all walks of life frequently connect in small groups to save lives. My favorite example took place in Logan, Utah, on September 13, 2011, in which sixteen citizens rescued a trapped motorcyclist under a burning BMW. I have watched a video of this rescue hundreds of times because it so clearly illustrates how people use the five-step Heroic Improv Cycle to save lives (Figure 6.1):

- Sharpening perception (Step 1: Alert)
- Finding resources and overcoming communication barriers (Step 2: Ready)
- Forming a team quickly (Step 3: Connect)
- Aiming attention to solve the problem (Step 4: Focus)
- Shifting into action together (Step 5: Move)

The entire five-step cycle can sometimes take seconds for a group to complete. As the cycle continues, the group will naturally know what the next right step is, even though they have never experienced

FIGURE 6.1 *Five-step Heroic Improv Cycle.*

this crisis before. The Heroic Improv Cycle is a rapid prototyping process for small-group problem-solving.

In the motorcycle rescue, the group went through the Heroic Improv Cycle four times, with different people signaling the action for each cycle. At the end of the fourth cycle, the group successfully pulled the motorcyclist to safety from underneath the burning car. Early in the rescue, Rescuer One (a man in an aqua T-shirt) runs up to the burning car to assess the action. Then, eight men and women try to lift the car but that attempt fails. Next, Rescuer Two (a petite woman in a black and white shirt) lays flat on the road to get a good look at the trapped motorcyclist. She signals the group that the motorcyclist is alive and communicating. Shortly after, eight more people show up to lift the car. This second attempt with sixteen people works. As the car is lifted, Rescuer Three (a man in a hard hat and neon yellow shirt) slips underneath the car to pull out the trapped motorcyclist. Next, Rescuer Four (a man with a white hat and green shirt) runs out to the injured motorcyclist on the road with a first-aid kit and starts treating him. All this action happens in just over two minutes (Garff 2011).

What I love about this rescue is how the citizens rushed into action. In my Heroic Improv workshop, we ask our participants to think about what they would do in the first five minutes of these high-stakes crises, before professional emergency responders arrive on the scene. In this motorcycle crash, the police arrived at minute five and the ambulance showed up at minute ten. The small group of citizens had already rescued the victim in the first two minutes. Time and again, a similar pattern shows up in rapid rescues. A group organically forms, the first rescue attempt fails, the group learns from that failure and keeps going using the Heroic Improv Cycle until the person is rescued. Inspiring!

Transferring Small-Group Abilities to All

My Heroic Improv programs are delivered as three-hour workshops, and led by one emergency response expert and one experienced improviser per every sixteen participants. If the workshop group is greater than sixteen, I add another improviser to the facilitation team to make sure participants are practicing their abilities in a small group. The emergency response expert (usually me) relates the Heroic Improv concepts to the exercises and real-life crises. The improvisers run the exercises for the group, as well as assist in customizing the disaster simulations used. This partnership offers a great opportunity to demonstrate to the group what emerging teamwork looks like.

Choosing experienced improvisers is key to the success of the Heroic Improv workshop. I pick improvisers who are passionate about serving others. They should have experience teaching improv games to nonperformers and improvising on stage with a troupe. They must be able to help me adapt the exercises to the workshop space, the participants' language skills, and physical abilities. They must also continuously demonstrate the small-group abilities we are imparting to our participants: how to bring your entire self to the exercise, how to sense the energy of the people in the room, how to initiate without overtaking the action of the group, and how to trust the group process to solve the emerging situation.

There are five sets of Heroic Improv exercises that connect to the five steps of the Heroic Improv Cycle. At the end of each set of exercises, the facilitation team asks a specific debrief question that focuses the group on the connecting step. For example: How were you "Alert" (Step 1) and using all your senses (or not) in this exercise? How were you "Ready" (Step 2) and using all the resources in the room? How did you "Connect" (Step 3) and give trust to your team? How did you "Focus" (Step 4) and choose the next right step in this emerging solution? How did you "Move" (Step 5) and commit to implement the action and build from there?

Each workshop also begins and ends with a short disaster simulation, which allows participants to self-assess how prepared they feel for unexpected crises. We do not use a traditional training introduction for this workshop, which would be, "Hi. We are your trainers and here are the training goals." Instead, we jump right into the disaster simulation, which the group is not expecting. An improviser reads a text alert aloud on her cell phone, for example: "There is a Category Five tornado coming toward this building! Your job is to keep this group safe together. Go!" Then our workshop team observes as the group creates a solution for a tornado shelter in five minutes. Because the improviser delivers the scenario with emotional conviction and orders the group to act immediately, adrenaline runs high and participants feel like they are in a real disaster. Often, the participants do not know each other or the training space, which is a realistic scenario for a high-stakes crisis. Based on the opening simulation, our team asks participants to reflect: How prepared do you feel for high-stakes crises. Did this simulation remind you of past experiences of disaster?

After the simulation discussion, the emergency management expert introduces the Heroic Improv Cycle and gives examples of how small groups use these five abilities to save lives and instantly innovate solutions. Then, the facilitation team starts the first set of Alert exercises. Alert exercises aim to help participants notice their bodies and the physical space around them. This may sound obvious, but people need to recognize when they are in a dire situation. You need information from your whole self, not just from your intellect in a disaster. Alert exercises aim to help people feel "in their bodies" and consist of basic warm-ups that get participants comfortable moving and making sounds together. For example, Snap-Clap-Stomp-Cheer is an Alert exercise that helps participants pay attention in a loud, dynamic atmosphere (Workbook 6.1). The second set of Ready exercises give participants experience with tuning into the people and resources around them, through practicing focus and clear verbal and nonverbal communication. For example, Snap Pass (Workbook 6.2) is a Ready exercise that shows participants how to pay attention nonverbally in a dynamic situation. The third set of Connect exercises helps build trust quickly. In regular team-building, you earn trust over time. In a high-stakes crisis, you must immediately give trust to the group to help save lives. In a dire situation, this is a big leap, especially with people you don't know. That same feeling of risk can be experienced with the Connect exercises. For example, Blind Lead (variation of Workbook 7.3) is a Connect exercise where a participant, with his/her eyes closed, is led through an obstacle course with verbal instructions given by the group. In the Connect exercises, participants learn the dynamic of giving and receiving trust and build confidence to try new things with the support of a group. The fourth set of Focus exercises gives participants an experience of group leadership, which we call "Fluid Leadership" in the Heroic Improv program. Participants practice Fluid Leadership through trading leadership in a dynamic situation. For example, Viola Spolin's (1963) basic Mirror exercises are Focus exercises, where pairs take turns initiating and then mirroring movement without words. Another Focus exercise we use is a variation of Spolin's (1963) Give and Take Warm-Up, where participants practice sensing the subtle patterns of action arising in the group and how to respond to them together (Workbook 6.3).

Finally, the fifth Move exercise set asks participants to put it all together and leap into the unexpected through two-person improv scenes. Unlike most improv classes where students self-select to perform, this part of the session is a surprise. Participants are not expecting to perform and this generates adrenaline and can replicate some of the out-of-control feelings a dire situation can prompt. Building on the previous four sets of Heroic Improv exercises, the group experiences the Move ability by making things up to move an emerging story forward. Each line in the scene informs the next action. With little introduction, an improviser picks a participant as their scene partner. We have used Remember the Time

(Workbook 8.1) to start scenes very successfully with nonperformers. Remember the Time asks the participants to "remember," in detail, an imaginary vacation they took with their scene partner. After doing scenes with a few participants, the improviser drops out and coaches participants through two-person scenes, until everyone in the group has performed.

Finally, after the last two-person scene is improvised, the improviser launches into another simulation disaster announcement, which sets up a situation more difficult to solve than the first one, such as an active shooter event. After the closing simulation, we ask participants to reflect again. Participants typically report that they feel more prepared after the three-hour workshop than they did after the opening simulation. Also, the workshop team usually notices the group working together more quickly and fluidly in this final simulation.

The Heroic Improv program is always adapted to a particular group and workshop space. In terms of which specific games to use for each Heroic Improv step, I often invite the improviser to suggest games that they are confident in leading, that meet the learning objectives of each Heroic Improv step. I have found working with theatre improvisers is like jamming with jazz musicians. More than once, I have met my improviser partner face-to-face just before the session, and we still work together seamlessly. We know where we want to go, and we know the basic format, then each musician brings their style to the music.

To keep these programs culturally sensitive and relevant, I always work with an improviser who is a member of the community I am serving, who knows the community sensitivities and can offer ideas for adapting the workshop to address potential concerns. For example, when I do workshops with Spanish-speaking groups, I use simpler, more nonverbal games, because the instructions need to be translated from English.

The function of each group also affects how we adapt the Heroic Improv program. With citizens, for example, we focus on games that can build social bonds quickly. With staff groups, we choose games that challenge teams to let go of their regular roles as they create solutions instantly together. For staff members that rely on standard operating procedures, we pick games that force the group to practice "out of the box" solutions and to go "off-script."

Improvising with the Heroic Improv Programs in the Philippines

Filipinos have more experience than Americans with natural disasters. The country is ranked third (after Vanuatu and Tonga) in UN University's annual World Risk Report (Garschagen et al. 2016) in terms of exposure to natural hazards, like earthquakes, typhoons, and volcano eruptions. Even for a country used to natural disaster, the Super-Typhoon was impossible for Filipinos to imagine when it arrived in the Central Philippines in November 2013. After 200 mph winds—the strongest in history—an unexpected two-story-high wall of water crashed on land, engulfing the harbor towns in dangerous floodwaters within minutes.

In early 2014, I was able to pilot my Heroic Improv programs in the Philippines. I was invited by Gabe Mercado, a native Filipino, a corporate trainer, and a man who has a passion for helping Filipinos help themselves. Gabe is the founder of Silly People's Improv theatre (SPIT) and Third World Improv (proud to be the first Asian theatre improv school) in Manila. In the wake of the Super-Typhoon, he wanted to use his theatre abilities to help fellow citizens prepare for the next disaster. He knew improvisation could promote disaster preparation and found me through the Applied Improvisation Network (AIN). A little over a month later, I was on a plane to Manila, paid for by members of AIN.

Gabe and his other colleagues at SPIT generated eighty days of volunteer effort and donations by Filipinos to bring the Heroic Improv programs to the Philippines. Gabe and SPIT coordinated the overall fifteen-day workshop program, with outreach to communities, travel details, and recruitment of volunteer trainers and translators. Each workshop was fresh because our lead improviser actors—Gabe, Ariel Diccion, and Dingdong Rosales—adapted our delivery depending on the workshop space and the needs of the participants in the room.

We ran the Heroic Improv programs multiple ways in the Philippines. First, we piloted the program with Manila-area trainers, who gave us feedback on how to modify the exercises for their communities and culture. Then, we ran the updated workshop with diverse groups of Filipinos in the Northern Philippines, including four groups of employees (airline, conference center, and school), one group of emergency responders and one indigenous tribe. Finally, we took everything we learned from these sessions to adjust the workshop for three groups of Super-Typhoon Haiyan survivors in the Central Philippines, 100 days after the storm. In total, we had over 200 Filipino participants, ranging in age from 10 to 70 years, complete the three-hour workshop. The ultimate goal of all of these sessions was to prepare the survivors for the next disaster.

Working with Filipino Citizens and High-Safety Workers

After piloting with the local trainers, we worked next with citizens and high-safety workers. In unimaginable crises like the Super-Typhoon, the barrier to action for citizens is: "I don't know *what* to do." In contrast, the barrier to action for professionals in high-safety environments like air transportation, child-care, emergency response, and medicine is: "I don't want to do the *wrong* thing." Both fears stop action. By putting both citizens and high-safety workers in emerging crisis situations in the workshop, they can practice working through their fears and consciously use the small-group abilities of the Heroic Improv Cycle.

In Manila, when I ran an earthquake simulation for citizens, all participants immediately went outside like they did in the school drills of their childhoods in the 1980s and 1990s. After the simulation, we explained that updated earthquake research tells us that most people who are killed in urban-area earthquakes die outside from flying debris. As a result, our workshop participants got very motivated to update their knowledge and skills for earthquake preparedness and response.

Unlike regular citizens, staff from high-safety organizations keep current with safety trends, but still have no practice with improvising because the consequences for going outside of standard operating procedures can lead to death or difficult results. But in unimaginable crises, there are no standard operating procedures, and *lack* of action can also lead to death or difficult results. We did the Heroic Improv workshop with two groups from a domestic airline staff in the Philippines, starting first with the senior managers. The improviser facilitator began the opening simulation by saying that a gunman had just killed the security guard 100 yards away and that they had five minutes to keep each other safe. This group of leaders stood in a circle together, staring at their smartphones and speculating on whom they could call to find out more information on the situation. In great contrast, the frontline airline staff performed differently when given the same active shooter scenario in the same training space. This group moved into action. They stayed away from the false, cosmetic wall of the training space, and barricaded the doors. Two men improvised weapons with their belts and chairs behind each door and the group sat in complete darkness and silence for the rest of the five minutes. Through the Heroic Improv exercises, the frontline staff uncovered how they were already equipped for high-stakes crises, with or without standard operating procedures, and by practicing together, could build agility and confidence.

Working with Disaster Survivors: The Importance of Confidence

How can a disaster preparedness workshop help disaster survivors 100 days after the storm? Our final three workshops with Super-Typhoon Haiyan survivors in Tanauan and Tacloban in the Leyte region of the Philippines showed us how—by building confidence (Figures 6.2 and 6.3).

For forty years, Filipinos have been sending visual, theatre, and music artists to disaster locations immediately after a storm, to help communities feel human again after they have lost everything. When we arrived at the disaster location, Gabe told our local collaborators that we were not here for trauma release and stress reduction. We were doing something different. Our purpose was to help survivors be ready for the next disaster.

By this point in our journey, we had fine-tuned the curriculum; nonetheless, we knew working with recent survivors would be different; so we left ourselves room to improvise and adapt the program as needed. Since participants had lived through a recent disaster, taking out the opening simulation was the first alteration made. When we landed in the disaster location and saw the devastation ourselves, Gabe suggested we start the workshop with a playful warm-up and followed by participants sharing their survivor stories in pairs. To our surprise, our workshop location was

FIGURE 6.2 *Participants in a Heroic Improv workshop gather in a local school in Tanauan, Philippines, February 2014.*

a roofless school without electricity, surrounded by a temporary camp of white UN tents filled with hundreds of families. I followed Gabe's lead and watched him work like an improviser, saying Yes, And to every offer we were given.

Without electricity and without roofs, we needed to complete the workshop by sundown, so we gathered the participants and got right to work. Gabe asked everyone to walk about the space. Then he asked them to find a partner wearing the same color clothes and talk about something they were looking forward to. Each pair then shared their dreams with the larger group. Next, Gabe asked participants to find someone "as good looking as you," which generated nervous laughter. Once new pairs were created, they talked about what they were afraid of, which naturally prompted the survivor stories. In this same pair, each member rated how ready they were to face their fears on a scale from one (not ready at all) to ten (extremely ready) and explained to their partner why they picked that number. I recorded the ratings. Next, Gabe explained how this

FIGURE 6.3 *Participants in the Heroic Improv workshop in Tanauan, Philippines, 2014. Gabe Mercado sitting next to Mary Tyszkiewicz in front row at center.*

workshop would help them face their fears together and experience the abilities they needed in disasters.

This "improvised on the spot" opening for the survivor workshop set a good tone for the Heroic Improv exercises. We noticed how much the survivors enjoyed the games. The laughter was louder than in our previous workshops in the Philippines. As we debriefed each exercise, the survivors would tell us they had *already* used these abilities in their own Super-Typhoon survival story. For instance, to avoid the storm surge flood, survivors had to improvise solutions to finding high ground when there were no roofs to stand on.

They told stories of how the unlikeliest leaders emerged to save lives, using the Heroic Improv steps. In one family, a shy, silent, teen-aged son became the family's leader during the storm surge flood. He kept everyone calm so the family could use all its energy to survive. His young sister was terribly upset about the danger around them. He calmly instructed her to stop screaming and to focus her energy on hanging onto the cables. The family also used large water containers as flotation devices as the water rose. The mother described her son's actions as an example of Fluid Leadership. In regular life, the mother, a teacher, was the leader of her family. Yet during the storm surge flood, her quiet son helped her family focus on the actions necessary to survive.

The key outcome for our workshop for survivors was the *attitude* of confidence. They created order out of chaos in the Super-Typhoon. They survived by harnessing their desire to help others and by moving into action. They realized they had accomplished a wonderful thing, and were confident they could use the Heroic Improv Cycle abilities again in a different high-stakes situation.

Moreover, after our time in the Philippines, we were confident we could facilitate the workshop anywhere, in any language. Our team of four facilitators and two facilitators-in-training had delivered the Heroic Improv programs in English, Tagalog (native language in the Manila area), and Waray (native language in the disaster area). Often, the exercises transcended language. We had no problems explaining the content and participants clearly grasped the five-step Heroic Improv Cycle and how to use it in crises.

At the end of our last three workshops, we asked disaster survivors, again, how ready they were for the next unimaginable event on a scale from one to ten. One participant rated herself as a three before we began one workshop, saying the Super-Typhoon effects were so horrific that she would prefer to die than go through all that again. However, at the end of the workshop, this same participant rated herself as an eight. She stated, "You gave me a weapon. I am ready for the next disaster. Bring it on!"

Heroic Improv exercises can help all of us get ready for impossible-to-imagine crises together. During difficult times, many people want to make a difference. They also want to feel confident in their ability to help themselves and others. Heroic Improv programs are a practical way to show how small groups can work together imaginatively in high-stakes situations. And improvisers are key to creating the right learning environment. The improvisers I have worked with have great imagination, inherent empathy, and the ability to control focus. They understand the connection between discovery and performance. They demonstrate listening deeply to all, presence in difficult situations, service to the participants, and curiosity about the human condition.

Note

1   For an example of a disaster playbook for communities, check out this earthquake playbook at https://www.fema.gov/media-library/assets/documents/98396.

WORKBOOK

6.1 Snap, Clap, Stomp, Cheer!

This exercise is done in pairs and is good for very large groups. It creates a loud, dynamic atmosphere in which participants lose concentration, as in high-stakes crises.

At the end of this exercise, participants will have ...

- experienced concentrating in a noisy environment that mimics the chaos of disaster;

- celebrated "dropped attention" by cheering and starting again, helping participants quickly release the feeling of failure;

- practiced starting over, critical for responding to emerging crises; and

- practiced performance improvement in a partnership.

Running the Exercise

1. Ask participants to form pairs, facing each other. All rounds are the same pairs.

2. **Round 1—One, Two, Three:** Take turns counting to three. Here is the pattern:

   a. Partner A says: One.

   b. Partner B says: Two.

   c. Partner A says: Three.

   d. Partner B says: One.

   e. Partner A says: Two ..., continuing the pattern until one partner "messes up" by getting confused and breaking the pattern.

   f. When either partner messes up, both cheer as if they've won an Olympic medal.

3. **Round 2—Snap, Two, Three:** Participants are asked to replace the word "one" with a snap of their fingers. This creates a new pattern: Snap, Two, Three. When anyone messes up, cheer with more enthusiasm.

4. **Round 3—Snap, Clap, Three:** Replace the word "two" with a clap of hands. This creates a new pattern: Snap, Clap, Three. When anyone messes up, cheer like rock stars.

5. **Final Round—Snap, Clap, Stomp:** Replace the word "three" with a stomp of one foot. This creates the final pattern: Snap, Clap, Stomp. When anyone gets it wrong, create thunderous applause for each other.

Debrief

- How did you feel in this exercise?
- What did you notice as you cheered for mistakes?
- What made it easier or harder?
- What did you notice about yourself and your partner, as the rounds got faster, louder, and more complicated?

Suggestion

If they are not making mistakes, go faster. If the group is small, play loud music.

Connections: For another fun and effective exercise that develops an individual's alertness to multiple incoming data, we recommend Spolin's (1963) Three-Way Conversation.

6.2 Snap Pass

This exercise is intended to help participants experience "situational awareness," tuning in to the people and resources around them, and what may be emerging, to solve problems in high-stakes crisis situations. If there are more than sixteen participants, divide them into groups of sixteen or fewer.

At the end of this exercise, participants will have ...

- practiced active awareness as to what is happening now and what is happening next,
- experienced rapidly moving into action, and
- experienced communicating nonverbally with group members.

Running the Exercise

1. Ask participants to form a circle, facing each other.
2. Ask everyone to practice snapping their fingers.
3. **Round 1—One Way Snap:** Partner A faces Partner B on their right and snaps their fingers. Partner B "catches" Partner A's snap by snapping their own fingers. Partner B then "passes" the snap to Partner C and the snap pattern continues around the circle in one direction. Each partner snaps twice. First to "catch" the snap and second to "pass" the snap.
4. **Round 2: Across the Circle Snap:** Partner A "passes" the snap across the circle to Partner X, who "catches" it with a snap. Partner X can pass the snap to anyone in the circle. Make sure there is only one "snap" crossing the circle at any given time.
5. **Round 3: Bounce the Snap:** Now, give the snap momentum by "bouncing" it off a surface in the room. For example, Partner A bounces the snap on the floor, giving clear eye contact to Partner X who then catches the snap as it "rises" from the floor. Advise participants not to bounce the snap off other people. Any other surface is fair game.
6. End the game with the game leader catching and swallowing the snap in her mouth.

Debrief

- What did you notice as you passed the snap, caught the snap, and watched it move around the circle?
- As you did the exercise, what happened that made it easier or harder?
- What did you notice about working in a group without words?
- What did you experience about "situational awareness" that you can use in high-stakes crisis situations?

Suggestions

If someone cannot snap, just have them say "Snap!" If working with a diverse group, invite players to demonstrate the unique way they snap fingers in their culture.

Connections: This exercise was originally taught to the author by Topher Bellavia. For additional "situational awareness" exercises, we recommend Spolin's (1963) Play Ball and Extended Sound.

6.3 Give and Take

Participants practice the "Fluid Leadership" concept by moving in and out of leadership in a group of sixteen or fewer. This exercise allows participants to experience how leadership can be given (i.e. a walker stops walking) or taken (i.e. a participant starts walking and the original walker stops) in a fluid way.

At the end of this exercise, participants will have ...

- experienced full group focus in an emerging situation;
- practiced paying attention to the action around them and decided, as a group, when it makes sense to start another action;
- experienced the improvisation tenet of "give and take";

- sensed the subtle patterns of action arising in the group and how to respond to them; and
- had the experience of taking the lead and being seen doing so.

Running the Exercise

1. Ask the group of participants to walk around the room, and then say "Freeze."
2. **Round 1—One Player Moves:** Instruct them to continue on their own—moving and freezing—but now only one person can move at a time, while the others stay frozen. Any single participant may now "take" focus (i.e. move or walk around the space) while all other participants "give" focus (i.e. hold their movement).
   - All players must pay attention to who is moving/freezing and decide, without speaking, when to move. The one taking (or "leading") may stop, requiring another player to immediately take over with movement or walking. Or another player can initiate the movement, requiring the one that was leading to hold and give focus to the new "leader."
3. **Round 2—Two Players Move:** Now two players can move around the room at any one time as "co-leaders." Monitor the action to ensure that only two players are moving at any given time.
4. **Round 3—Three Players Move:** Finally, three players can move around the room at any one time.

Debrief

- What did you notice that made it easier or harder for you?
- How did it feel to pay attention to the all players in the room?
- How did it feel when you made a choice to move in the room?

- How was it easier or harder for you to move or watch for movement?
- How was it easier or harder to focus when more than one person was moving?

Suggestions

If the group is having trouble with only one person moving at a time, ask participants to slow their walking. Watch out for players creating a pattern of "taking turns," like at a couple's dance. Challenge players to move and stop more randomly.

Connections: Adapted from Spolin's (1963) Give and Take Warm-Up. For other exercises that focus group members on engaging all of the senses in emerging situations, see also Boal's (1992) "Space Series" games.

PART THREE

Leadership Development

7

Tiffany & Co. Says Yes, And

Caitlin McClure

Caitlin McClure designs and facilitates experiential learning leadership development programs worldwide. Her formative years were spent studying at BATS Improv and with Keith Johnstone. She later received her MA in Adult Learning and Leadership at Columbia University. From 2011 to 2017 she led and helped redesign Tiffany & Co.'s core leadership development programs.

The iconic blue box of Tiffany & Co. is associated with luxury, perfection, and beauty. Improv is associated with spontaneity, failing with good nature, and leaping before you look. This is the story of how Tiffany started to incorporate Applied Improvisation (AI) into its core leadership development programs.

By the time I joined the Tiffany's Organizational Effectiveness (OE) department in 2011, Charles Lewis Tiffany would have been amazed that 174 years after founding his stationary and small goods store in New York City, the name Tiffany & Co. would still be synonymous with quality, craftsmanship, and extravagance, and that his family business was now publicly traded, vertically integrated, on the forefront of sustainable environmental practices, and had expanded to more than 250 stores and 8,000 staff worldwide.

To thrive for so long, the people at Tiffany have had to identify and cast off whatever was no longer serving the company while maintaining the core aspects of what made it successful. In 2011, the OE department was at just such a point with their very successful three-day Management Development Program (MDP). It was Tiffany's first company-wide leadership development program, created by the OE department in 2003, to address the needs of a rapidly expanding company, but by 2011 those needs had again changed. Tiffany's chief human resources officer described it this way:

> The leadership opportunities that excite us center on reducing the challenges and capitalizing on the advantages of globalization, which has become increasingly embedded in the framework of the organization. We have more people in more places, giving ideas, changing the fabric of Tiffany, bringing their energy to it. Generating ideas is not a challenge—it is how to bring those ideas to fruition.[1]

A greater emphasis was now going to be placed on Tiffany leaders' ability to respectfully disagree, collaborate effectively across silos,[2] time zones, and cultural differences, and to unlock the potential of their staffs.

As the original creator of MDP, the director of Global Leadership Development wanted to revisit not only the core theories in the program but the teaching methodology as well. At my interview for the job, she said, "I feel that if our managers could *play* with our management theories they would incorporate them more into their work lives after MDP." Did I hear her correctly? Play? Oh, I can do that. Conventional wisdom says that educational programs must feel serious to be taken seriously—if you feel good when you leave a workplace learning experience, then it must not have been a worthwhile program. Yet for eleven-plus years I had been incorporating play in my work as an external consultant: developing and leading programs for onboarding, leadership development, strategic thinking, coaching and communications, with world-class companies, using AI as a key methodology.

I made the leap to work internally rather than externally for several reasons. Most of my jobs entailed working with a client or team only once or for a short amount of time, making it impossible to support them over the long term or address the full climate.

As an external consultant, it always seemed so mysterious the way companies organized their learning and development functions, and I wanted to know the secret. (Answer is, there is no secret!) Ultimately, I'd always believed it was possible to positively transform a full organization using the tools of AI if there were a will to do so, and the job at Tiffany & Co. would give me a chance to test out that idea.

The Theory of Organizational Climate versus Organizational Culture

Our OE team had to deconstruct and reconstruct MDP, learning what elements of the program were still relevant to Tiffany and should be kept, and which were now obsolete. It was agreed that the primary logistics would stay the same: three-day off-site program, the target demographic was first- and second-level managers from all areas of Tiffany (including retail, corporate, operations, and supply chain), twenty-four participants per session, offered six times a year.

As we dug into the redesign, the theory of Organizational Climate as opposed to Organizational Culture became the backbone of the revised program. We liked the simplicity of defining "climate" as "what it feels like to work in a place" (Davis et al. 2010). An organization shares one culture—traditions, values, history—and multiple climates, each the result of individual team leaders. Culture is typically inferred and difficult to change. Climate, however, is easily observable, can be readily changed, and a positive climate directly correlates with productivity and innovation. Climate can be analyzed through several different conditions such as the degree to which employees feel emotional safety in their relationships, how much they understand the organization's goals and how their job responsibilities help meet those goals, and to what extent they interact with spontaneity and ease.

To teach the theory of Organizational Climate, I knew that my job as an instructional designer and facilitator was to create an optimal classroom climate for our participants, and make explicit the behaviors that led to that climate. In that way, these leaders can return to their workplaces and intentionally use those behaviors to create optimal climates for their teams. In MDP, I would need to model those same behaviors and help participants practice them. This would be especially necessary for those whose leadership journeys may never have included the experience of working in an optimal climate.

Key messages within the program:

1. Great climates do not exist by chance; they are intentionally created.
2. There are many things you as a manager can do to create a great climate for your team.
3. Climate directly correlates with productivity and innovation. To improve your team's productivity, improve your climate.

Creating a High-Performing Climate in a Classroom

By design, the first hour of MDP opens like many corporate training programs. When these twenty-four first- and second-level leaders from different areas of Tiffany & Co. enter the conference center training room, the climate is generally friendly, polite, somewhat excited, and a bit tense. They see toys like building blocks and pipe cleaners on the tables and music is playing. Some of them know each other, most do not. They are about to spend three days together, in a program facilitated by me, a colleague most of them have not met. I stand at the front of the room with a PowerPoint deck. We introduce ourselves, engage in full-group and small-group discussions to help clarify their expectations for the program, and watch a short video of senior Tiffany leaders sharing their views of leadership. This opening definitely starts the process of creating a psychologically safe climate, but the real transformation happens after they return from their first break.

I welcome them back and say something like, "Since the goal of this program is for you to actually *behave* differently when you get back to your workplace, not just gain an awareness of different management theories, let's start by practicing some new behaviors."

The first activity is called Quick Draw, created by Keith Johnstone (1999) and originally called The Eyes. I learned Quick

Draw years ago from Alain Rostain, one of the founders of the Applied Improvisation Network. I often use it at the start of a program because it is a very safe way for participants to begin the shift from judging themselves and their surroundings to being open and curious about them. Participants are still seated (safe) and they are working in pairs (safe).

I ask a volunteer to join me at the flip chart at the front of the room to help me demonstrate the activity.[3] I make a point of thanking the volunteer when she comes up—we do a lot of thanking in our programs because it is one of the easiest ways to positively impact a climate. I draw two dots on the flip chart, side by side, then explain that Janice, the volunteer, and I are going to draw a face together using these two dots as a starting point for the eyes. We will then take turns adding features to the face—she will add one feature, then I will add the next. We will follow two rules: (1) as soon as one of us hesitates, the drawing is done, no matter how complete or incomplete it is. When her pen comes off the page, mine must go down, and vice versa; and (2) we will proceed without talking.

Usually the first volunteer is an eager drawing partner, so typically I am the first one to "hesitate" and interrupt the drawing. I make it explicit, "It's obvious that Janice and I could have continued to add more details to this drawing. I interrupted the drawing by hesitating so we can demonstrate the next part of the activity." Then we proceed to give the face a name in the same fashion, I add one letter and she adds the next. No matter how unpronounceable our name, I do my best to proudly read it aloud to the room (Figure 7.1).

After the demonstration, they all play Quick Draw at their tables in pairs, creating two drawings per pair. Immediately the room is full of laughter and other emotional sounds of surprise, confusion, and delight. Their body positions soften, with the pairs leaning in toward each other. You begin to see people's personalities come through their drawings—some are tight and detailed, others loose and flowing. Some participants may make sarcastic remarks to express their discomfort, but most of the participants don't speak and are visibly enjoying themselves, shoulders beginning to loosen, their smiles less forced. As they complete their drawings, I invite them to walk around the room to see the different pictures their colleagues have created.

FIGURE 7.1 *Quick Draw drawings by McClure and a participant.*

What differentiates Quick Draw from a regular icebreaker is what comes next: I propose a series of open-ended questions to prompt them to consciously make meaning from their experience.[4]

How would your drawing have been different if I had asked you to draw it yourself rather than with a partner? *Less creative, more controlled, I could predict the outcome, I would feel pressure to make it look good.* Who was in charge of the picture? *No one—it was shared.* How did it feel to not be able to control the final outcome? *Fun!* Usually in life we want to feel in control, but you just said that this was fun because you were not in control. Why?

For some Tiffany leaders, this may be the first time they have become aware of their willingness or resistance to share control. They begin to see that their preference to control their surroundings may result in missed opportunities to learn from their teams and produce stronger solutions.

A NOTE ABOUT EXPERIENTIAL LEARNING

Learning theorists, like David Kolb (1984), make explicit that an activity by itself is not experiential learning if participants don't have the chance to reflect on their experience (using any method: on paper, in movement, discussing in pairs or in the full group). "Learning is the process whereby knowledge is created through the transformation of experience" (38). When I was a new AI facilitator, it was easier for me to set up and lead activities than it was to lead debriefs, so I tended to rush the debrief. Besides, it appeared that my participants were making clear connections between the activities and their own ability to manage, but invariably they would walk out of a session saying merely, "Thanks, that was fun." It took me many years to learn to be as skillful leading a debrief as I was in setting up and running an activity, and to trust that my participants' real meaning-making would come from processing the experience rather than the experience itself.

After our initial conversation about Quick Draw, I point to a flip chart with six Collaboration Principles that will guide us throughout the three days (we changed some of the terminology of the improv tenets to feel more Tiffany specific):

1. Commit
2. Make your partner look good
3. Build with what you're given
4. Treat mistakes as gifts
5. Be curious
6. Be obvious

Where did you observe any of these principles in action? *We had to build with whatever the other person drew.* What happened if you didn't like or understand what the other person drew? *You just had to keep going and add to it. I drew a neck but my partner thought it was a body and added arms! So, I added hands.* Which brings up "treat mistakes as gifts." Did your partner make a mistake? *No! She didn't know I thought it was a neck.* Okay, so imagine you're back at work and you've just made a mistake. What would be different if you could think of that mistake as something to build upon?

A NOTE ABOUT MODELING IMPROV PRINCIPLES

When I train other trainers to lead this program, what I observe most carefully is their ability to model the principles, not just talk about them. These principles are drilled into improvisers every time we take a class, perform, teach, or direct. This may not be the case for facilitators and teachers without an improv background. This ability is especially necessary when an activity does not go as planned (which also provides some of the best learning for the facilitator and the participants). We are seeking authentic responses, whatever they may be; and the more a facilitator can Yes, And even the most skeptical, frustrated, or sarcastic participant response, the more they and the rest of the participants will learn. Our job is to guide participants through an experience, help them put into words whatever they are feeling, and help them connect that feeling to whatever the current learning objective may be.

In the second activity, called Snap Pass (Workbook 6.2, Round 2), we stand in a circle, I make eye contact with someone across the circle and snap my fingers in their direction, then that person makes eye contact with someone new and "passes" the snap to this person, and so on. The psychological risk feels greater in Snap Pass than in Quick Draw because now the whole class is watching, but the fear dissipates almost immediately as the participants discover their own games (e.g. two people will snap back and forth to each other, sending nonverbal signals that they want to keep playing), and the whole class laughs, plays, and builds a sense of connection.

After the activity, a typical debrief may look like this: Which Collaboration Principles did you see? *Commit.* Specifically, where did you see commitment? *Well, we all played.* What does the opposite of commitment look like? *Maybe they wouldn't look at you, and act like they don't want to be there.* Do you ever see that at work? *Yes!* What does it feel like to work with someone like that? *Groan.* On the other hand, what's it like to work with someone who's fully committed, involved, taking the ball and running with it? *Great!*

A NOTE ABOUT REPEATING GAMES

If you have a multiday program, it can be quite satisfying to repeat activities on consecutive mornings, which we do with Snap Pass. On Day 2 of MDP when we are standing in a circle, without preamble, I pass a snap to someone across the circle and they quickly figure out it's their turn to make eye contact with someone new and pass the snap along. Repeating the activity builds a sense of camaraderie from the shared experience, as well as a sense of accomplishment when they compare how well they played the third day to the first. The objective at the start of MDP is to help participants connect with each other and be present in the room. On consecutive days, we use it to explore communication and climate. Participants will often comment that they have become more aware of how to "read" the climate of a room; or they become aware of the impact in the workplace of their tendency to be thinking three steps ahead (whom do I pass a snap to) rather than be present and fully attentive to the person in front of them (be open to receiving the snap).

The final activity we play in the morning is I Am a Tree (Workbook 7.1), which increases the risk even more because now they are asked to create a series of three-person pictures in the center of the circle, building on each other's ideas and naming themselves "I am a squirrel" or "I am a leaf." Some participants readily jump in because they have discovered it's more fun to play than worry about their inhibitions. Their commitment is contagious and invariably infects even the reticent players. As a facilitator, I try to find a balance between letting the reticent players choose for themselves when, or whether, to join in the action, and when to nudge them with a reminder to "make your partner look good," and not to leave their partners alone and uncomfortable in the middle of the circle.

We end the activity with the entire class forming one final picture together. When everyone returns to the edge of the circle, I'll often ask them to look around the room and describe the climate now, as compared to when they first walked in. They will say, *open, friendly, easy* ... Again, we discuss where the six Collaboration Principles were apparent in the activity, how following these principles supported the group's ability to work together in this way, and how these principles connect to their work lives.

By 10:45 a.m. on Day 1, the climate of the room has palpably changed. They have laughed together, made eye contact with their colleagues, safely taken psychological risks, they've acted like squirrels and created drawings together, and, most importantly, they have been introduced to a foundation of new behaviors—the Collaboration Principles. As a facilitator, I have also identified things about the participants, such as who tends to be hesitant, who will jump in, who is noticing others' emotions in the room, and who is focused mostly on themselves. Armed with these insights, I can better tailor activities or discussions to help them celebrate their individual strengths, see their blind spots, and "play" with new behaviors.

They sit and write for a few minutes, reflecting on the following:

1. What did you learn about yourself in these activities?

2. What did you learn about collaborative learning climates?

3. How can the collaborative principles be applied to your work climate?

To use Keith Johnstone's terminology, our "circle of probability" (Dudeck 2013: 10) has been created. In this case, they now know that they will be expected to engage fully, and playfully, in their learning rather than coast through the three days passively.

Applied Improv throughout the Three-Day Program

Approximately one-third of MDP involves AI activities. Each was strategically designed to bring to life key theories and best practices around topics such as collaboration, trust, motivation, assertiveness, active listening, and giving feedback. We typically start each new topic with an AI activity, then discuss the theory in depth. Starting with an activity helps make that theory tangible, ideally heightens participants' self-awareness, and gives them the chance to practice new behaviors.

To broach the topic of collaboration, we start with an activity called What I Like about That (Workbook 7.2). This is one of my favorite Yes, And activities because, for facilitators, it so clearly reveals which participants are still struggling with listening and building on other's ideas. Once you know this is a challenge for someone, you can better help them explore the reasons why sharing control is hard, and support them in practicing new ways of doing so.

In small teams, participants must design something mundane, like a toaster. The first person suggests a characteristic of the toaster, such as, "I'd like the toaster to have six slots for toast." The person to her left responds by saying, "What I like about that is ..." and finishes the sentence explaining why having six slots is valuable. *What I like about that is that my husband, my son, and I can all have toast at the same time.* Then she adds another characteristic, "And I would like the toaster to be blue." The person to her left responds in kind, "What I like about that is ..." and finds something to say about why blue is a good color. *What I like about that is that blue matches my eyes, and ...* When I set up the activity, I also add two more key variables: They have an infinite budget and the rules of physics do not apply! Typically, the first round of ideas for the toaster stays within the realm of the practical. By the end of the activity, the toaster has the ability to levitate and follow its owner around, travel in time, and fold up to fit in your pocket.

After each team describes their fabulous creation to the others, we discuss this process of creating together. What was it like to offer an idea knowing the person next to you will find something they like about it? *It made me feel safe to say even goofy ideas because I knew they'd accept them.* And what did you have to do if the person to your right made a suggestion you didn't really like? *I knew the rules instructed me to finish the sentence, "What I like about that," so even though I really wanted the toaster to be multicolored and not blue, I had to throw away the multicolored idea and go with blue. Once I let go of my own idea, I realized it was more fun to build together than to show how brilliant I was. Plus, the others made me feel brilliant because they kept saying what they liked about my ideas!*

Additional activities in MDP include doing a Trust Walk (Workbook 7.3) to address the topic of which behaviors build or undermine trust as a leader. And to heighten their self-awareness of how well or not they actively listen, and to practice Building with What They Are Given, we do Word-at-a-Time Stories.

A NOTE ABOUT DIRECTED IMPROV

If a facilitator has experience directing and side-coaching improv in formats like Keith Johnstone's (1999) Gorilla Theatre and Maestro, you have an even greater set of skills to draw on at any point in a program. You can spontaneously ask a couple of volunteers to improvise a "role-play" and side-coach them, enabling them to better illustrate topics like ways to give feedback. You can take it even further and freeze the role-play, ask the observers what they think should happen next, just as you would with an audience at a show, and continue the role-play from there. You can swap out one of the "performers" with someone else, or require someone to speak in sentences that are a maximum of five words long or only using questions. Consider all the techniques you use in performance and how they can be used here.

Impact

All Tiffany leadership programs are grounded in the belief that self-awareness is the foundation of good leadership. One of the signature benefits of AI is that participants continually practice, in the safety of the classroom, behaviors we want them to apply to the workplace. This gives them opportunities to immediately experience how well or not they did something, try a behavior in a new way, get immediate feedback from others, and deepen their self-awareness, all while developing skills.

One participant, I'll call Sue, proceeded to draw the entire face by herself in Quick Draw, leaving her partner with nothing to do. Her partner commented on it during the debrief discussion and Sue sheepishly said she just got "lost" in the drawing. Then in Snap Pass, twice she did not notice when someone had passed her a snap nor did she make eye contact when she passed it. Later that day when we played What I Like about That, she added her feature to the toaster without first saying what she liked about the previous offer. Her teammates corrected her, and she admitted she didn't fully listen to the instructions, nor to the previous person's offer. In the discussion that followed, Sue very candidly shared that she was becoming aware that she does not share control easily or listen to the contributions of others. This was on the afternoon of the first day of MDP. By Day 3 she was still challenged by sharing control and listening, but she was consciously trying these new behaviors, and laughing with her colleagues when she didn't always succeed.

Another benefit of a psychologically safe climate is participants are free to spend more of the class time exploring real management issues of concern, rather than assessing if they can trust their colleagues to support them—and not judge them—when they reveal shortcomings, such as a fear of giving feedback to a pushy direct report or the inability to handle emotional outbursts. This safety, and the laughter generated from the games, usually helps form strong bonds between the participants that often last beyond the classroom. This is an intense three-day program, and participants often comment on how surprised they were that they stayed engaged the whole time.

For facilitators, AI activities provide multiple opportunities to discover which participants might be struggling with specific leadership challenges by observing how they participate in the activities. Looking again at Snap Pass, occasionally I get a participant who looks in one direction but passes the snap in another, calling attention to himself (see how clever I am) and causing confusion. I might deduce that this person tends to be more concerned about himself than his team, perhaps he is hungry for attention, or he may not be comfortable trying new things. I may augment or direct later discussions or activities to help him work on these challenges, or meet with him one-on-one later to share my observations and explore ways to support him.

Another benefit of integrating AI into your program is, if facilitators feel that the participants' attention is waning, it's very easy to get everyone on their feet and engaged in an activity, regardless of the agenda. AI activities and improv principles also create a sense that all parties, including facilitators, are invited to be leaders of their own learning. And finally, when co-facilitating, it is a joy when a colleague is doing their best to "make you look good" and you are doing the same for them.

I frequently get unsolicited feedback from former participants months or years after a training session saying they still find an empty room and do superhero poses before leading a difficult conversation, or how playing with being assertive, as compared to aggressive, opened their eyes to how they were being too aggressive at work. Many participants lead these same activities with their teams, and I have heard of more than one Tiffany store whose morning huddles have included Snap Pass. Phrases such as "What I like about that" have become commonplace at one of our service locations (to the point where they now use it in a sarcastic fashion—undermining its value?). Additional feedback includes gratitude that Tiffany invested this kind of time and attention in their development. And I am always delighted when MBA graduates tell me that they learned more about themselves and how to lead in these three days than they did in their graduate program.

Impact on the OE Department

My colleagues in the OE Department were already a very Yes, And kind of team when I arrived, so the improv tenets merely reinforced what they were already striving to put into practice. To my eye, the two biggest changes that have happened with this team since being exposed to a regular diet of AI is the expanded toolkit of options they can draw from, and the precision with which they think about creating their learning opportunities. I watch my colleagues verbalize a learning objective, then explore a whole raft of experiences that might help their participants better achieve that objective. They think about how the setup of the room supports or limits their objectives, and they make sure to craft rich debrief questions to help their participants make meaning from each experience. They courageously ask participants to try new things. In a word, they are fearless!

I am especially pleased with the work that our team did to craft experiences for the Tiffany Leadership Development Program, a four-day offsite for a select number of senior leaders. Because of the high-stakes nature of the program, the activities we used were carefully chosen, modified, rehearsed, and set up. Activities included Walk/Stop (inspired by Augusto Boal's [1992] Space Series) and storytelling exercises like Story Spine,[5] and ended with the leaders writing haiku about each other's successes. One of the participating leaders is now working with our department to create a year-long initiative using AI activities to help her 140-member team communicate and collaborate better.

Among my OE colleagues and former participants, the conversation has shifted from, "Why would we play games to help people learn?" to "What games can we use and how?"

Tiffany Today

In the past five years, AI has been incorporated into three of Tiffany's four core leadership development programs, the eighteen-month rotational program called the Tiffany Academy for Excellence and Diversity in Retail Leadership, as well as customized initiatives for finance, HR, distribution, and other departments. Close to 1,000 employees have experienced an improv game at work, whether they know it or not.

My hope is that these leaders will be able to draw on their experiences and implicitly or explicitly influence their colleagues to courageously be vulnerable and share their stories and assumptions (Be Obvious); to model what it looks like to collaboratively solve problems (Build with What You Are Given); and if appropriate, even throw up their hands in celebration of learning from a mistake and say, "whoo-hoo" (Treat Mistakes as Gifts). I believe this will influence the 12,000 people currently at Tiffany to better navigate the challenges that every company faces and welcome the opportunities such as embracing diversity, fostering a sense of inclusion, improving cross-cultural communication, creating the ultimate customer experience, developing colleagues, and nimbly adapting to external economic challenges. It all starts by saying Yes, And …

Notes

1   V. Berger-Gross, personal communication, November 2011.
2   "Silos" in this context meaning separate business units that typically do not communicate well with each other.
3   We decided to use the term "activities" rather than "games" at Tiffany. "Games" have a connotation of being for fun only. Not only is the term "activities" more formal, and Tiffany is a formal organization, we wanted to be clear that each activity serves a specific pedagogical function. Nor do I mention that an activity will be "fun" when I set it up, because my goal is to give them an experience and help them learn from it, regardless of whether they had fun or not.
4   Common participant responses throughout the chapter are in italics.
5   Story Spine was invented by Kenn Adams. Daniel Pink (2012) calls this "The Pixar Pitch" because this structure has been adopted by Pixar as their "4th Rule of Storytelling."

WORKBOOK

7.1 I Am a Tree

This is a very effective way to teach Yes, And to groups of six to twenty-four. It is playful and fun, great for people who are getting to know each other or learning to work together in a new way. The language requirements are minimal (good for groups who do not speak the same language) and because it is physical and not just verbal, when used in a corporate setting, it sets an expectation that the participants will not be passive, but must actively participate in their learning.

By the end of this exercise, participants will ...

- have interacted with each other in a state of play;
- have created a more psychologically safe climate, as evidenced by laughter, open body postures, eye contact, and supportive interactions with each other;
- have had a visceral experience with the concept of Yes, And;
- be able to discuss the metaphor of I Am a Tree relative to Yes, And for use during the remainder of a session; and
- have had a shared experience and will be able to refer back to moments in the exercise (e.g. "When Joe added to the picture of the rain by being an umbrella ...)

Running the Exercise

1. Ask the participants to stand in a circle. Go to the center of the circle and ask a volunteer to do the following: Join you in the center, pose in such a way that looks a bit like a tree, and say, "I am a tree."

2. Thank the volunteer. Explain that the group is going to create a series of three-person pictures. The first picture will start with a tree.

3. Ask the group, what else might be in a picture with a tree?

4. When another participant responds, saying, for example "nest," acknowledge that that is a great example of something that could be in a picture with a tree and ask that person to join the tree, and say, "I am a nest" (or whatever they suggested).

5. Invite one more person to add the final element to this first picture and state what they are (e.g. I am a baby bird).

6. Give instructions that the first person to *start* the picture is the first person to *exit*, and will take one of the other participants with them by saying, "I will take the nest" or "I will take the baby bird."

7. The first volunteer (i.e. the tree) will take either the nest or the bird and both return to the edge of the circle. Ask the remaining participant, still in the center of the circle, to state again what they are, "I am a baby bird." Then ask two more participants to come in, one at a time, to create a new three-person picture starting with the baby bird.

8. Rotate through until everyone has been in the center at least once.

9. End by creating one final picture that includes everyone in the room (e.g. if the picture starts with a football player, the additional elements may be a stadium, a coach, a fan, a football, etc.)

Debrief

- What did you notice? About your colleagues? About yourself?
- What was easy about this exercise?
- How would you describe the climate of the room?
- How has the climate of the room changed, if at all?
- Call out one word to describe how you feel?
- Where did you see Yes, And? Commitment? Being obvious?

Suggestions

For those participants who may be reluctant to participate, suggest that they can always join the picture by matching an item (e.g. if one participant is a rabbit, a second participant could be a second rabbit). Urge everyone to go in at least once—the focus here is on trying new behaviors and keeping momentum, not on being the most brilliant "tree"—but allow those who do not join to observe.

Connections: The author learned this exercise at BATS Improv from cofounder Rebecca Stockley who learned it in Australia from someone who learned it in Edmonton who learned it from a German improviser! With an especially brave group, you can take I Am a Tree to the next level. After the group builds/deconstructs/builds pictures for a while, ring a bell and say, "Begin a scene," and the three people in the picture (e.g. the tree, nest, and baby bird) must begin a scene animating their characters whether human, nonhuman, or inanimate. Then go back to building pictures again. *It is not recommended to play scene after scene,* instead wait until you feel a dynamic picture with interesting relationships present itself before animating it. At this level, I Am a Tree becomes a wonderful story-building exercise.

7.2 What I Like about That

This exercise can awaken in participants the joy of discovery when using Yes, And, while also revealing how it feels to actively listen. By slowing down the communications process—requiring participants to first say what they like about another person's idea before they can say their own—participants develop greater self-awareness around their own tendencies to actively listen to others, or not.

By the end of this exercise, participants will have …

- experienced collaborating with others in a climate in which all ideas are built upon;
- reflected on their own tendencies to actively listen, or not; and
- used their imaginations to expand on what is possible.

Running the Activity

1. Ask the participants to form small groups (of three to eight people).

2. Tell them that each group is now a product design team. They will design a new product, such as a toaster, using a specific procedure:

   a. One person adds one feature to the toaster (e.g. I would like it to have six slots).

   b. The person to their left will say, "What I like about that is ..." and finish this sentence based on something in their partner's offer (e.g. What I like about that is my husband, my son, and I can all have toast at the same time). Then they add another feature to the same toaster, "And I would like the toaster to be blue."

   c. The person to their left will say, "What I like about that is ..."

3. Demonstrate with one of the teams.

4. Instruct them that there are two additional variables: They have infinite resources and the laws of physics do not apply.

5. Ask them to all design a sofa, and continue until everyone has had two or three chances to contribute.

Debrief

- What was easy/difficult about having to say, "What I like about that ..."?

- What surprised you?

- What is the difference between accepting and agreement?

- What did your group have to do to be successful?

- How does this process compare to how you communicate at work?

- What would be different if you spent one day responding to everything you hear with "What I like about that is ..."?

Suggestions

Demonstrate at least three What I Like about That exchanges
before they play—participants tend to skip the "what I like about
that" step and move straight to adding their own feature to the
item. Visit each group and observe how well they are supporting
each other, or not, and who is paying more attention to their own
ideas than focusing on their teammates. In the debrief, when some
individuals struggle with building on their partner's idea, make
sure that that behavior is not characterized as bad or wrong—for
some people, learning to listen like this is a challenge. Finally, you
can ask the group to suggest the item to be designed—ideally,
keep the item mundane so that the suggestions start simple then
become more fanciful.

Connections: The author learned this exercise at BATS Improv.
Several variations exist, for example, for generating ideas on specific projects, try using the prompt "YES, what I like about that
idea is ... AND we could ..."

7.3 Trust Walk

This exercise is great for building trust between participants
and illustrating the importance of building and communicating
trust as leaders. There are many variations of this exercise—
this version, using only a person's name, also makes it easy to
explore nonverbal communications techniques, such as tone
of voice.

By the end of this exercise, participants will have ...

- reflected on their own ease or discomfort with adjusting
  their communication style to meet their partner's needs,
- experienced fundamental ways to give and sense trust, and
- reflected on their actions as leaders and the extent to which
  those actions build or undermine trust.

Running the Activity

1. Ask the participants to form pairs and remind each other of their names.

2. Explain that, in a moment, one person will close their eyes while their partner will lead them around the space, using only their names.

3. Make clear this is not the Run Your Partner into the Wall exercise. The intention is to make your partner look good, take care of them, and give them a good experience.

4. Ask a participant to help you demonstrate—they lead you, with eyes shut, around the room for thirty seconds, calling only your name.

5. Thank the volunteer and ask the group, what did my partner do to successfully lead me around?

6. Instruct them to build on the strategies they just named and invite them to discover their own. Remind the people with their eyes open that they will probably be walking backward and should be alert for others walking backward. The number one rule is to take care of their partners.

7. Ask the first person to lead their partner. After two minutes, ring a bell signaling they can switch roles and continue for another two minutes.

Debrief

- Who preferred having their eyes closed/open and why?
- What did you and your partner have to do to be successful?
- What did you discover about yourself as a leader?

Suggestions

Prepare the room beforehand by clearing obstacles on the floor and, if possible, opening doors so participants can move in or out

of the room. If you are timid when you demonstrate, the participants will be timid when they play, so demonstrate boldly. The
debrief can include connections to neuroscience, such as describing amygdala hijacks and the idea that psychological risks trigger
the same physiological reactions as physical risks.

Connections: For another fun exercise that builds trust through
positive reinforcement, try Dolphin Training. This is an exercise
that Keith Johnstone often plays with his students. It is similar
to the traditional game Hot and Cold, but in this version, only
positive reinforcement is allowed, that is, the group offstage side-
coaches the player onstage by repeating the word "ding" louder
and more frequently as the player gets closer (i.e. "hotter") to the
task the group has secretly decided they want the improviser to
fulfill (e.g. to put on a hat, do a cartwheel, sit in someone's lap,
etc.). No one is to say "No" or give any negative feedback what-
soever. All side-coaching must be in the form of positive "dings!"
Can be played in pairs, too.

8

Action! Transforming Executives through Improvised Theatre

Teresa Norton

The founder of StarMaker, **Teresa Norton** brings a lifetime of professional theatre experience and over thirty years living in Greater China to her coaching, training, and consulting of executives in how to inspire confidence, lead with authenticity, communicate with impact, and engage across cultures.

Imagine having the courage to get up in front of a paying audience without a script and co-create stories in real time. In my view, this is precisely what business leaders do at work every day in meetings, during performance reviews, and in discussions with their own clients. In the late 1990s, I began to develop training programs in Hong Kong using tools I had gathered from a career in the theatre. Convincing human resource managers that executives could learn about communication from actors, theatre directors, and playwrights was not an easy sell.

In my pitches, referencing American actor and teacher Sanford Meisner's techniques of "the reality of doing" helped enormously. I would point out that if "acting is living truthfully under an imaginary set of circumstances," executives could be trained to "act" in ways that would better serve them under the real circumstances at work. Applying my experience as an actor, director, and playwright, I knew I could help executives prepare for their role of "Leader," and for the past twenty-five years I have had the great privilege of helping them perform in more emotionally intelligent, thought-provoking, and dynamic ways in the workplace.

Some of my coachees seek out my support independently, but in most cases I am approached by someone from a business Talent Development department to work with a manager on a communication-related issue. The general request is to develop their leadership skills, often with a more specific directive to focus on influencing stakeholders, presentation skills, demonstrating gravitas, engaging team members, or adapting their communication style to the audience.

My bimonthly, ninety-minute sessions with my coachees mirror the relationship between a director and actor. We typically meet nine times to explore different strategies for overcoming their communication challenges using a variety of theatre techniques and activities. Some of the most valuable of these tools in my kit come from improv, allowing us to recreate real-life interactions that identify the gap between what feels most natural and what will be most effective when performing as a leader. And because improv exercises are basically games, they help create a nonthreatening coaching environment where my clients can practice new behaviors, and I can start and stop the activities to provide them with ongoing feedback.

Walking into my office for the first time, clients are surrounded by artwork, theatre posters, and a carpeted stage upon which two wingback chairs look out on the South China Sea (Figure 8.1). After getting them their tea or coffee, we begin by reviewing the results of the WorkPlace Big Five psychometric assessment,[1] which they would have completed online. This is the only personality-profiling tool that I've ever effectively integrated into my work. It is a tool for understanding the difference between personality and behavior, the basis for my director/actor approach. It provides an in-depth, highly researched, and globally recognized introduction to an individual's

FIGURE 8.1 *Norton at work in Hong Kong.*

character, which enables me to see the inner workings of my clients as compared to how they are being perceived in the workplace. Together we look at where their instinctive reactions to stress, or the degree to which they are hardwired to accommodate others, may be manifesting itself in behaviors that interfere with their performance as leaders. Along with their Big 5 scores, we discuss whatever objectives have been identified for the coaching engagement, often in conjunction with their boss. This further illuminates any links between their default behavioral tendencies and how these could cause issues at work.

I introduce improv games at various points during the coaching process, using them like gardening tools to cultivate self-awareness. Responding to a communication issue that has surfaced for them since our last meeting, I might want to employ a game that unearths reluctance to collaborate with coworkers or a game that encourages a more open mind-set. If a coachee has had a disagreement with a colleague and it is clear to me that part of the problem is an unwillingness to accept the other person's point of view, playing a simple Yes, And game like Remember the Time (Workbook 8.1) is a nonthreatening way to expose an aversion to ideas that aren't self-generated.

Whenever I introduce an improv game, I am assessing how much they are willing to play, take risks, and how open they are to new ways of doing things, giving me ideas of how best to work with them going forward. It is fascinating to see how their response to the improv games correlates to identified behaviors in the Big 5. A score that is low on trust or high on worry often manifests as a desire to control or a reluctance to take risks while playing the games.

One of the improv games I use most often is Color/Advance.[2] This terrific tool is as useful as a Swiss Army knife because of its wide variety of coaching applications and ability to help clients change hardwired behaviors. Below, I have detailed two of my coachee's journeys through the use of this game. I will also describe how and when I bring in an outside actor to help my coachees strengthen key behaviors and to give them practice making new choices that are more effective than their default tendencies.

Color/Advance

The premise is simple: One person tells a true story about a person, place, or thing. Their partner, *The Listener*, can stop the story at any time by saying, "Color that for me." At that prompt, *The Storyteller* needs to pause and give as much descriptive information as he or she can on that person, place, or thing. When *The Listener*'s curiosity is satisfied, they say, "Advance" and *The Storyteller* picks up the thread of the story where they left off. When I introduce the game, I ask them to describe a trip they took; remembering a holiday provides them with something that is not work related and pleasant to recall. We play a round where the coachee is *The Storyteller* and another round where they are *The Listener*. There aren't any complicated rules and this game offers immense benefits relating to communication skills.

One of my coachees, Leo, a director of budget control, had a sharp mind and a great capacity for critical thinking. However, at work he came across as passive, overcautious, and lacking in leadership presence. Our work together focused on getting him more comfortable with shedding his passive ways and presenting himself more as a thought-provoking and dynamic leader to his manager, peers, and direct reports.

Acting assertively, especially with one's boss, can be a slightly more complicated topic in Asia than in the United States. In Hong Kong, there is a saying in Cantonese that translates as, "Don't interrupt your father when he's speaking." The implication is that it is disrespectful to interrupt or contradict anyone who is more senior to you—parent, boss, teacher, client.

In our first session, we played Color/Advance to explore how Leo could probe the rationale of his boss's thinking without making either party feel uncomfortable. I asked how he felt when I asked him to "color" something in the story he told me about a family holiday. He said, "It feels good to know that I have shared something that interested the listener." I suggested that in my experience, most people enjoy expanding on a subject when we feel the listener is curious to know more. Leo and I also switched roles so that I told stories and he asked me to Color or to Advance them, putting him in the position of "interrupting" me. Then we came up with a variety of ways to say, "Color that for me" that could apply easily when in a professional setting: "Can you say more about …," "I'd like to better understand how …," and "I'm interested to know …"

At our second session, Leo said he was seeing opportunities to use his new Color comments with his colleagues and had tentatively begun to employ some of them. We then explored how these inquiries might be framed so that he, as finance director, could include some of his own thinking on a subject. We came up with the questions, "Can you say more about how this will affect the budget?" or "I'd like to better understand when you think we might see a return on this investment." Leo found these questions to be helpful, and these probes helped to connect the underlying principles of Color/Advance to real-life scenarios. More about Leo again, later in this chapter.

Unlike Leo, another coachee of mine, Wendy, had no problem speaking her mind. Wendy was an experienced senior manager and self-confessed perfectionist. At work, she earned a reputation as a critical, controlling, difficult, and demanding micromanager. At her team meetings, she often gave orders to her direct reports, providing them with few opportunities to ask questions or share any thoughts.

After four coaching sessions with me, Wendy was starting to become more self-aware of her behavior and how her micromanagement tendencies affected others. I observed her making a switch in her thinking from *this is the way I want it* to *this is what is needed.* Wendy was starting to develop an awareness of what her team was capable of delivering, and I wanted to capitalize on this moment in order to elicit more advanced thinking about putting herself in her team's shoes.

I told her about an activity that I had seen when presenting a business school leadership development workshop. The fellow who was leading the session had expanded the role of *The Listener* in Color/Advance to include all seventy participants. Each person received a red and a green card and were instructed to hold up the green card when they wanted clarification from a colleague (Color). If the colleague was belaboring a point and they wanted them to move on (Advance), they could hold up a red card.

Wendy, taking this idea to heart, distributed red and green cards to her team, and reported back at our next session that the exercise gave her team a voice while also reminding her when to incorporate their opinions. She had been leading a meeting and was outlining the marketing plan for the upcoming quarter, when one of her team members tentatively held up a green card. This, in turn, inspired a few others to hold up their cards as well. Her team wanted clarification on a change in direction for one of the stores and they were able to communicate their need to Wendy in a nonthreatening way. She was amazed they actually used the cards and said it was a wake-up call for her that she'd been "talking at" rather than sharing information with a team that had questions and ideas of their own.

When we met the next time, Wendy said it wasn't just the cards themselves that enabled this communications breakthrough. Over the previous two months, she had been actively observing, listening, and interacting more intentionally with her team. She was not always successful, but she felt that, at a minimum, her team saw that she was committed to engaging with them more constructively. Wendy was becoming self-aware and as a result developing the actor's "third eye"—that ability to observe oneself in action, while simultaneously recognizing the effect she was having on her audience.

During the last of my nine sessions with Wendy, we recapped what we had been uncovering over the six-month period and talked about the changes she was making in her leadership style. We agreed that managing her natural tendencies for extraversion and perfectionism was going to be an ongoing challenge but, to quote an advertisement from the 1970s, she had "come a long way, baby." In parting, I asked which tool she had found most useful from the coaching engagement. "Color/Advance," she replied, without hesitation, "I use that one all the time." I didn't ask her to color that statement, I didn't ask her to advance, I merely said, "Perfect."

Coaching from the Director's Chair

The middle and the last of the nine sessions I do with each coachee includes directed role-play scenarios with an outside improviser/actor, where my clients can put the techniques and insights from our sessions into action as we replicate the kinds of conversations that most challenge them. It is a powerful opportunity for my clients to explore that varied palette of responses and to hear feedback from the actors on how they are being perceived by others. When do we ever get to read the thought bubbles as they surface in the other person's mind during a difficult dialogue?

We begin these sessions with the client briefing the actor on the real person he or she will portray, the context of the conversation, and any other relevant background information. I also encourage my clients to share any mannerisms, often used phrases, and their perspective on how they feel the other party will likely react.

Critical to the success of improvised role-play is my responsibility for creating a safe space for experimentation. I always begin by saying that whatever isn't working is a cause for celebration because it affords us the opportunity to try something new—to dip into a different color on the palette of optional responses. The actor, regardless of how generous and open, is a stranger to the coachee, which is a departure from the intimate to and fro of our regular coaching sessions.

Once a sense of trust has been established and the actor feels they have sufficient information, we begin. I first ask the coachee what they want to achieve out of this exchange. If the scenario involves a direct report who has not been performing to expectation, I might probe a bit by asking, "What does she need to understand from the start of the conversation? Do you want to understand why she is underperforming? Are there any examples you might be able to share with her?"

What I enjoy about bringing in an actor to improvise with the coachee is having the opportunity to switch my role from active participant/fellow improviser to director. As the director, I am able to take a step back to assess the coachee's progress and can help drive the interaction in a more productive way. My focus is always on my coachee and how the dialogue is progressing based on the verbal and nonverbal cues I pick up from observing the actor.

A key function of the director is to stop the action when I feel the exchange is heading in the wrong (or right) direction. When I stop the scene, I ask the actor what he or she, as that character, is experiencing. The on-the-spot feedback—"I feel like she's trying to sell me something" or "I don't understand the point of what he's trying to say" or "I feel like he is setting some sort of trap"—is taken onboard as simply an opportunity for the coachee to explore a different approach. In improv terms, the coachee has an opportunity to Yes, And the feedback. The response might be a change in body language: leaning in or sitting back, taking some notes, consciously making more or less eye contact. Or it is an opportunity to experiment with the choice of words: being more succinct, asking a question, and giving a direct answer. Vocal tone and pace are assessed as well, and I can encourage the coachee to be less aggressive, slow down, interrupt, and/or stop interrupting.

In some cases, particularly if my client is struggling to find the right words or tone, I ask the actor—who has heard all the feedback I have given the client—to switch roles. This provides a unique opportunity to help the coachee sit in the seat of the other person and to hear the conversation from their perspective. I need to say here that I work with a select few very talented, sensitive, and experienced corporate role-play actors to make sure that the role-playing does not become some sort of caricature of the coachee. Rather, this authentic role-playing offers a unique opportunity to help the client see a different approach to how my notes might be embodied. And, powerfully, it allows the coachee to sit in the seat of the person they have almost certainly considered "difficult," and hear the conversation from that person's perspective.

Whenever we have identified an approach that feels truthful and effective, I have the coachee, again playing their own role, run the scene at least twice. There is no fixed script so the scene is improvised and slightly different each time; but the muscle memory that comes from rehearsal is invaluable for arming my clients with the confidence to go back into the "real world" and participate in difficult conversations.

Once the actor has been thanked and departed, I reserve the last twenty minutes of the session to talk about the experience with the coachee. Without exception, the experience is one of empowerment and insight. Do these simulations guarantee a positive outcome? No, but helping my coachees gain awareness that people can manage their behaviors under pressure and in real time is the gift of improvised role-play.

Leo's Experience with the Actor

With my previously mentioned coachee, Leo, our goal was to help him feel comfortable presenting himself in more of a leadership capacity with his colleagues. I knew that bringing in an outside actor would give him the chance to practice behaviors that would help him be seen as more of a leader, and help him see how his passive tendencies were perceived by others.

During the first role-play with the actor playing Leo's boss, the managing director (MD), Leo, true to self, sat very still, listening intently as the actor dominated the conversation. After a few minutes, and not seeing Leo making any active efforts to insert himself in the conversation, I interrupted the scene to ask the actor what he was experiencing as the MD. He said, "I feel like Leo isn't in the meeting with me."

I suggested that Leo take notes when the actor was speaking, nod his head when in agreement, lean in and take in a breath to indicate he had something to add. We ran the scene again. The actor paused when he clocked that Leo might have something to say. An opening! Leo used one of the phrases from Color/Advance we had developed to get clarification. The actor expanded on the point. Leo inserted a question that provoked discussion between the two of them. Suddenly there was momentum in the conversation. The results were transformational. Leo had exercised his voice and inserted himself effectively in the conversation. The role-play is a form of rehearsal and as such, when we hit on something that is working well, I ask that they run the scene again, just as they've played it. Invariably the improvised dialogue will change somewhat during progressive run-throughs but all three of us now know what we are after and the experience is exhilarating for everyone.

At the conclusion of the ninety-minute session I asked the actor how he was feeling as MD. "I feel like I'm in a meeting with some-one who is listening to my ideas, but now I feel like he has ideas of his own." Leo walked round the table to shake hands with the actor as he rose to leave the session. I noticed a visible spring in Leo's step. He demurred when I congratulated him on his performance, but there was not a doubt in my mind, or his, that his success in the improvised role-play had set something important in motion. The next time we met, Leo said he had begun incorporating what he had learned at work. He was no longer sitting back and letting his superiors do all the talking, but instead sat forward at meet-ings and made anticipatory suggestions, actively contributing to the team dynamic.

Conclusion

I have worked with clients for nine sessions only, and with others for years. We meet individually, with representatives from the cli-ent's HR team, or in groups. One of my clients—one of the world's largest property developers—engages me to work with cohorts of seven of their leaders at a time. Because the coaching with them has been cascaded over several years, the bosses are generally men and women who have been through the process themselves and appre-ciate first-hand the challenges involved in changing one's behav-ior, and they are familiar with many of the tools I employ to that end. The "graduates" support each current cohort as they try out their new techniques back in the workplace. The company's manag-ing director is so supportive of the work and the leadership team's response to it that he has encouraged us to form an "alumni fellow-ship" to continue learning and sharing as an even larger group as new graduates emerge.

In all of my coaching, the focus is on workplace relationships. I am not a therapist, psychologist, or life coach, but I have seen the transformative effects of this theatre-based approach and have been told it has even changed the way clients communicate with family members, partners, and friends.

I feel incredibly grateful to have contributed to the success of my coachees through the power of theatre. Improv, on stage and off, is a tool for putting theory into action and can be used to increase self-awareness through reflection, build more collaborative relationships, and increase our ability to communicate with confidence and clarity. Interactions in the workplace are simply a series of improvisations, and learning to mindfully access a palette of responses, instead of being bound by habitual reactions, makes us better able to contribute at work and in the unfolding story that is our one precious and finite life.

Notes

1   Created by the Center for Applied Cognitive Studies (www.centacs.com).
2   This exercise shares characteristics with Viola Spolin's (1963) Explore and Heighten and with Keith Johnstone's (1999) Advancing (And Not Advancing). Color/Advance is also described in Fotis and O'Hara (2016).

WORKBOOK

8.1 Remember the Time

This simple Yes, And exercise develops myriad skills—making and accepting offers, letting go of outcomes, making your partner look good, and staying within the story circle. These skills are easily translatable to workplace communication: contributing in meetings, listening actively, building on ideas, collaborating rather than controlling, building trusting relationships, and staying on point.

By the end of this exercise, participants will have ...

- experienced how to Yes, And in scene work,
- practiced responding in a connected and appreciative way to offers, and
- practiced generating ideas without judgment or censorship.

Running the Exercise

1. Tell your coachee/partner that you are going to build (or create) an imaginary memory together. You will start by suggesting, "Do you remember the time we ..." and finish the question with, for example, "... we went to Tahiti?" or "... sailed a boat to Spain?" or "... went to your cousin's wedding?"

2. Explain that for the rest of the conversation, each sentence must begin with Yes, And. For example:

   A: Remember the time we went to Tahiti?

   B: Yes, And we got a little hut on the beach.

   A: Yes, And the little hut was up on stilts and looked out over the water.

   B: Yes, And we watched the sun set over the water every evening.

Partners should go back and forth exchanging lines. One player should not dominate the story or go on too long.

3. Find an ending then create a few more imaginary memories together, switching who starts.

Debrief

- Who was in charge of creating this memory?
- What did we have to do to succeed? How would you define a successful conversation?
- Where did we get stuck?
- Where did you feel momentum in the story? What did we do that helped build that momentum?
- What would be different if you listened at work the way you listened here?

Suggestions

This exercise can sometimes turn into a "disaster story" where things keep going wrong, so invite players to make it a *good* experience and encourage them to add specific, sensory details instead of focusing on the plot. You can also start with a positive relationship and a topic, such as:

- Best friends in college, on graduation day, remembering the first day of school
- Loving grandparents, remembering when they saw their first grandchild
- Happily married couple remembering their best vacation

When doing this exercise with groups, ask them to form pairs, run the exercise for two minutes then switch partners and run it again, at least three times. This helps focus the debrief on the process of the exercise rather than on what their partner did or did not say.

Connections: The author was introduced to this when she co-facilitated a Leadership Lab with Patricia Ryan Madson, who had learned it earlier from Rafe Chase. For additional one-on-one exercises that could be used for coaching, see What I Like About That (Workbook 7.2) and Picture Story (Workbook 12.1).

9

The Fish and the Fishbowl: An Adventure in Using Applied Improvisation to Unleash Collaborative Intelligence

Julie Huffaker and Karen Dawson

Julie Huffaker and **Karen Dawson** are collaborators at Deeper Funner Change, a consulting collective dedicated to unleashing collaborative intelligence. As "pracademics," both are wildly curious about what transpires when organizational and leadership theory meet the reality of complex day-to-day business challenges.

Jenelle is a dynamic, red-headed CEO of a fast-growing real estate agency. Her vision for the agency was to reinvent how they do real estate. We were surprised and delighted when she called to share how she had used what she had learned with us during a one-day workshop. "This is a total transformation of my ability," she said, "an 'Aha!' of how to show my commitment and to share where I'm coming from *and* listen without getting so defensive."[1]

The workshop Jenelle attended was about shifting team and organizational culture to enable co-creative change. We had donated the day as a fundraiser for Living Yoga, a Portland-based nonprofit that provides yoga to people in prison and drug and alcohol rehabilitation centers. The workshop was open enrollment at $500 per seat, all of which went to the organization. Other supporting businesses donated the venue, food, and champagne for a closing toast.

Unlike the heart of our work with clients, where we engage deeply over time, this workshop was for a single day. Not knowing the participants beforehand, we emailed them three weeks prior and invited them to arrive with a real change challenge, personal or professional, through which to explore a radically collaborative approach to change. Twenty people gathered from across a wide professional spectrum: senior leaders from large, global companies, nonprofit executive directors, a lawyer exploring how to shift his practice, and Jenelle.

For the previous year, Jenelle had been struggling to gain her company's commitment to her vision for the future, but the harder she pushed her ideas on them, the more resistance she encountered. She hoped the workshop would help her use her upcoming annual State of the Union speech as an opportunity to get her company on board.

She shared with us that after the workshop, her State of the Union was more like a conversation than a presentation. She asked her company members powerful questions, allotted time for discussions, and distributed markers to collect their ideas on flip charts. Jenelle engaged them in the beginning to create a shared vision for the future. "Last year, when the presentation was all about me, it was, 'This is the bus, and you can get on or off.' This year, it was, 'This is our bus.'"

We use the workshop Jenelle experienced in many different forms, all aimed at unleashing the collaborative intelligence of a team, department, or organization.

Our Big Shift in Applying Improvisation

For the past twenty-plus years, we have been using the tools of improvised theatre to help clients make behavioral changes. If participants could only learn how to listen deeply, make bold offers, let go of controlling, and expand their attention ... surely, we thought, this would support more collaborative interactions and generative relationships back at the office. It made sense: our clients often described their challenges in terms of the behaviors that weren't working for them. They hired us to help interact and relate differently so they could get different results. Part of the magic of improv is that the methods are pretty darned accessible to non-improvisers. Yet even when participants left our sessions raving, the translation back to their real worlds rarely met their (or our) goal to enable groups to work in a profoundly different way over time. Our intention all along was to catalyze lasting change.

Our big shift came from considering that in improv, like in any emergent system (Lichtenstein 2014), the *interaction* of system elements may be what enables creating a whole that's greater than the sum of its parts. The behavioral practices we were teaching were just one element of the overall system.

What if we looked beyond behavioral practices and focused on the vital interplay *among* system elements? What if we included not just *behaviors* but the *beliefs* underneath them, and even the organizing *structures* of the games? By "behaviors," we mean the practices of improv: accepting offers, noticing more, playing big, letting go, and supporting each other to look brilliant. By "beliefs," we mean the mind-sets improvisers bring to the stage—like "we've got each other's backs." By organizing structures of the games, we mean the rules that both support and constrain participants' activities—like each person adding just one word in a word-at-a-time story. In our use of applied improv, we had never before focused in a meaningful way on the interplay between these aspects. We are now making each of these elements visible and deliberately playing at their intersection.

If we think of team members as fish, the way they organize themselves is the fishbowl. Interestingly, as humans we are rarely aware of the structures we're swimming in—let alone how we ourselves participate in creating them. The focus of our work now is to help participants see this fishbowl, and then intentionally make the most meaningful fishbowl possible.

What follows is an overview of the one-day workshop and how an applied improv experience can be translated to day-to-day organizational worlds. Then we share a bit of who we are and how we came to this work and explain our emerging point of view in relation to the wide world of organizational thinkers. After that we provide more detail about the key components of the workshop. We wrap up with a few burning questions currently on our minds, hoping you'll join us in exploring them over time.

The Fish and the Fishbowl in One Day

We play with combining three primary components in a core experience. First, we start by helping people begin to see their own fishbowl. Second, we facilitate first-hand experience with a collaborative leadership culture that is a big step away from their organizational world (no surprise to anyone reading this book, we use improv theatre). Through rich debrief, we make visible the mind-sets, practices, and structures that enable this way of working. Third, with laser focus, we expose people to everyday tools that help translate these mind-sets, behaviors, and structures directly back to their world.

We think of the day in six distinct phases: creating a learning community; proposing our point of view; curating an experience of a new way of working; translating that experience to participants' real worlds; practicing with sample tools that make a difference; and finally, supporting each other (using the new tools) to take the experience back to work. Participants describe the journey as exhilarating, challenging, and deeply personal (with a side helping of pure fun). In a nutshell, here's what unfolds between 8:30 a.m. and 5:00 p.m.

Creating a Learning Community: As participants arrive, funky music is playing, colorful charts are hung to frame the day's activities, and chairs are arranged in a semicircle, a journal on each one. After a warm welcome, we plunge into a rapid-fire speed dating game, starting with, "Tell a story about your quirkiest relative" to "Share a one-minute story of your life that ends with the sentence 'and that's why I signed up for this workshop!' " We watch participants physically loosen up as they strive to learn each other's names in a zippy name game, delighting in a few wild "failure WHOOPS!" as mistakes are acknowledged, not punished. And then, just as quickly as the play begins, we transition to silent reflection and journaling as participants dig deep to explore their burning questions about organizational change and describe their very real work challenges to each other.

Proposing Our Point of View: In a no-more-than-ten-minute lec-turette, we share the axes and arrow diagram (Figure 9.1; described in detail on page 187) and George Box's (1979) reminder that all models are wrong and some are useful and that we think our model is quite useful.

Participants are invited to lean into a neighbor and explore how the axes and arrow model connects to their worlds. This is when things really get cooking, the room buzzing with lively stories of the participants' own organizations. We struggle to interrupt the conversations as participants begin to share questions about how to actually create a collaborative leadership culture described in our model's upper right quadrant. We've got their full attention and it's barely 9:40 a.m.

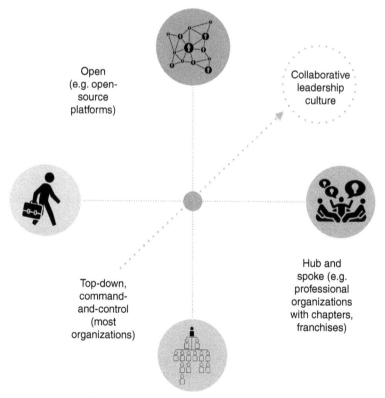

FIGURE 9.1 *The Axes and the Arrows: Four Organizational Fishbowls.*

Curating an Experience of a New Way of Working: It is at this point in the day that we deliver what some participants call a bombshell. We explain that we are about to take a huge step away from the world of work, with a promise that we will build on the experience to help make direct connections to their very real change challenges. "There are groups of people who work together in an 'upper right quadrant' way passionately and consistently," we say, "and one of those groups are theatre improvisers." We tell them that in approximately two hours an audience will arrive to watch a thirty-minute improv show. We announce: "You are the actors who will be performing that show. We define a successful show as one that has your audience leaning forward in their seats, delighted by your performance." Gasps of disbelief, furrowed brows, looks of dismay, and mutterings of "You've got to be kidding" erupt.

We introduce Jess Lee, our cherished collaborator and one of the world's finest teachers of improvisation. In a clear, confident voice Jess promises the group that they will have everything they need to perform beautifully in two hours and that she is there to support them to do just that. With a blend of fierce "Let's get 'er done" and warm acceptance of whatever questions and concerns participants have, Jess introduces the practices of improvisation through exercises and skill drills that build improv muscles fast. Side-coaching like crazy, focused intently on the quickly approaching performance, Jess nimbly reinforces improv practices and affirms how the players will relate and support each other to co-create within a generous improv ensemble. The show lasts less than thirty minutes, is comprised of four performance games, and every workshop participant plays in at least two of the games.

In every workshop we've done, participants astound themselves (and each other) with their collective capacity to perform; our invited audiences (composed of friends and colleagues whom we thank with chocolate) applaud loudly, appreciating with delight the deep, courageous learning they are witnessing.

Translating the Experience to Their Real World: The "big turn" in our day happens after a delicious lunch as we invite participants to unpack the shared experience they have just had. Journals in hand, participants sink into silent reflection. What was your journey? How did you feel? How did you relate with each other to co-create the performance? What did you notice Jess doing that allowed you to perform so well together? How did the structures of the games (the rules) invite you to play big, let go, and notice more? After participants have shared their (often emotional) reflections, we invite them back to the axes and arrow model.

The time is finally ripe to make visible the interrelated dance among the mind-sets, structures, and practices of improvisation, and how all three elements are integral to the extraordinary improv performance they have just created together. The big idea, and the idea on which this workshop is based, is our suggestion that this way of relating—the magic they have just experienced together— is indeed possible in organizations. We promise them that we are going to spend the rest of the day looking at the integrated dance of behaviors, structures, and mind-sets that, when incorporated mindfully and deliberately, can help shift how people organize themselves to do real work, and that we will do this together by diving into their very real change challenges.

Practicing with Sample Tools That Make a Difference: We are so grateful to have discovered the beautiful work of inventive practitioners Henri Lipmanowicz and Keith McCandless (2013). Henri and Keith offer a toolkit of facilitation structures, which they call liberating structures. The liberating structures we introduce in this one-day workshop offer "rules of the game" just as improvisational activities have rules. One common rule in many of the structures, for example, is for participants to write for one minute in silence before turning to a partner to speak. A simple rule? Yes. Does the rule shift how a group behaves in response to a provocative question? Definitely. The most important aspect of this phase of the workshop is that we quickly hand over facilitation duties to our participants (these structures are easily facilitated and practicable). They dive in, wholeheartedly. Participants get to take these structures for a test drive on their very real questions about change in this newly co-created learning community (think fishbowl) crafted to practice new ways of being together. Our intention is twofold. First, we aim to nourish the growing awareness of the similarities between liberating structures and the rules of the games in their improvisation experience (and the behaviors that are invited by those structures). Second, we aim to nurture their confidence in facilitating these liberating structures by demonstrating that they too can quickly and easily create a fishbowl that unleashes collaborative intelligence back in their workplaces. This is the sweet spot in which the likelihood of meaningful translation comes alive for participants.

Supporting Each Other to Take This Back to Where They Have Influence: The day ends with a liberating structure called Troika Consulting that allows each participant to create greater clarity regarding their own change challenge and how they might move forward more effectively. Participants depart with a clear, go-forward next step for finding a situation in which they will give one of their "new structures" a whirl, just as Jenelle did with her fresh approach to her State of the Union.

Who We Are and How We Came to This

Like everyone, our respective backgrounds influence what we can see and want to explore. Julie is a cultural anthropologist who fell into business by accident, working as a marketing strategist for Starbucks Coffee Company in the early 1990s. Later, taking a class with dynamic improviser Gary Hirsch (see Chapter 1) as part of an MBA program, she became fascinated by the links between improvisation and the high-performing teams she had seen and been a part of. For the next fifteen years, Julie worked with Gary and others to build On Your Feet, a global boutique business consultancy that applies improvisation as its key methodology. Karen had been a flying instructor in the Canadian Military Air Cadet program, a high school theatre teacher, university business school faculty, and had fifteen years of experience as an executive coach. When our paths crossed at an Applied Improvisation conference in 2003, our interest in collaborating began. Julie brought Karen in to help leaders in a fast-paced global organization get better at difficult conversations. In partnership with talented theatre director Ian Prinsloo, Karen invited Julie to the Banff Centre to help incubate a week-long Creating Positive Change Program. We had a hunch then that exploring the creative processes of theatre and improvisation would help organizational leaders create change more effectively. We explored that hunch through five years of vigorous experimentation at the Banff Centre and with our own clients, alongside our respective doctoral journeys focusing on leadership development and organizational change.

Now, we are evolving this work as part of a fabulous (and fun) consulting collective, Deeper Funner Change. We facilitate game-changing collaboration initiatives to build culture, leadership, and teams (Figure 9.2).

FIGURE 9.2 *Dawson and Huffaker working on-site with a Seattle-based client as part of a nine-month project focused on collaborative co-creation of the company's strategy.*

What We're Assuming

We know today's organizations must meet the challenges of rapidly shifting environments. Across all sectors and in all shapes and sizes, organizations are encountering complex problems that no single thinker or decision-maker can solve on his or her own. Geography, the speed of changing markets, advancements in technology, and demands for increased transparency combine to demand shifts in the way we organize. Our newest generations joining the workforce are better educated than ever before. They seek meaning, purpose, and values-driven organizations in which to contribute, learn, and develop. In our minds, all this makes organizations ripe for new mind-sets, practices, and structures as they explore new ways of organizing themselves. We see unleashing collaborative intelligence to develop new, collaborative leadership cultures as a potent place to focus.

Leadership Is a Process That Happens between People

We define "leadership" not as what an individual in a position of power is or does. Instead, thanks to Bill Drath and his colleagues (2008) at the Center for Creative Leadership, we define it as a relational, social process that produces direction (where we are going), alignment (how our work fits together so we make progress), and commitment (how we stay inspired by a shared goal, above our individual interests).

Aligning with psychological anthropologist Barbara Rogoff (2003), we define "culture" as the common ways a group pursues a shared goal they care about. This definition assumes that while culture influences individuals, individuals also influence culture. An organization's *leadership* culture can be defined as the common ways organization members work together to create direction, alignment, and commitment.

The Must-Have Is Relentless Learning

Individual and collective learning is essential to co-creating. Learning is not always comfortable. Working collaboratively demands rigor and discipline. A myth that deserves busting is that collaborative cultures are wishy-washy and loose-y goose-y. One of Robert Kegan and Lisa Lahey's (2016: 35) clients, for example, describes their deliberately developmental organization committed to *both* continuous learning and business results: "Growth and development does not always equal 'feeling good.' Our culture is not about maximizing the minutes you feel good at work. We don't define flourishing by sitting-around-campfire moments. We ask people to do seemingly impossible things … and you won't be given any time to sit on the sidelines and observe."

Organizations all over the world are breaking new ground, living into the intersection of adaptive learning and collaborative co-creation. Few people are arguing against transforming the ways we organize. The challenge, it seems, is figuring out *how* to do it and where to start.

Seeing, Experiencing, and Creating a New Fishbowl

As mentioned before, this workshop combines three primary components in a core experience: (1) Helping people see their own fishbowl, (2) creating a first-hand experience with a truly collaborative leadership culture, and finally (3) exposing them to tools to help translate these mind-sets, behaviors, and structures directly back to their world. Below we describe each component in detail and how combining them unlocks their power.

1. Help People See Their Fishbowl: The Axes and the Arrow

We use two axes to characterize the four types of organizational fishbowls we typically see (see Figure 9.1). Imagine a line in front of you, stretching from your left to your right. This line represents a spectrum, the distribution of voices (how many and which voices) invited to weigh in and make significant decisions. At the left end of the line we have one voice, the boss. On the opposite end, to your right, we hear from all voices: frontline workers, administrative assistants, people from up, down, and across the entire organization. This left-to-right spectrum of one-to-many voices is the horizontal axis of our model.

Now, imagine another line that runs vertically, bisecting that first line, from ceiling to floor. This line also represents a spectrum, the way information is shared within this organization. At the bottom of the vertical axis is a traditional organizational chart in which information flow is controlled and typically moves down from the leader at the top, from layer to layer, toward the rest of the organization at the bottom. While information may also move up from the bottom, in our observation it rarely gets more than halfway up to the senior positions at the top. When it does, it's often been misconstrued, censored, or watered down. Back to this axis, at the top of the vertical axis the traditional organizational chart has been replaced with a webbed network in which information flow is fluid. Information passes through the network in all directions and in many different ways, evenly distributed and interconnected. People have immediate, easy access to all data and information, whenever they need it.

Where do most organizations you know operate most of the time? Of course, these axes are not binary. They each represent a spectrum. Depending on the project, role, or context, input on decisions might be gathered from one or a handful of people (left) or a large group (right). Information may flow formally and hierarchically (floor) or in a networked way (ceiling). In our minds, no quadrant is inherently bad or good. Each is, however, well-suited to a specific set of circumstances.

Top-Down Command-and-Control Leadership Culture (Lower Left)

Like Jenelle, most of our clients self-identify as living somewhere in the bottom left quadrant. We refer to this quadrant as a traditional way of organizing: top-down, centralized command-and-control. One or a handful of people make key decisions, and most organizational information flows downward from the top. This approach was an improvement over the days of divine rights and getting your head chopped off if you didn't do what you were told. The bottom left quadrant is not bad or wrong; there are contexts in which it serves quite well. Think of environments that are relatively stable and known, the "only game in town" without pressure to innovate, or that attract members who like the structure and predictability of a top-down approach.

This doesn't describe what most of our clients want. Instead, they come to us with hopes of creating the conditions for ongoing change. They want to operate in a more collaborative, agile, and innovative culture.

Collaborative Leadership Culture (Upper Right)

As we've described, some fear that organizing in an upper right quadrant manner implies loose-y goose-y laissez faire workplaces in which few decisions get made and chaos is the norm. Early exploration of these forms (e.g. McCauley et al. 2008; Laloux 2014; Huffaker 2017) shows quite the opposite! Collaborative behaviors, expressive of certain mind-sets and invited and reinforced by specific structures, when systematically and rigorously practiced *do* allow groups to create and evolve in response to their rapidly changing environments. Many people have a say in the decisions that affect them, and authority for making decisions is distributed across the system to those close to the work. Information flows fluidly across networks of relationships; cross-functional groups regularly come together to cross-pollinate perspectives; and individuals proactively share and solicit information and insights with and from others for the sake of collective success (Laloux 2014; Huffaker 2017).

Open-Boundary (Upper Left) and Hub-and-Spoke (Lower Right) Organizations

We don't spend too much time on these quadrants because—at least at this point—we see them as less critical to understanding the change in leadership culture most helpful for contemporary organizations. Understandably, a few investigative participants come up to us during a break to ask about them.

We think that the upper left quadrant can best be typified by open-boundary communities where information flows fluidly and proactively across a network, yet one or a few people control ultimate decisions. A venture like open-source software Linux is a good example. The lower right quadrant is typified by a franchise organization with a hub-and-spoke configuration. License-granting headquarters sit at the center, making key decisions and pushing them out to member franchisees. Most information flows outward from HQ to the franchisees.

2. To Understand a Different Leadership Culture, You Must First Experience It

Playing improv games and observing herself in real time enabled Jenelle to notice more about her drive to control a situation. She loved being able to jump in to a game, but it was hard for her to share control and wait her turn, or watch others stumble and not be able to fix it. Then hearing others reflect on how it felt to play with her opened her eyes to the impact her style might be having on those around her. She had always thought that her ability to get things done was a strength—now she was seeing that it often resulted in others not feeling heard. Jenelle described the improv as "totally getting out of myself and onto the other side, their side, the other peoples' side." Our improv coach extraordinaire, Jess, put it this way:

> The performance gives them real feedback because it's a test. Not a pass/fail test, but they can't help but learn from this. They will have new information about themselves after this perfor- mance ... about how ensemble works, how they feel as part of it, what it's like to play big and trust each other under pressure. "I think this will be easy" doesn't wash; strengths and weaknesses are now laid out.[2]

To prepare participants, Jess side-coaches to focus everyone on the fast-approaching show. "What went well? What helped it go well? Let's do more of that in your performance!" She encourages, teaches, and challenges all at the same time: "Every one of you will be out there performing together, soon, and we have a job to do. High stakes. We are doing these drills and honing these skills for something real, not abstract. We have one project to work on— your show. And, by the way, we are going to be wildly successful together."

Participants are consistently far more successful than they thought they would be. As Jess reminds us, "It's not possible to sim- ply tell people that this improv way of relating is doable and that they can all be great—they must experience it. When they do, it's a game changer."

3. Translating Integral Elements of Improv to Day-to-Day Organizational Life

We are exploring how to translate one discipline that does collaborative leadership culture exceedingly well, theatrical improvisation, to one that does not yet, organizational life. Again, we believe we can best help organizations by focusing on the multiple parts of this complex dance: the behaviors, certainly, but also the beliefs and structures. We believe it is their interplay that results in an agile, responsive, continuously evolving organization.

For us, the linchpin of translation was illuminating the structural elements, or rules of the games, that invite and reinforce collaborative behaviors: liberating structures from Lipmanowicz and McCandless. What we recognized in liberating structures were the same rigorous structural design elements built into basic improv theatre games: articulation of a clearly shared purpose, every person encouraged to participate, turn-taking, working rapidly within a constrained timeframe, and no single person seen as more important than any other person. (For a step-by-step example of a liberating structure, see Workbook 9.2.) Of course, liberating structures from Lipmanowicz and McCandless. For example, many of Sivasailam Thiagarajan's (TheThiagiGroup) energizing frame games include them. There are multiple, existing toolkits that use similar structural design elements to invite collaboration during real work tasks such as giving feedback, sharing responsibility, and strategizing.

The aim is to unleash the collective capacity of a group to co-create. When these structural elements are present, the interpersonal challenges of hierarchy, style, lack of skill or self-awareness so common in organizations (and wherever there are human beings) are less likely to get in the way of integrating diverse perspectives into shared solutions.

So, this third component of our core workshop is experience with toolkits that invite improv practices every day at work. By giving these a spin on their work challenges, participants see that improvisational ways of working help them get better results on their real stuff. With a little practice and courage, these toolkits also provide scaffolding for taking this way of working back to real projects and colleagues. This is making a bigger difference than our work ever has. A client put it like this: "Working this way is like having a whole new superpower."

Conclusion

There's no doubt that teaching improv practices with a fabulous debrief gives people a new sense of what's possible. It stretches and frees them, and begins mind-set changes for some. What we are suggesting is that if sustained change in a group's way of working is the goal, this is not enough. Organizational culture *also* includes structures and mind-sets. Structures can be particularly helpful—especially simple, fast-paced structures—for translating collaborative leadership culture from improvisation to the change challenges of day-to-day work.

In our core one-day workshop, we make visible three aspects of leadership culture: mind-sets, behaviors, and structures. We use improvisational theatre to give people a visceral experience of what it's like to engage in a leadership culture where the mind-sets, behaviors, and structures support and enable radical collaboration. Finally, we help people translate collaborative leadership culture to their day-to-day work, at a scale appropriate to their circle of influence.

Is this approach a slam-dunk? Of course not. Does it still take courage on the part of participants? Yes! Is it for everyone? The mysterious algorithm of readiness for developing a collaborative leadership culture is a topic more suitable for a long conversation over a good glass of wine than for the end of this chapter.

Moving forward, we have three big questions on our minds. One question is connected to the open enrollment nature of the workshop in which Jenelle participated. How might we help participants see that the change they long for requires deliberate collaboration with the people actually *creating* change with them? We want them leaving feeling both hopeful and challenged. We know that their new learning has a high evaporation rate unless they can invite their colleagues back at work to engage with them in this new kind of fishbowl. Another question we're excited to explore is how to help intact teams or cross-functional groups from within an organization use this kind of one-day experience to self-assess where they are as a group of collaborators. By identifying their strengths and weaknesses, we'd like to learn how to help them determine what needs to come next to develop their capacity to unleash collaborative intelligence in response to an organizational priority. Our third big question revolves around how much openness, readiness, and explicit support is needed from senior organizational leaders for this new kind of collaborative fishbowl to flourish in an existing organization.

We know that it makes a difference when big shots with money and mojo are on board. We also believe, and we've even got some proof, that profound organizational change can start anywhere—it does not need to begin at the top. So, we will leave you with this: how do we debunk the myth that the person who is large and in charge must lead co-creative change? We know that change *can* start anywhere. We believe that our world needs collaborative leadership cultures, now more than ever.

With this approach, we think we are onto something. Our story is still unfolding. We are learning our way forward with our clients—people like Jenelle—and we invite you to be wildly curious with us. Our hope is that you will connect these stories and our strategies with your own questions and observations. It will be at this junction we all learn the most.

Notes

1 All quotations from Jenelle Isaacson excerpted, with permission, from a phone interview on February 5, 2014.
2 All quotations from Jess Lee from an interview, August 12, 2016

WORKBOOK

9.1 Three in the Middle

This exercise focuses on supporting one another to make our partners look brilliant, playing big, and expanding one's focus to others.

At the end of this exercise, participants will have ...

- had an experience of using their bodies and voices to create abstract creatures (usually outside their comfort zone);
- realized how hard it is to play a game if everyone does not help each other out and have each other's backs;
- paid attention to their own tendencies: Do I leap in first or do I tend to follow? and
- felt more psychologically safe (as shown by the laughter generated and supportive interactions with each other: it takes courage to let go of looking sophisticated and cool).

Running the Exercise

- Ask a participant to stand in the center of the circle with a movement and accompanying sound—a monster creature that no one has ever seen before. Quickly ask two other participants to join in, all making similar styled movements and sounds.
- Explain that the three in the middle cannot relax back into the standing circle until another trio has boldly stepped in with a new, completely different movement and sound.

Debrief

- What helps us be excellent at this game?
- What did it feel like if there was a lag in being replaced by three others?

- How did the rhythm change if there was a rapid succession of creatures?
- What may have kept you from jumping in to be a creature?

Suggestions

Side-coaching includes saying: "Stay away from words; use abstract sounds"; "Remember, we have each other's backs, so don't leave one of your colleagues on their own"; "Notice each other and play together"; and "Are you holding back from jumping in or are you jumping in too often?"

Connections: Deeper Funner Change collaborator, Jess Lee, learned this exercise from John Breen.

9.2 1-2-4-All

This is a full group exercise intended to engage participants in generating questions, ideas, and suggestions. 1-2-4-All is a basic, very useful brainstorming structure.

At the end of this exercise, participants will have …

- insight into what changes occur in people when a structure is utilized to organize conversations;
- realized how fast ideas can be generated using "rules of the game" that are like the rules of improvisation; and
- begun to see the connections—in structures, mind-sets, and practices—that influence how we relate to one another.

Running the Exercise

- Ask a question that is open-ended. For example, "What are your biggest questions or concerns about this change?"
- Ask participants to journal their responses for one minute in silence and then share in pairs for two minutes.

- Ask groups of four to compare responses for four minutes looking for the big ideas that emerge.
- Solicit one idea from each group and capture responses.

Debrief

How is this 1-2-4-All structure different from the ways you typically talk in meetings? How do the rules of this structure invite you to let go, play big, and notice more?

Suggestions

If facilitating in pairs, avoid the temptation to visit with one another during the minute of silent journaling. Use a chime to indicate when it's time to move from journaling to pairs, and then into fours. Say as little as possible.

Connections: This liberating structure is from Lipmanowicz and McCandless (2013).

PART FOUR

Higher Education

10

From Hell, No to Yes, And: Applied Improvisation for Training in Conflict Resolution, Mediation, and Law

Barbara Tint

Barbara Tint is a psychologist and professor of conflict resolution at Portland State University and works at many other universities worldwide. She is also a global trainer, facilitator, and consultant in areas of conflict resolution, dialogue, gender relations, intercultural dynamics, power and status, leadership, and change. She has been studying and applying improvisation since 2009 and serves as the president of the Applied Improvisation Network. She wonders if there's still hope for her performance career.

Introduction

In October of 2009, I went to Sri Lanka to work on issues of communal conflict and to attend a meditation retreat. The meditation teacher, Deva, was a grounded and insightful man, someone I had worked with before, someone who knew me well, and someone I trusted. During one afternoon of private time together, we were sitting quietly, when he suddenly turned to me and said, "Could you teach something else?" I was surprised by the question, yet knew Deva well enough to know there was something behind it and to pay attention. "What?" I asked, with my attempt at avoidant irony, "Math? You want me to teach math? Why? *This* is what I do."

For the previous twelve years, I had been a professor and practitioner of conflict resolution, specializing in issues of communal, social, and political conflict. I had worked in Australia, Ethiopia, India, Israel/Palestine, Rwanda, Sri Lanka, and the United States. My work stemmed from my roots as a clinical psychologist; now, instead of working with individuals or families struggling to move past personal challenges, I was working with individuals and groups of people who struggled with small- and large-scale conflict. I was also teaching and training others to do this work in academic, organizational, and community settings around the world. I knew I was doing what I was called to do and could not quite imagine where Deva was heading.

"Well," he said, "your energy is very heavy. I'm getting the feeling you're absorbing the trauma of the people you work with." At this, I began to cry. He was right. My latest project had been working with refugees of the genocides in East Africa and I had moved from one heartbreaking story of displacement and loss to another. While he saw that the work was creating a psychological burden for me, I could not imagine abandoning it. And I also knew that for my sake and for the sake of the people I worked with, I needed to find a path that would allow me to move forward with more sustainable energy.

At that same time, I had serendipitously discovered the Applied Improvisation Network (AIN) and, as luck would have it, their next international conference was the following month in my hometown of Portland, Oregon, United States. Having always used experiential methods in my teaching and being a latent comic and performer,

I decided to give it a try. I cautiously signed up for only one day, concerned that I might be met with people in fairy costumes, magic wands, and clown noses with no viable connection to my work. Well, there were a few clown noses, but four days later, I came out a changed woman. The heaviness I was carrying was lifted by the spontaneous, joyous, generous, freeing collaborative work and spirit of improvisation and its participants. Those of you who are already involved in improv know what I'm talking about. Those of you who don't … go find out!

In my attempt to figure out how to connect improv to my work, I initially felt that I had two *seemingly* disparate realities: the "important," difficult, and heavy world of international conflict and the "frivolous," playful, and joyous world of improv. How could I bring them together? I couldn't exactly approach genocide survivors or my students with clapping games or word-at-a-time exercises. Or could I? I slowly began to see that these principles and methods provided some of the most transformative and healing potential I had ever experienced. They were anything but frivolous and were useful in working with individuals and community members in conflict as well as those training to be conflict resolvers. I also learned that much improvisational practice originated from the work of Viola Spolin (1963), sometimes referred to as "The Mother of Improvisation," who developed these tools to work with social issues like inner-city and immigrant youth challenges. And so, at the next AIN conference in Amsterdam, I presented a workshop on the use of improvisational methods in working with conflict and conflict resolution and have never looked back. I now use improv in all my work and have written about it as well (Tint et al. 2015).

This chapter explores the use of Applied Improvisation (AI) for training conflict resolution professionals, mediators, and lawyers who are already schooled in the fundamentals of conflict resolution. AI training in this context focuses on improvisational principles and methods that align with those of conflict resolution.

Thoughts on Conflict Resolution

I have often said that one of the best things in my career would be to run out of work. That is, to live in a world where the need for effective conflict resolution training and intervention were no longer necessary; a world in which we all had the tools to approach personal, organizational, and community conflict in constructive and transformative ways; a world where we find the means to stem the tide of long-term and violent conflict. Sadly, there seems to be no risk of closing shop any time soon. Locally, we continue to struggle with issues of conflict at home, at work, and in community contexts. Relationships, resources, and collaborations are fractured because people are unable to move past the real or perceived differences between them. Globally, we continue to see and experience communities struggling with conflict at the Track One (official, governmental), Track Two (unofficial community and organizational leadership) and Track Three (grass-roots, citizen to citizen) levels of engagement.

Among the hundreds of definitions that have emerged around the term "conflict," the one that we can use as our operational definition is: An expressed struggle between two or more interdependent parties, revealing real or perceived differences in values, needs, and interests between the parties which lead to the belief in incompatible goals (Hocker and Wilmot 2014). The aim of this field is not to eliminate conflict; this is neither possible nor desirable as conflict of some sort is regarded as an inevitable dimension of life. Rather, our goal is to find more constructive means by which to address it, so individuals and groups can meet their respective needs in collaborative ways preserving relationships, communities, resources, and enhanced possibilities for the future. When addressed well, conflict can be an opportunity for growth, intimacy, and both personal and societal transformation.

While the causes and consequences of small-scale and large-scale conflict may be different, many of the underlying issues are the same. All conflicts have some dimension of objective features (the dishes, the money, the project, the land, the immigration laws) and some dimension of subjective features (the perceptions, the identity, the relationships, the history, the emotions). A successful conflict resolution approach will effectively address both of these dimensions. Ignoring one for the sake of the other will often lead to limited resolution. All issues of conflict are also informed by embedded systemic forces such as racism, gender bias, or class inequity. These forces are very powerful, difficult to remediate, and always at play. Awareness of and ability to address them is a critical dimension to this work. While it is not possible to discuss all of the core components of conflict resolution practice in this chapter,[1] I present foundational principles that are relevant at both the micro level of small-scale personal, organizational, and community conflict, and the macro level of large-scale societal conflict. The approaches outlined in this chapter are not necessarily able to remediate objective and societal systemic forces informing conflict; however, with better skills in the subjective realm, we are more able to successfully respond to the forces at play.

Training Processes and Methodologies

In training, I use differing formats such as half-day, full-day, twenty-hour weekend, and ten-week to fifteen-week classes. One day or less is really a taste of what is possible. A training should be a minimum of twenty hours, and ideally more, if the goal is to create a cohesive group that can productively approach issues in-depth. Here, I feel the need to offer some words of caution. While some of the approaches shared in this chapter can be used effectively by trainers new to this methodology, training for conflict resolution is complex and should ideally be facilitated by those with foundational knowledge and experience in this area. It is critical to understand the multiple issues that inform and resolve conflict and to be able to hold the space for people whose own experiences, memories, emotions, or challenges may be stimulated. I encourage those of you wanting to use these techniques to be experienced in this area or partner with others who are.

While I come prepared with goals, a loose structure, and a variety of activities, I typically select what I do based on the group, their energy, their flow, and what seems most necessary in the moment. In no small show of irony, I share here a war metaphor and quote from Eisenhower who said, "In preparing for battle I have always found that plans are useless, but planning is indispensable." Therefore, for each skill or content area that I focus on, I come prepared with a range of activities that can cultivate that particular skill. As it is impossible to share every activity that I use, the reader is encouraged to consult a variety of resources when focusing on a particular content area.[2]

At the beginning of training, I work to build a safe and cohesive group environment. There are a variety of improv games and activities that can achieve this. I work to get people into their bodies, to get to know each other, and to increase the comfort level in the group. I use sociometry (McWaters and Moore 2012) to help people find out who is in the room, to observe the constellations and connections that emerge, and to develop the beginnings of group cohesion. I choose a variety of formats that include whole group, small group, triads, and dyads to get people connected to as many others as possible. At this early stage, we will also address the discomfort around risk-taking, making mistakes, and getting up in front of others, which can impact the freedom or inhibition that people bring to the process.

In working with conflict resolution content, I follow a basic framework that includes the following sequence: (1) Identify the specific conflict resolution principle or skill we will be working with (i.e. listening, collaborating, responding to emotions, solution building, etc.); (2) do a variety of improvisational activities that focus on that concept; (3) debrief the activity related to the participants' immediate experience; (4) explore how the participants' experiences relate to conflict and conflict resolution practice; (5) introduce a conflict scenario or conflict activity where these principles or experiences can be applied and practiced directly. Time will not always allow conflict scenarios for each principle, so sometimes I will cover several principles and then incorporate them into one conflict-related activity. We often think of this work as building the muscles we need for conflict resolution. One colleague likens this work to cross-training. Marathoners spend a lot of time lifting weights, doing push-ups, and so on. They may not be running, but they are building their muscles so they are ready when it is time to run.

After all activities, debrief is critical. Dr. Sivasailam "Thiagi" Thiagarajan, a renowned expert in interactive learning in organizations (TheThiagiGroup), suggests that learning comes less from an activity itself, and more from reflecting on an activity. Some activities will be debriefed more immediately and directly than others— that depends on time, group flow, and content needs. Debrief ideally should be conducted in multiple formats (i.e. in pairs, trios, small groups, large groups, verbally, through art, reflective writing, and playful expression). The more you can utilize different methods for both activities and debrief processes, the more you will tap into different learning styles and needs. The key is balance—not to debrief every little thing so it becomes repetitive and not to overlook critical aspects of learning. Basic debrief questions include: What happened? What did you notice? What did you experience? What did you feel? What surprised you? How does this apply to conflict? How is this useful to your role as a conflict resolver? How might you use this idea, experience, principle?

Improv and Conflict Resolution Skills

Conflict resolution and AI go together like a pair of gloves. Working to address disputes requires the very principles and skills that are core to improvisation. Former US Ambassador Richard Holbrooke said, "Negotiation is like … improvisation on a theme. You know where you want to go, but you don't know how to get there. It's not linear" (Wheeler 2013: 97). For anyone who works with conflict, skills such as listening with deep focus, authenticity, accepting and building upon offers, collaboration, creativity, spontaneity, quick thinking and decision-making, risk-taking, flexibility, adaptability, engaging emotions, addressing issues of power and status, and working with multiple narratives are foundational to successful practice. These are the same skills improvisers use to help them perform on stage. The following section delineates seven core conflict resolution skills and demonstrates how improvisational methods are used to address them in training processes. They are presented here in the order in which I introduce them, as the development of skills in one area prepares participants for greater success in subsequent ones.

Listening

Conflict resolution work is founded upon good listening. The greater ability we have to focus and be present with others, the more effective we are at dealing with conflict. Harold Saunders (1999: 82), a former US diplomat who spent much of his career doing citizen-to-citizen diplomacy in conflict zones such as the Balkans and the Middle East, suggests that dialogue is "a process of genuine *inter*action through which human beings listen to each other deeply enough to be changed by what they learn." When we are in conflict, our patience, tolerance, and desire to listen are severely challenged.

We block and feel blocked by others. Conflict resolution work trains people to sit with their discomfort, and to suspend their own inclination to discount or interrupt others. We also train people to listen for themes, values, feelings, and needs rather than listening only for words or content. Cultivating empathy, perspective taking, and connection are critical elements of this process and are difficult to do when we are in conflict.

Improvisation is fundamentally about listening—being able to attend to what's happening in the moment and to respond with presence and authenticity. When we listen and notice more, we are able to incorporate information in more connected and meaningful ways (Poynton 2008). The best improvisers are excellent listeners who repeatedly let themselves be changed by what they hear. There are a wide range of activities that cultivate listening and attention skills. A few I like are Pass Clap, Sound Ball, Word Ball, Patterns, Mirror, Zip Zap Zop, and Last Word. Once we have worked these muscles, participants pair off and take turns sharing concerns from a real conflict scenario in their own lives (people are invited to share as little or as much as they are comfortable with). As a listener, each participant works to convey presence, empathy, and to reflect back an understanding of the needs, values, and interests of their partner.

Agility, Adaptability, Responding to Uncertainty

Conflict resolution practice relies upon the ability to deal with the unexpected (Kriesberg and Dayton 2017; Wheeler 2013). While conflict resolvers may have theories, methods, or frameworks that they use, the heart of the work lies in their ability to respond agilely to the unique scenarios that emerge with people in conflict.

Improvisation depends upon agility and adaptability in the face of the unknown. It is vital to get participants engaged in exercises that work these muscles before introducing them to other aspects of the curriculum that require those skills. Activities that I use to increase agility and adaptability skills in a short period of time include Half Life (Workbook 12.2), Swedish Stories (Workbook 1.1), Category Die, Alphabet Scene, and Memory Loss. Next, we role-play a conflict scenario. Conflict content is drawn from the group and typically from a real-world conflict that someone knows about. Sometimes group members all participate in the same role-play (in small groups), and sometimes we have a demonstration up front. I will spontaneously insert words, ideas, or situations (i.e. the mother-in-law shows up; the boss walks out, etc.) so that partici-pants have to deal quickly and gracefully with the unexpected. It is at this stage in the training that participants typically begin to let go of their need for as much control, a predetermined agenda, and attachment to a particular conflict outcome. They begin to experi-ence the benefit of how being present and working the muscles of agility gives them greater resources in the moment.

Accepting, Building, Collaborating

Conflict resolution work focuses on collaborative processes that eliminate a win/lose, competitive mind-set (Fisher et al. 2011; Hocker and Wilmot 2014; Saunders 1999). This requires that we fully understand the interests, values, and needs of all parties to unlock what appear to be polarized positions in a conflict. Often when we dig more deeply into people's needs and motivations, we find common ground and more flexibility in how to work together. Resolution in seemingly polarized conflicts often calls for creative collaboration that transcends the "you vs. me" nature of much conflict. Developing processes that allow parties to work together toward a shared goal of mutual benefit is one of the most critical and challenging dimensions of good conflict resolution work.

Improvisation is a collaborative modality with the core princi-ples of Yes, And and Make Your Partner Look Good. Good impro-visation is built on acceptance and mutual support for each other's ideas and solutions. Competition goes out the window when peo-ple build something together and realize that their shared construc-tion is greater than a particular outcome to which they may have been previously attached. Johnstone's (1979) work on Accepting and Blocking Offers provides rich description of this phenomenon for improvisers. Activities like Johnstone's (1979, 1999) Giving Presents and Group Yes; I Am a Tree (Workbook 7.2); and Yes, But and Yes, And scenes make it very clear that the principle of Yes, And does not mean that you have to agree with everything in real life. It is more about having a spirit of receptivity and acceptance, which can help conflicts shift even when we disagree. After a number of

Yes, And activities, we work with conflict scenarios and practice the Yes, And principle as mediators, conflict resolvers, and as conflict parties. Parties work in pairs with a conflict drawn from the group. In the first round, parties literally have to respond to everything with the words Yes, And. In the second round, parties have to bring the *spirit* of Yes, And into the scenario without using the words. This is a challenging exercise, as it requires affirming your "opponent." What is revealed in the debrief is that the nature of the Yes, And spirit actually transforms how people consider new ideas and find solutions.

Emotions

At both individual and collective levels, emotions are a critical aspect of what keeps people stuck; ignoring them will almost guarantee that a conflict will not be resolved (Fisher and Shapiro 2006; Goleman 1995; Nair 2008). Constructive attention to the emotional realm can help people find resolution to seemingly intractable conflict. This includes awareness and identification of emotions, ability to express emotions safely and productively, and empathic acknowledgment and recognition of emotions by the mediator or the other conflict parties. I steer away from the concept of "positive and negative" emotions, and rather, look at all emotions as a natural spectrum of human experience. It's what we do with our emotions that makes them constructive or destructive.

Improvisation invites us to allow our emotional experience to spring forth spontaneously. Often, we are blocked emotionally and the thought of spontaneously expressing ourselves can be terrifying. But increased comfort with a wide range of emotions is useful in our personal conflicts as well as for facilitating conflicts of others. I encourage participants to play with a range of emotional expression by having them choose an emotion in a conflict simulation and then randomly assign them numbers from one to ten (where one is low and ten is high), and they have to experiment with what happens as the emotions fluctuate in degree of intensity and expression. We also do activities such as Emotional Carpool or Emotional Mediation (Workbook 10.3) as a way to examine the contagion and reciprocal influence of emotions in human interaction. In the debrief, it is important to reflect on how people felt and how their choices impacted the relational dynamic. Which emotions were they comfortable with? Which ones were more difficult? Deep exploration of these issues will allow participants to understand the challenges they face when strong emotional content becomes part of a conflict scenario.

Power and Status

Conflict resolution work must always examine issues of power. Power exists in many forms—it can exist at the individual level (beauty, money, education, strength, knowledge, positional rank, networks, etc.); at the structural level (organizational, governmental, military); and at the societal systemic level (race, gender, class). These differing forms of power inform and impact each other in extremely complex ways. All conflicts will have issues of power at play (Coleman et al. 2000; Rouhana and Korper 1996). Dynamics of power are sometimes in the consciousness of conflict parties and conflict resolvers and sometimes not. Typically, it will be the parties with smaller amounts of power who are more aware of the power differentials (Baker Miller 1995). Conflict resolution work must always include some sort of assessment of the power dynamics among the parties and attempt to address or balance them in some way for the good of the parties and the overall goals of the conflict process.

Power also comes in the form of status dynamics, that is, interactional, visible, and audible behavior related to dominance and submission. Status dynamics are also always at play and are critical for understanding and working with individuals and groups in conflict. While understanding status behavior can't change systemic power influences such as race or gender, we can explore status interactions as they relate to these systemic issues. For example, women often feel silenced in organizational contexts with male superiors. The physical and verbal choices for both men and women in this dance reflect longtime conditioning in "status appropriate" behavior across gender. Increased awareness of and training around these dynamics can provide more flexibility and choice in relational behavior.

Improvisation practice has long explored status dynamics on the stage. Status is a core element of Johnstone's (1979, 1999) work and has been one of his most significant contributions to this art. Being able to shift interactional status dynamics is critical to changing relationships, scenes, and stories. It is important to make clear, again, that the term "status" here does *not* refer to ascribed status, but to interactional patterns of behavior. I often start with getting people to try on different status behaviors, walking around either large and loud, or small and quiet. I frequently use a deck of cards so people randomly get a number that symbolizes their status number relative to the others. I then have them interact in different combinations (pairs, triads, groups) to see what happens with the combination of different status roles. I also teach verbal status moves that can include elevating (i.e. complimenting) or diminishing (i.e. insulting) either oneself or the other, which we are all doing much of the time. Once people are comfortable playing with status, we create scenes and simulations that build on Johnstone's Status Party, Status Battles, and Master/Servant exercises. We then layer this in conflict scenarios, shifting status behaviors and hierarchical rank as a way to play with different conflict possibilities and solutions.

Culture and Identity

Conflict resolution practitioners must understand that everyone has cultural conditioning that informs their worldview, their behaviors, and their values. Culture and identity are at the root of almost 80–90 percent of worldwide conflicts (Kriesberg and Dayton 2017; LeBaron and Pillay 2006; Rothman 1997; Ting-Toomey and Oetzel 2001). This means that at both the micro and the macro level, people are fighting deeply for the right to be who they are, to be affiliated with whom they want, to freely practice their preferred ways of being in the world, and to be recognized and acknowledged in ways that are meaningful to them (Bush and Folger 2005). Any effective conflict resolution process must attempt to understand the cultural worldviews that inform the parties and their conflict, and practitioners must work to acknowledge and support the identity needs of all parties.

Improvisation invites us to explore differing characters and identities. Building scenarios allows us to attempt to step into the shoes of others different from ourselves. Being aware of and sensitive to the stereotyping that inevitably arises when we are playing different characters, particularly ones with which we don't have much direct experience, is a critical aspect of this work. In developing characters, identities, and stories, I work with participants to explore how that person might *feel*, what they *need*, what they are *motivated* by. By exploring the inner world of potential characters, we minimize the trap of playing a stereotype that is typically informed by external behaviors. However, there is no way to avoid assumptions when we play others different from ourselves. Safe examination of these issues must be a part of the debrief process. I ask participants what it was like to play a certain character, what they learned about themselves and their assumptions, what it felt like to encounter the characters they interacted with? At this stage in training, we have built strong group cohesion and trust and it often leads to group dialogue on people's real culture and identity in relation to conflict. Other ways to explore the insights that emerge from role-playing can be through nonverbal games, mask work, mime, gibberish, and object work.[3] Physical activities that transcend language can cut across cultures, particularly when there might be language differences within a group.

Stories and Narratives

Conflict resolution depends upon perspective-taking and exploration of differing narratives. Stories are a big part of conflict scenarios—the stories we hear, the ones we tell ourselves, the ones we remember. Retelling stories—imagining different motivations, outcomes, and relations—becomes a critical aspect of conflict resolution. Frequently, conflict parties have different narratives of the same event. Accepting and integrating the stories and perspectives of others, rather than holding on so tightly to our version of the narrative, allows us to imagine our collective stories as a path toward resolution.

Improvisation practice is often focused on creating and co-creating good stories. Johnstone has created many exercises and techniques for collaborative creation and structuring of narratives. I get participants to work on their story muscles with Word (or Sentence) at a Time Stories, Story Spine, New Choice (Workbook 4.3), and Color/Advance.[4] We practice with stories about anything and then move into conflict stories, often drawing from participants'

FIGURE 10.1 *Tint (center) facilitating a workshop at the Global Improvisation Initiative Symposium, 2017.*

real experiences. I might facilitate using this structure: First, we play Word-at-a-Time Conflict (Workbook 10.2) and then debrief that experience. Next, I pair up participants and give each partner a different perspective on the same conflict scenario. The pairs work with a third-party mediator (who knows nothing of the scenario) and they have to tell the story of the conflict one *sentence* at a time. It is a good way for participants to experience the tension between trying to control a story in a certain direction or allowing it to be created from shared perspectives.

Conclusion

Time and again, participants express that they have never been so impacted by a conflict resolution training before. Because the learning happens on so many levels—cognitive, emotional, physical, relational—participants often report being freed up in new and empowering ways, counterbalancing the more traditional structures and expectations of law school, mediation agencies, and conflict resolution programs. The power of improvisational methodology is vast and the enduring dimension of the learning is such that it percolates long after a training experience is over. Sometimes I hear from participants six months, a year, or two years later telling me how the training transformed their work and their lives. One student wrote: "Thank You. This was my last class in three years of Law School and I finally feel like I have gotten my life back."

In writing this chapter, it occurs to me that it's difficult to convey an interactional experience on paper. I just want to come and *do this* with you (Figure 10.1). But until then, I hope this has been useful. Using improv for training in conflict resolution is important in several ways. First, anyone taking conflict resolution classes or trainings has conflicts of their own. Philosophies such as acceptance, support, adaptability, and creativity allow people to lovingly and radically transform their approach to conflict. Second, as was evidenced by my own burdened experience, improv is useful for the health and well-being of anyone working in the area of conflict resolution, which is work that can be difficult and stressful. Third, with these methodologies, anyone working as a conflict resolver suddenly has a greater ability to be flexible, agile, creative, adaptable, and quick thinking with their own clients, greatly enhancing their ability to help others. Fourth, some of the activities, philosophies, and approaches that we use in the training can be used directly with clients, therefore, providing more tools for the conflict resolution toolbox. And last, for anyone wanting to train others in the area of conflict resolution, these tools are powerful strategies for training. Again, I cannot stress enough that this is challenging and complex work. I encourage all practitioners and trainers to know their capacities and limitations; partner with others who might have the skill and knowledge base that complements your own.

Improv has changed my life in ways that I cannot fully explain. My own capacity for attention, joy, collaboration, and creativity has been so fully enhanced that it is hard to remember life beforehand. When I have an opportunity to share it with others, I feel as if I am opening a door to a mysterious and transformational world. I invite you to walk through it.

Notes

1 For greater insight into this work, see Fisher et al. (2011); Hocker and Wilmot (2014); Kriesberg and Dayton (2017); LeBaron and Pillay (2006); Lederach (2003; 2005); and Trujillo et al. (2008).
2 Many exercises are recommended throughout this chapter. Some are described in the Workbooks. Most of the others can be found in one or more of the

following: Boal (1992); Fotis and O'Hara (2016); *Improv Encyclopedia*; Koppett (2013); Jackson (2003); Johnstone (1979; 1999); Hall (2014); Madson (2005); McWaters and Moore (2012); Spolin (1963); TheThiagiGroup.

3   Also called "space object work," this is the practice of "using" imaginary objects to make them appear real.

4   For Color/Advance, see Chapter 8.

WORKBOOK

10.1 Creative Solution Building

This two-part exercise builds the capacity to think quickly and creatively with limited, available information. It begins with a warm-up followed by applying skills to a conflict scenario. The ultimate objective is to imagine as many out-of-the-box solutions as possible for a conflict.

At the end of this exercise participants will have …

- learned to think quickly and (momentarily) let go of rational thinking,
- experienced developing creative approaches to ordinary things and scenarios, and
- collaboratively discovered creative solutions to conflict.

Running the Exercise

1. Part One: Ask the participants to form pairs or small groups. Give each group an ordinary object (e.g. a board eraser, sponge, telephone, or marker) and a few minutes to take turns "using" the object in as many imaginary ways as possible, for example, a pencil could be "looked through" as if it were a telescope, or waved as if it were a conductor's baton. Encourage participants not to limit themselves to "reality." Yes, an eraser can be a flying carpet for a mouse!

2. Part Two: Give participants a conflict scenario (e.g. neighbors arguing over the position of a property line; coworkers having a conflict over a project or resources). Ask participants to now work backward, and imagine all the possible solutions for this conflict. Ask participants to share their solutions and see how many new ones emerge.

Debrief

- What did you experience?
- What did you notice?
- What surprised you?
- What was different in trying to find solutions?
- How does this relate to your work/life?
- What will you see or do differently because of this experience?

Suggestions

These exercises work best when presented in sequence. In conflict resolution, we encourage people not to rush toward solutions. Until people feel heard, validated, and the issues are explored sufficiently, it is typically too soon to offer or encourage solutions; people may not be ready, or the solutions may not sufficiently address important underlying needs.

Connections: Part 1 of this exercise is an adaptation of Boal's Homage to Magritte (See Chapter 11) and/or Johnstone's (1999) Changing Real Objects. See also Johnstone's (1999) Changing the Object, Spolin's (1963) Transformation of Objects, and What Are You Doing? (Hall 2014; Fotis and O'Hara 2016) to build the skill of seeing new possibilities in what is familiar.

10.2 Word-at-a-Time Conflict

This exercise allows participants to explore a conflict scenario as told from different perspectives. It builds on the idea that all conflicts have multiple narratives and perspectives and that attachment to one's own perspective or "agenda" can be limiting.

At the end of this exercise, participants will have ...

- viewed a conflict scenario from multiple perspectives,
- experienced the tension that arises when people hold on to only their version of the truth, and
- practiced letting go of their attachment to a narrative.

Running the Exercise

This exercise can be run in pairs, trios, or small groups. Try different versions to explore the different outcomes and combinations.

1. As a warm-up, ask participants to stand in a big circle. Say "Let's construct a story by adding a word each. I'll begin." Start with a simple word, a name, or even with "Once" as in "Once upon a time" so that you can guide the player to your right to say "upon" and the player on their right to say "a" and so on. Create several stories this way, encouraging participants to go as fast as they can, and to pay attention to the story unfolding. Remind them that there's no way to control the future (i.e. to plan what word they will use), because this exercise demands that they wait to see what the person before them offers.

2. Then introduce a conflict scenario to the group. This can be done spontaneously (i.e. ask for an idea of a conflict) or provide a prepared scenario.

3. Divide into groups, trios, or pairs. Ask the group/trio/pair to tell the story of this conflict (as if they were telling it to someone who didn't know it) with each participant adding just *one word*, taking turns.

4. Each group/trio/pair will know, or decide together, when the story is over.

5. Have the participants debrief with each other before discussing the exercise in the larger group.

Debrief

- What did you experience?
- What did you notice?
- What surprised you?
- What happened to your story?
- What was it like when the story went in a different direction than you intended?
- How does this relate to your work?
- How might you see or do things differently after this experience?

Suggestions

Encourage the participants to speak quickly, without thinking about the "right" word. Coach them to be grammatically correct in their telling so that the people following them have something to work with. You may choose to offer alternatives by having participants give two, three, or four words at a time. Or expand to one sentence at a time.

Connections: This activity is adapted from Keith Johnstone's (1979; 1999) Word-at-a-Time.

10.3 Emotional Carpool or Emotional Mediation

This exercise explores the experience and impact of emotions in a conflict scenario. It works in large groups, with people getting in and out of an imaginary car, or in small groups of four to eight. Ideally, it should be played in different phases to build on the learning.

At the end of this exercise, participants will have ...

- explored a range of emotions they might encounter within a conflict scenario,

- experienced the contagious or polarizing dimensions of emotions in conflict, and
- experimented with strategies that effectively address a challenging emotional situation.

Running the Exercise

1. Ask the group to brainstorm a list of emotions that could come up in a conflict, writing them on a board or flip chart. Coach the group to go further than likely initial responses such as *anger* or *fear.* Stop only when there is a wide range of emotions listed.

2. Ask each participant to select an emotion from the list. Get their commitment in advance not to change their mind.

3. Set up four chairs in the center of the room to simulate four seats of a car. Ask for a volunteer to begin by sitting in the driver's seat.

4. Tell the group that in this exercise the driver will pick up hitchhikers (other participants), one at a time. Everyone in the car must interact with others utilizing the emotion they chose. Let each interaction continue for a while before adding a new hitchhiker. Once the "car is full," have the driver find a reason to get out, everyone shift one seat, creating a new driver, then pick up a new hitchhiker.

5. There are different variations, each with its own purpose. If time allows, scaffold the work with each of the following rounds. If not, choose the one or two that best serves what the group needs:

   a. **Round One:** Everyone in the car adopts the emotion of the person getting into the car. This will magnify and demonstrate the impact of a single emotion. This is a good first activity; it tends to be more playful and exaggerated. It will get people more comfortable with trying on different emotions.

   b. **Round Two:** Each participant stays true to their own particular emotion, regardless of the other emotions that arrive in the car. This conveys the experience of differing emotions existing in the same context; it adds more tension and reveals the influential interactions of differing emotions.

c. **Round Three:** Each participant starts with their own emotion and lets it naturally shift to whatever feels congruent in response to the other emotions in the car. Participants allow themselves to be impacted/altered by the others. This begins to simulate real scenarios where one's emotions are influenced upon interacting with others.

6. Following the car simulation, divide the participants into small groups and have them role-play a conflict. The scenario can be developed in real time, or come prepared with a scripted role-play. Depending upon the topic, a mediator may be invited as well. This is helpful for understanding the role of the mediator, who is to remain neutral, but invariably comes in with their own material.

Debrief (after Each Round)

- What did you experience?
- What did you notice?
- What surprised you?
- What does this tell you about emotions in conflict?
- How does this relate to your work?
- What will you see or do differently as a result of this activity?

Connections: This exercise was adapted from a popular game called Hitchhiker, and according to Theresa Robbins Dudeck, a game that her first teacher, Avery Schreiber, played often. Schreiber was an early member of The Second City in Chicago.

11

Decolonizing "Diversity" on Campus Using Applied Improvisation

Annalisa Dias

Annalisa Dias is a citizen artist, theatre maker, community organizer, and educator. She is a producing playwright with The Welders, a DC playwright's collective; and is co-founder of the DC Coalition for Theatre and Social Justice. Annalisa frequently teaches Theatre of the Oppressed workshops nationally and internationally and speaks about race, identity, decolonizing practice, and performance. She is a TCG Rising Leader of Color, and also works in diversity and inclusion full time at the American Political Science Association. She has an MA in theatre history and criticism from the Catholic University of America and dual BA degrees in English and religion from Boston University.

"Diversity" Education at Predominantly White Institutions

This chapter is about how Applied Improvisation (AI) can develop skills in dialogue facilitation and empower students on college campuses to instigate change toward social justice. I draw from my experience working for three years (2013–16) as the program coordinator in the Office of Campus Activities within the Division of Student Affairs at the Catholic University of America (CUA) in Washington, DC. To begin, I want to reflect on the term "diversity" as it has been used within the context of higher education in the United States before thinking about how improvisation might be used to challenge both theoretical and practical modes of dominant discourse and practice.

"Diversity" has been thought of as a mixed composition (mostly) of bodies within an institutional space which creates opportunities for confrontation with difference. Briefly, after the Civil Rights Movement of the 1950s and 1960s, colleges and universities began creating institutional spaces for nonwhite students (e.g. centers for multicultural affairs or residence halls designated as cultural affinity spaces). For the most part, and ironically due to the successes won by the Civil Rights Movement which often perpetuate the false notion that racism has been conquered in the United States, "diversity" in institutions of higher education is no longer sought after as a civil rights and justice issue. Instead, diversity is sought after for the purpose of increasing the economic value of institutions, which are still primarily owned and operated by white individuals, particularly at private institutions. For decades, even though empirical research has shown the positive cognitive and affective outcomes of learning environments that aim to promote inclusivity, diversity, and intercultural competence (Harper 2008), educational diversity has been conceptualized increasingly in terms of the value it can provide to institutions. Leigh Patel (2016: 91), in her book *Decolonizing Educational Research*, puts it another way: "Diversity is desired, but to improve the institution through representation, through heuristics, not to fundamentally alter or dismantle the settler logics of white supremacy and heteropatriarchy." The ideal of "diversity" has been divested of its radical power in the service of neoliberal goals.

My interest in this history stems from my position at CUA. The Division of Student Affairs was hoping to identify new strategies for "diversity" initiatives, and I was brought on and given the freedom to build programming to address institutional needs around intercultural communication and intergroup dialogue. Although I was hired to address student needs, I was still answerable to quantifiably measurable institutional operational goals from an economic standpoint. This tension was palpable between the institutional demand to meet neoliberal, intervention-style goals that conceptualized the low persistence rates of students of color as a problem to be solved (ultimately due to the economic impact of lost tuition dollars), and the student demand for the institution to be answerable both to their lived experience of daily oppression and their consistent, simultaneous yearning for transformational learning. Nonetheless, I was excited about the position and its potential to affect some degree of sustainable change at the institution.

Intervention versus Praxis, Educational Methodologies

Neoliberal educational research frames education, and its purpose, as a social instrument by which learners are thought of as productive, bourgeois workers for the state.[1] "At the base of neoliberalism are privatization, standardization, and accountability systems that are affecting the ways in which universities are structured, including how moneys are allocated, how tenure and promotion is determined, and how the curriculum in our classrooms is determined" (Monzó and Soohoo 2014: 161). These structures pervade universities at every level and make them accountable to business and economic outcomes, rather than teaching and learning (e.g. by putting focus, prestige, and resources behind academic programs that produce high-paying jobs, and undervaluing academic programs that focus on critical thinking, creativity, or relational ways of knowing).[2]

For many years, the project of educational research in service to the state has been to identify failures in the systematic production of effective workers, and thereby hypothesize potential "interventions" that might improve outcomes. Researchers measure successes and failures in education by quantitative test scores that reduce learning to numerical inputs and outputs. Then they orchestrate interventions to address "at risk" students whose test scores are lower than the dominant (predominantly white) peer group. This prevalent systematic approach positions students from non-dominant groups as objects of study, while simultaneously recentering students from the dominant group as the norm (Patel 2016: 41). This tends to have a dehumanizing effect.[3] In an article looking back on the legacy of Paulo Freire's revolutionary ideas about educational liberation, R. D. Glass (2001: 16) wrote: "Dehumanization makes people objects of history and culture, and denies their capacity to also be self-defining subjects creating history and culture." The authors of the essay "Culturally Responsive Contexts: Establishing Relationships for Inclusion" suggest: "Failure to acknowledge inequities in education and the wider context of society between those that fit within the parameters of the normal dominant and those who are defined as being different from normal is to ignore a fundamental social injustice and to be complicit in an oppressive regime" (Berryman et al. 2015: 44).

Beyond individual dehumanization, research interventions tend to address surface issues of representational equity while still implicitly and complicitly maintaining colonial logics of white supremacy. Colonial logics function on the premise that materials and knowledge should be drawn toward a stable center (empire), there to be transformed, and then redistributed outward to the periphery (colony). The logics of coloniality are built on stratification and difference, but always position the center as dominant (Smith 1999: 58–72). Neoliberal educational research maintains the logics of stratification in order to frame its questions and then hypothesize interventions. An intervention might "solve" a problem in the moment, but the system that creates the stratification in the first place is permitted to remain.

A decolonial alternative to educational interventions is what Paulo Freire and Augusto Boal conceptualize as "praxis," or a continual and mutual process of action and critical reflection. The ongoing and complementary cycle of reflexive action opens space for transformational process-based learning. Pedagogies based on praxis are less concerned with educational inputs and outputs (that position students as objects of an educational system), and more with process, dialogue, and encounter (that position students as subjects and agents in their own education) (Freire 1968). A critical question for educators, and particularly of interest to me in my previous position at CUA, is how to manifest decolonial, praxis-based pedagogies on college campuses. What strategies are actually effective?

Moving toward Praxis and Peer Education

Patel (2016: 1–9) calls on educational workers to pause, to halt the drive toward knowledge production, and to reflect on their relationship to the systems that perpetuate colonial logics of ownership. I am thankful for the opportunity now to pause and reflect on the work we accomplished over the years that I worked at CUA as a program coordinator for intercultural programs. During my time at the institution, I worked alongside CUA's student leaders of color to found a student peer education program called the DREAM Team. The road to developing and implementing this peer education model was hardly straight.

When I first began my position coordinating intercultural programs, then housed within the Office of Campus Activities (which oversaw things like new student orientation and student government associations), I worked in coordination with another colleague of mine who was then responsible for CUA's leadership development programs. Together, we built a yearlong workshop curriculum to develop student skills in intercultural leadership. Unfortunately, within one semester of the program's launch, it became clear that it was a failure. We never had more than three students attend the sessions, and some only came to cover it for the campus newspaper. After the semester (and in the spirit of praxis!), we decided to cancel the program in order to reassess needs and how to meet them.

In the following weeks and months, I had a series of mostly informal meetings with my student staff members and several student leaders of the cultural student organizations on campus that I was advising. During these meetings, I was able to get a better picture of the students' struggles to feel heard and valued by the institution and by their peers. For example, they expressed their frustration with ongoing microaggressions in their living and learning environments. Students told stories about peers and professors who would make marginalizing comments in classrooms or in other campus spaces that harmed these students' ability to engage with their learning, because they were so focused on their frustration. Often simultaneously, they would express great hope and ambition for making lasting change at the institution. They wanted to know what they could do. In fact, these conversations led directly to the creation of the DREAM Team.

I was also able to gain a better understanding of how these particular students were already networked socially across year, course of study, cultural group affinity, and residence hall community. From a traditional multiculturalist perspective, one might expect students in cultural affinity groups like the Black Student Alliance or the Student Organization of Latin@s not to have relationships with each other. As I built relationships with these students it became clear that most of them were members of more than one cultural affinity group. As language around identity changes and expands, students often shift faster than educational programming. As we continued to meet and discuss strategies for moving forward, eventually the idea emerged to create and implement an intersectional, intercultural peer education program. And I knew AI would be an ideal methodology for this program given its capacity to spontaneously respond and adjust to continuously shifting landscapes.

The DREAM Team was founded for two purposes. First, it was an attempt to answer the institution's consistent low persistence rates for students of color in comparison with its white students.[4] The second purpose was to meet student demands for equity in their educational experience. The team would be responsible for planning and executing peer engagement and education events on campus throughout the academic year, either independently or in collaboration with other campus entities. Each event would be followed by a dialogue, led by the DREAM Team, designed to create space for students to take ownership of their learning beyond the classroom by determining topics important to them and by building relationships with their peers, with professors, and with administrators.

In the fall of 2015, we put out a campus-wide call for anyone interested in being on this peer education team. One of my student staff members in the Office of Campus Activities, who I will call Justin here, took on a primary role in assembling the first DREAM

Team with me. We were intentional about seeking diverse representation in the group on a number of levels; therefore, after a rigorous application process, we were thrilled that the ten top candidates (all undergraduates including Justin) representing all four class years, were from several different major courses of study (e.g. sociology, nursing, vocal performance), and from a variety of racial identities (including two white students), gender identities, sexual orientation identities, and socioeconomic class backgrounds.

Next, Justin and I divided the team into co-facilitator pairs, giving each pair a core area of focus: (1) racism; (2) oppression; (3) stereotypes; (4) privilege/power; (5) perception and prejudice. During training, I began by sharing research and information on these core areas of focus and processing with the students how the research related to our lived experiences. Then, we moved into dialogue facilitation training using improvisation games and techniques. I intentionally did not put "improvisation" or "theatre" in the call or application because I have found that students (outside of theatre and performance programs) rarely see the educational value of learning improvisation techniques and think of theatre/improvisation as nonserious. Or students self-select out of "theatre" groups because they are intimidated by students who have "training" in theatre. When I introduced the DREAM Team to improvisational games, some of them were confused as to what games like Boal's Homage to Magritte had to do with our work.[5] Briefly, in Homage to Magritte participants sit (as they are able) in a circle, and the facilitator takes an object (e.g. a spoon, a shoe, a chair, etc.) and places it in the center. The facilitator asks participants to pick up the object, one at a time, and without using words show the object as something other than it is (e.g. picking up the spoon and making a motion to comb your hair or brush your teeth). The participants in the circle take turns guessing what the object has been transformed into until they get it right. I use this game in almost every workshop I teach, because in social justice work, we have to be able to imagine the world as other than it is before we can do anything. Once students began to dialogue about their experience playing, they quickly saw the utility of "theatre games" and improvisation as a methodology for dialogue facilitation training.

My objective was to give the DREAM Team the tools they needed to plan and facilitate a series of engagement events on campus around topics of their choosing. The events ranged from movie screenings to panel discussions to presentations from professors. Each event was followed by a dialogue that was co-facilitated by two DREAM Team students. For the rest of the academic year, we met once a month for two-hour sessions (Figures 11.1 and 11.2). This ongoing training had three primary goals:

1. To build *knowledge* around issues of oppression, racism, stereotypes, prejudice, and privilege

2. To develop *skills* in facilitating dialogue and instigating change toward social justice

3. To cultivate positive *attitudes* about the value of social justice and solidarity

We worked on building knowledge by reading social justice literature together and developing definitions and vocabulary around issues of oppression. I found *Teaching for Diversity and Social Justice* (2nd ed.), to be remarkably useful for this. At each monthly meeting, we would break down another topic from the book, think about its social function, and then work on building personal narratives around that topic. Critically, when students were able to build personal narratives about their relationships to different issues of oppression, their attitudes about themselves as agents of change began to take shape.

Most of the dialogue facilitation practice we did during training was framed through a series of improvisational games that come from the lineage of, if not directly from, Augusto Boal's *Theatre of the Oppressed*. None of the work we were aiming toward with the DREAM Team had anything to do with creating "theatre," applied or otherwise, but Boal's games and their principles are remarkably useful for training dialogue facilitators. My application of Boal's improvisational games was toward training students to facilitate and respond to the moment like improvisers, in other words, to pay attention to the process unfolding, say Yes, And to offers, to gently nudge the process/story forward, and to be self-aware (e.g. of their status). The Boal games we played included several iterations of the Rhythm Machine game (Workbook 11.1–11.3); a game called Homage to Magritte, which I have explained above; and several iterations of Image Theatre, which at its core asks participants to go beyond intellectualized constructs to (wordlessly) confront lived realities.[6] Beyond the actual content and structure of the games, we discovered that the three most salient features of improvisation that were most relevant to this kind of praxis were accepting what others have to offer, lowering status, and valuing silence, each explored in detail below.

In terms of theory, improvisation techniques like accepting offers, lowering status, and valuing silence eliminate structural social hierarchy when in conversation, which allows dialogue participants to share their voices and represent their perspectives more freely. Improvisation also negates the need, particularly within the highly codified space of an institution of higher education, to rely on intellectualization of difficult topics. Rather than teaching students to explicate and rationalize using the structured language of the Academy, improvisational techniques allow students to encounter not only each other but also faculty and staff members on a more equitable footing. Improvisation encourages spontaneity and imagination, which creates spaces where all ideas (or offers) are worth consideration. This is particularly necessary when engaging with and building knowledge around the issues listed in goal number 1 above.

Accepting Offers

Most improvisational systems involve some form of accepting offers. As Theresa Robbins Dudeck (2013: 8) explains in her biography of Keith Johnstone, creator of the Impro System: "One improviser will make an 'offer' (i.e. any physical or verbal input) and the other improviser will 'accept' or 'give' credibility to that offer and then 'offer' something else, 'taking' the initiative, without cancelling any previous offers." This principle is common in many improvisational methods, including the work of Viola Spolin, Augusto Boal, Robert Alexander, and others. I have found that when a dialogue facilitator enters with a real openness both to giving and accepting offers from participants, the participants' experience is vastly improved. Openness is characterized by flexibility, which is to say, it is important not to enter a dialogue with a need for a specific outcome. A good facilitator makes an offer and then inhabits the physical space with dialogue participants and encourages participants to make their own offers.

A particularly difficult dialogue the DREAM Team hosted in 2015 involved discussing the continued use of the Confederate flag and its symbolic and cultural meanings. The dialogue was attended by a wide variety of students, including many white students (primarily from southern states) who spoke impassionedly about the flag's positive cultural meaning for them, many other white students (from both northern and southern states) who expressed negative attitudes toward the flag, several students of color from different regions who spoke about their fears of its symbolic value, and one student of color who spoke about a personal trauma she experienced at the hands of white men flying the Confederate flag from their truck. The widely varied and personal views made for a tense dialogue. Reflecting on the dialogue Justin facilitated, he articulates the tension between accepting offers neutrally and maintaining an ethical framework as a facilitator:

> The technique that should have been used was to challenge ... perceptions in order to dig deeper in the conversation, in addition to providing informative context that could have aided in seeing a different view. On the other hand, if digging deeper did not go very well, it would have been best for the facilitator to redirect the dialogue and complete a temperature check of the room.[7]

The temperature check is a method for asking for offers from dialogue participants. It can be an extremely useful tool for assessing difficult spaces, and is in itself a method of "give and take." The facilitator can set up the expectation of a temperature check by "taking the temperature" at the outset of a dialogue. The verbal cue can be: "I'd like to take a temperature check by asking anyone to say one word or make one gesture that indicates how you're feeling about being here right now." Later in the dialogue, the "temperature check" can be particularly useful in assessing whether or not to go forward with planned activities, and whether or not to continue dialogue at all. It can be used as a way of building room for spontaneity into facilitated spaces.

Dialogue facilitators can train for accepting offers by playing games that focus on, to borrow a term from choreography, accumulation. Games of accumulation set up situations in which participants build together. The Rhythm Machine game is a game of accumulation. Many Image Theatre games are games of accumulation. Concretely, accumulation is apparent when one participant starts by making an offer, another participant builds on that offer by making an offer of their own (without negating the first offer), and another, and so forth. These types of games allow participants the opportunity to build skills in active listening and collaboration, while simultaneously destabilizing the need for there to be a single narrator or arbiter of truth in any situation.

Lowering Status

Keith Johnstone doesn't understand why colleges of education do not teach social status skills to future teachers. Status is learned physical and verbal behavior that, for social animals like us, determines our placement in hierarchical structures (Dudeck 2013: 12–13). Successful educators and dialogue facilitators fluidly lower (or raise) their status in almost any situation as the need arises. This skill usually necessitates training. I have drawn the practice of lowering status mainly from Boal's Joker System[8] and from Paulo Freire's ideas regarding critical pedagogy, though other improvisation practitioners, especially Johnstone, practice this strategy as well. At CUA, I was able to use my position as a student affairs practitioner to have a more flexible, less formal relationship with students while still acting as a "professional" representative of the institution. In order to cultivate a more equitable relationship with my students, I began practicing lowering my "professional" status as frequently as possible. For example, when students would come to my office for one-on-one meetings, I would practice simple adjustments to my physical posture like sitting with both my legs crossed in my chair, in a sort of childlike position; or, when facilitating more traditional educational sessions, I would arrange the seats in a circle if possible, and if not possible, I would place myself in a lower status position by sitting on a desk, again, often with both legs crossed in a childlike posture. These kinds of physical signals begin the unconscious process of breaking down the perceived social hierarchy between educators and students. They can also be used as a point of departure for conversations with students about the need to be critically aware of performative social signals we send to each other on a daily basis through the choices we make, and particularly, how these choices relate to socialized expectations about gender, race, and class.

Within the context of facilitating dialogue about difficult topics, the same principles of lowering status apply. Facilitators need to develop a keen sense of awareness of socially coded behaviors and language patterns, and the ability to adjust spontaneously as needed. When asked to reflect on his facilitation style, Justin said:

> As a facilitator, I go into the dialogue with a neutral attitude and demeanor. I have had people tell me that my mannerisms come off as upper-class, or bougie even, which I think comes from living day to day as a black male that has to prove white America wrong that all black men are not bums, drug dealers, or users, or useless to society.

Here, Justin articulates his understanding of his own social identity within an intergroup space and his awareness of how dialogue participants' perceptions of him influence their relationship to the dialogue and their ability to participate. He also articulates how his approach to facilitation revolves around creating a "neutral" demeanor, which hearkens back to Boal's Joker System. Awareness of one's own status and the ability to spontaneously adjust physical behaviors and speech patterns is critical to facilitating dialogue about issues of oppression. And further, this self-awareness functions as a decolonizing practice, as it attempts to break down rigid social stratifications and relationships.

I was particularly fond of using the Rhythm Machine game as a method for practicing lowering status with students because it asks students to relinquish their need for socially codified behaviors. The first level of the Rhythm Machine game is played entirely in gibberish and discrete repetitive gestures, forcing participants to lower their own social status. When everyone is ridiculous, participants have permission to take risks and to fail. In fact, most "icebreaker" games that student affairs practitioners use, whatever the lineage from which they come, are games that invite participants to lower their statuses.

Pedagogy of Silence

A final strategy for decolonizing practice and dialogue facilitation training is developing a pedagogy that values silence. Silences in improvisational contexts allow participants to develop heightened senses for nonverbal communication. Silence allows time and space for observation of self and for encounter with others. As Viola Spolin (1963: 45) wrote, "A close-working group in improvisational theater often communicates on a nonverbal level with uncanny skill and swiftness." In Boal's games, particularly at the introductory level, participants do not use verbal language. Instead, students are asked to pay attention to the information they give and receive with their bodies, and to expand their physical choices beyond the learned rigidity of contemporary life—sitting in classrooms in the same posture all day long, typing on computers, or tapping screens. The thinking goes that if students can decrease their reliance on hyper-intellectualization, they can gain access to the profound wisdom of their own bodies. The untapped knowledge stored in the bodies of students of color and students with other historically oppressed identities is especially deep. Additionally, on a theoretical level, valuing silence challenges hegemonic needs for ceaseless production of words and exemplifies what Patel refers to as "pauses" in the educational process.

In a culture oversaturated with words, silence has become increasingly difficult not only to value, but often even to find. On college campuses, students are asked over and over to be productive (that is to say, literally to produce writing, analysis, and papers) in their classes, in their student organizations, other leadership positions, and in their internships and work experiences. I have found that practicing what I call "a pedagogy of silence" in institutional spaces can challenge the dominant discourse of production and open spaces for reflection. A pedagogy of silence focuses attention not on the production and replication of objective knowledge but on embodied encounter between learning subjects. Educators can create spaces within their curriculums for reflexive pauses (i.e. moments of silence) on a number of levels—pauses within the semester to personalize learning, pauses within a class session to elicit both reflection and analysis from students who might not otherwise speak up, and pauses within individual interactions with students for whole body listening and learning on the part of the educator.

Practically, as I was teaching students how to facilitate dialogues around difficult topics, I asked them, again harkening back to Boal's ideas of the neutral Joker figure, to begin practicing sitting in silences. As a dialogue facilitator, it can often be tempting to move the conversation along by inserting your own opinion when a question goes unanswered. However, I asked my students to practice allowing silences to have value in the room. Often, particularly when dealing with deeply personal topics such as forms of oppression, silences are needed for processing.

In a conversation reflecting on the DREAM Team training with my student, Justin, I asked him what valuing silence meant to him. He responded with the following:

> Valuing silence in the room was important when we completed the Privilege Walk exercise. This exercise was very eye-opening due to the fact that one begins to reflect that no matter what race/ethnicity, gender, or sexual orientation, we all have some type of privilege and at some point in our lives we all live with oppression ... *I believe it made us all realize that none of us have the right to think that we are better than the next person.* (Emphasis mine)

The Privilege Walk exercise is a fairly common one in the realm of anti-oppression training on college campuses. Briefly, facilitators ask participants to stand in a single line, shoulder to shoulder. Slowly, facilitators read a series of statements that indicate either a privileged identity or an oppressed identity, and participants either take a step forward (privileged statement) or backward (oppressed statement) according to each statement that applies to them. At the end of the series of statements, usually participants are in physically disparate places in the room. The activity can be triggering for participants if mutual trust has not been gained, however, when done in a trusting environment, as Justin articulated, it often builds intersectional solidarity. No verbal analysis is used during the activity, which allows participants to focus on their embodied experience and changing physical relationships to other participants, and the debriefing dialogue after the activity is frequently characterized by long periods of silence and internal processing.

Layering Improvisational Techniques for Dialogue Facilitation Training

In the Rhythm Machine game, as in so many improvisational games and activities, layering of all three techniques—accepting offers, lowering status, pedagogy of silence—is required. For example, this game asks participants to accept whatever gesture and sounds are offered by the rest of the group and to build a gestural machine together. Due to the apparent absurdity of the game at first, the need to accept all offers effectively breaks down perceived social barriers that might be present within the group. Everyone is essentially on the same level of status. The first stage of the game functions as a social icebreaker. Once the game gets to its second and third stages, the game functions as a means by which all offers of social critique become valid, even if the offer is challenging or controversial. Accepting offers becomes increasingly important when participants offer a perspective that may in fact be oppressive. It can be difficult in those tense moments for facilitators to maintain neutrality (without losing their own perspective) and to accept the participants' offer *of participation* without accepting the introduced oppression. The Rhythm Machine exercise gives dialogue facilitators opportunities to practice accepting all offers.

Further, within the context of the Rhythm Machine game, at all its stages, but perhaps most so when using it to analyze systems of oppression, the participants experience the value of silence from at least two perspectives. First, as a facilitator, I make certain to leave room for participants to process information. I keep vocal cues to a minimum and save any and all verbal analysis for the reflexive dialogue portion of the game. College students are inundated with lectures and reading in addition to the contemporary twenty-four-hour news cycle, and are often surprised by a pedagogical choice to remain silent. Second, on a more technical note, when the Rhythm Machine game slows down and speeds up and the actual rhythm of the sounds participants make shifts, silences or lack of silences become all the more evident. Awareness of silences and noise in the context of the game helps students practice comfort with silence in other contexts, in addition to listening and trusting others. I have found that when facilitators are aware of silences as part of a natural rhythm of communication, they feel less anxious about needing to fill silences by pushing conversation forward before participants might be ready.

Coming Full Circle

Over the course of one full academic year, I saw my ten DREAM Team students become more and more skilled in dialogue facilitation and active participants in their own education. I watched students who joined the group, in some cases out of a desire to be activists on campus, or frankly, out of anger at their experiences of systemic oppression, become agents of transformation not only for their peers, but also for themselves. Students who would frequently meet with me one-on-one at the beginning of the year in response to oppressive events with questions like, "What can we do?" would, toward the end of the year, come to me with questions like, "Where can I learn more?"

AI techniques like the ones I have discussed in this chapter (accepting offers, lowering status, and pedagogies of silence) allowed me to work from a very specific time and location to disrupt and challenge the entrenched logics of settler colonialism at a specific historically predominantly white and patriarchal institution. Patel (2016: 94) suggests, "Educational researchers who seek decolonial praxes would do well to remember, from their specific social locations and places, that knowledge is always place-specific." I encourage anyone who might use the techniques I have discussed in this chapter to adapt them as needed to their own specific social and physical locations. As I mentioned, my specific location within the division of student affairs permitted a degree of flexibility in my relationship with students that I may not otherwise have been able to attain. I encourage you to think about how accepting offers, lowering status, and pedagogies of silence might be situated within the coordinates of the epistemological and ontological lineages associated with your individual and institutional locations. I encourage you further to use these techniques intentionally as a method of speaking back to and resisting the oppressive structures of neoliberalism as they manifest in institutions of higher education and elsewhere.

Finally, I leave you with these words of encouragement in the hopes that this chapter will open up new spaces for you to contextualize this work in your own practice from your own location. On principle, in any workshop I give, I always end with a short game that signals not the end, but the new space that has been created for work to continue. In this game, with participants in a circle, I ask everyone to clap three times while counting out loud "one, two, three." However, on "three," the final clap never lands and we hold our hands apart. The silent clap and the space used to create it are reminiscent of the notion that, as Boal used to say, "the work

FIGURE 11.1 *DREAM Team members taking part in training session.*

FIGURE 11.2 *DREAM Team members taking part in training session.*

never ends." As you move forward with your work, my hope is that you will be able to take and adapt the improvisational techniques I have shared here, to pause and reflect on their significance for you and the spaces you inhabit, and to use them to continue the work of moving toward a decolonized and more just society. One, two …

Notes

1 See also Giroux (2017).
2 See also Lilia D. Monzó and Suzanne Soohoo (2014) for extensive discussion of critical pedagogies, diverse epistemologies, and the colonial legacy of the language and structure of the Academy.
3 See also Derald Wing Sue et al. (2007).
4 CUA is, historically and currently, a predominantly white institution. For the past five years, roughly 62 percent of undergraduate students at CUA have identified as white or Caucasian, and persistence rates for students of color have remained consistently lower than persistence rates for white students. Statistical profile. The Catholic University of America Office of Financial Planning, Institutional Research and Assessment.
5 See Part One of Workbook 10.1 for another use of Homage to Magritte.
6 See Boal (1992) for descriptions of these games. Also, I use the term "games" following Boal's terminology rather than "exercises" or "techniques." The language of "games" and "play," for me, gets at the open-ended, spontaneous purpose of the activities, rather than suggesting, as "exercises" or "techniques" do, that these activities are designed to have a prescribed outcome and formulaic implementation.
7 Quotes by Justin are from personal communication emails to author from July 2016.
8 Boal's Joker System consists of facilitators referred to as "jokers." The appellation is drawn from the joker in a deck of cards—the neutral, flexible figure who can change suits and thereby fit into any hand. The joker's goal is principally to upset or destabilize any normative reality and point out multiple interpretations of any singular event or situation. This destabilization provokes in participants a critical awareness of reality.

WORKBOOK

11.1 Rhythm Machine, Part One: The Blank Machine

This is a small- to medium-size group exercise, in three parts, adaptable for unpacking difficult subjects and to instigate dialogue. It works best in groups of eight to twenty. The exercise asks participants to relinquish assumptions about social presentation, to practice active listening with their counterparts, and to accept offers made by others. Part One (The Blank Machine) operates as an icebreaker and as a "hierarchy-breaker" and builds a base for deeper dialogue in Parts Two and Three.

At the end of this exercise, participants will have ...

- had an embodied experience of accepting other's ideas and building on them,
- made physical complex abstract ideas, and
- given each other permission to take social risks in a group setting.

Running the Exercise

1. Ask participants to sit in one area of the room, facing an empty area designated "the stage."
2. One volunteer stands and faces "the audience."
3. Ask this first volunteer to make a repeatable sound with a gesture. The sound should not be a word, just a vocalization. Aspirated sounds usually don't work well; short vocalizations work best.
4. Ask the first volunteer to continue repeating their chosen sound and gesture.
5. Ask another volunteer to join the first one on stage and add to the image by making up their own repeatable sound and gesture and interacting with the first volunteer.

6. Keep adding participants, each with their own repeatable sound and gesture, until there are only a few "audience" observers left. This is "the Blank Machine" effect.

7. Allow the machine to work for a few moments.

8. Side-coach the machine to slow down and speed up. This can be done by instructing the whole group or approaching the first volunteer and whispering, "See what happens if you slow down or speed up your rhythm."

9. Thank all participants and observers for their work.

10. Repeat steps 2 to 9 enough times for everyone to participate and to get comfortable with the process.

11. Begin Debrief.

Debrief

After each part of the exercise, ask participants, "What was challenging or surprising?" This requires them to reflect on their experience by analyzing their own obstacles and moments of potential growth. In Part One, most participants usually observe challenges in overcoming social behavioral norms, and surprises in others' risk-taking. The group may also begin to analyze the difficulty of listening together while remaining physically and verbally active. They might also discuss assumptions made about how they could or should use their bodies in relation to the space.

Suggestions

- Participants may be hesitant to try this exercise because of the significant social risk associated with expressing simplistic sounds and gestures over and over. It can be helpful to cue, "Notice if you're hesitating, and ask yourself what that's about. There will be an opportunity to discuss this later."

- Remind participants to think about using levels of space, at floor level, mid-body, and above-the-head level. Observe if participants use only a single level. Repeat Part One of the Rhythm Machine game several times before the debrief.

• While useful for facilitating dialogue around issues of oppression, this exercise can be adapted for other outcomes.

Connections: Adapted from Augusto Boal's (1992) The Machine of Rhythms.

11.2 Rhythm Machine, Part Two: The Image Machine

Running the Exercise

1. Use the same spatial setup as for Part One (The Blank Machine).
2. Ask one volunteer to stand and face "the audience."
3. Say to the whole group, "Now we're going to see what happens if we throw an image at the machine."
4. Explain that this is going to be "The Machine of ..." and choose an abstract word like "love" or "despair" or "peace."
5. Ask the first volunteer to make a repeatable sound and gesture that relates to the abstract image or word you've given, for instance, the word "despair" may elicit a groan and a collapsing of the head and spine. Encourage the volunteer to move to action without overthinking—there are no wrong sounds or gestures.
6. Repeat steps from Part One.

Debrief

Ask participants, "What was challenging or surprising?" Participants usually observe challenges in sustaining their momentum and surprises and similarities between gestures and sounds. The group may also discuss how alternate interpretations of an image affected the group's understanding, and interpretations of parts of the machine that seem disconnected to the rest.

Suggestions

This can be repeated several times using different abstract images. It may be helpful to say, "Don't think too much. Your body probably understands the image better than your brain." The Image Machine can help concretize abstract ideas since participants are asked to confront and discuss different interpretations of the same image.

Connections: Adapted from Augusto Boal's (1992) The Machine of Rhythms.

11.3 Rhythm Machine, Part Three: The Oppression Machine

Running the Exercise

1. Use the same spatial setup as in Parts One and Two.
2. Ask a volunteer to stand and face "the audience."
3. Say to the whole group, "Now we're going to see what happens if we use the machine to unpack an issue of oppression."
4. Explain that this is going to be "The Machine of …" and choose a system of oppression to analyze (e.g. racism, sexism, able-ism, heterosexism).
5. Ask the first volunteer to make a repeatable sound and gesture that relates to the chosen system of oppression.
6. Repeat steps from Part One.

Debrief

Ask participants, "What was challenging or surprising?" In Part Three, depending on the issue addressed, the group may experience challenges around concretizing abstractions and surprises in images previously not conceptualized as part of the system of oppression. Participants will discuss how different components of the system of oppression are interlocked. They may discuss their emotional responses to being parts of the machine.

Suggestions

It may be helpful to allow participants a few moments to call up images of the chosen system of oppression before they jump into the machine. Part Three can be repeated several times, though it is not recommended to analyze different systems of oppression in one session. The more concrete the group can make one topic, the better.

Connections: Adapted from Augusto Boal's (1992) The Machine of Rhythms.

12

Making Sense of Science: Applied Improvisation for Public Communication of Science and Health

Jonathan P. Rossing and Krista Hoffmann-Longtin

Jonathan P. Rossing and **Krista Hoffmann-Longtin** have dual backgrounds in educational fields and in communication studies. Jonathan studied higher education administration for his master's degree and then pursued a doctoral degree in rhetoric and cultural studies, with a minor in critical pedagogy. Krista received her master's degree in communication and then studied education leadership and policy for her doctorate with an emphasis on faculty development. Their combined training in education and communication theories have influenced their strong commitment to Applied Improvisation as a pedagogical technique and form of experiential learning.

Applied Improvisation (AI) workshops focused on communication, storytelling, and audience engagement have great potential to address the scope of the challenges faced by scientists and physicians when speaking with public, nonexpert audiences. For instance, instead of assuming traditional research roles in higher education, many scientists turn toward employment opportunities—in business and industry, public policy, science reporting, and science museums—requiring public communication skills.[1] These emerging roles and demands require the ability to communicate specific scientific knowledge to broad audiences.

For professors and graduate teaching assistants who stay in academia, they face the challenges of communicating effectively with students and igniting interest in scientific research. These audiences require professors and graduate student teachers to present complex information in ways that help the students learn particular course content, get them excited about scientific disciplines, and inspire interest in scientific discovery.

Increasingly, physicians and scientists face the need to tailor their communication for a variety of audiences who are not scientific experts or researchers. When speaking to patients, for example, physicians must deliver a clear message while building empathy and trust. In a recent Pew Research Center study on public and scientist's views on science and society, 84 percent of the scientists who responded said that limited public knowledge about science was a "major problem." The study also revealed significant gaps between scientists' and the public's understanding on key issues. For example, the study found that 57 percent of the general public believes genetically modified foods are *unsafe* and only 37 percent believe these foods are safe. In contrast, 88 percent of the scientists in the survey said genetically modified foods are *safe*. The study revealed similar knowledge and opinion gaps for issues such as climate change, nuclear power, offshore drilling, and vaccinations. Likewise, both research scientists and healthcare professionals must communicate vividly to funders and policymakers about why their work matters (Funk and Rainie 2015). Moreover, scientists ranging from researchers to professors at research institutes and universities increasingly participate in science education and outreach programs designed to promote better understanding of science among the public.

In every context, scientists and physicians must tell engaging stories, respond spontaneously to the needs of the moment, and explain their work in terms non-scientists can understand. AI training helps scientists and physicians find ways to make sense of science with a wider range of audiences. AI offers an experiential technique that alters thinking away from "My goal is to deliver this information" toward "My goal is to create understanding in partnership with another person."

Scientific experts need the skills of empathetic imagination, perspective-taking, and responsiveness to an audience's needs and interests (Brownell et al. 2013). Successful scientific outreach and communication with audiences requires experts to listen attentively to discover misunderstandings and preconceived notions that might thwart meaning-making conversations. AI reframes the audience as a co-creator of meaning and emphasizes communication *partnerships* that equalize the power differentials between expert and public.

Program at IUPUI and IUSM

To meet these needs, we developed a three-part workshop series at Indiana University Purdue University, Indianapolis (IUPUI), and the Indiana University School of Medicine (IUSM). We are not the first to do work of this kind. Organizations across the country are applying improvised and scripted theatre methods to address the communication gap between scientists, physicians, and the public. The Alan Alda Center for Communicating Science at Stony Brook University, New York, has developed innovative curricula based on Viola Spolin's theatre games that help scientists transform their approach to talking to the public about complex research. The Medical Improv program created by Katie Watson at Northwestern's Feinberg School of Medicine and Belinda Fu at the University of Washington works with healthcare providers to help them communicate more effectively within their teams and with greater empathy and clarity with their patients. At the University of Michigan, the CRLT Players (Center for Research on Learning and Teaching) perform interactive sketches facilitated by theatre teachers and medical school faculty to help medical students practice the art of delivering bad news to patients.

In our program, participants came from a variety of disciplines, but most were technical or scientific in nature (medicine, nursing, life science, engineering) and included professors, professional scientists, physicians, and graduate students training to become science researchers. The university recognized that grant writing, patient satisfaction, and teaching effectiveness would be improved if current faculty members and graduate students in these disciplines developed skills in science outreach and communication. IUPUI and IUSM are affiliates of the Alan Alda Center for Communicating Science at Stony Brook University. We adapted the workshop curriculum based on a series of academic credit-bearing courses offered at Stony Brook and on a similar three-part series offered at Boston University School of Medicine, also an Alda Center affiliate.

Each workshop in the three-part series ran for two hours. Because our participants were primarily physicians and clinical professors, their busy schedules did not allow for workshops longer than this. The workshops also had to be scheduled months in advance, and although we requested that participants commit to all three sessions, we could not require attendance as clinical schedules are so unpredictable. The workshops were capped at sixteen participants so that all could take part in activity debriefing discussions and to allow for more one-on-one feedback time.

We co-facilitated all of our workshops and, beforehand, discussed and assigned who would lead each game or activity, that is, who would explain the rules, and guide and side-coach participants through the activity. The primary facilitator for an activity also began the debrief discussion; however, as debriefing proceeded, we shared equal responsibility for asking follow-up questions and for encouraging participants to reflect on different behaviors and responses that we observed. Following each workshop, we made note of the highlights, strengths, and areas for continued development.

In the following sections, we describe the three-part workshop series format and outline some of the challenges and opportunities we faced in implementing this curriculum at a large research university. It is important to mention that, in speaking generally about these issues below, our aim is not to stereotype the scientific and medical community or their training. Rather, we hope to provide useful context and additional considerations for those AI practitioners working with this audience.

Workshop One: Connecting with Your Audience through Applied Improvisation

All the exercises in Workshop One have been selected to help participants practice skills such as connecting with an audience, paying dynamic attention to others, reading nonverbal cues, and responding to questions with sensitivity to the context and questioner (Figure 12.1). Importantly, the first workshop must also mitigate the fear some faculty members and physicians may have about playing games that invite participants to take risks and to change their attitude toward failure, vulnerability, and emotional expression. In our experience, it was difficult for some participants, especially for those concerned with prestige and professionalism, to consider taking risks in front of their colleagues. Interestingly, we observed that it was even more difficult for graduate students to let go and take risks, perhaps due to a need to prove their worth or belonging among peers. However, in most cases the participants were willingly participating by the end of the first workshop session. Facilitators should be aware of the levels of risk required for

FIGURE 12.1 *Participants in the program.*

every improvisation exercise. The first workshop should begin with low-risk exercises that build trust, comfort, and success. Be prepared for faculty to opt out of participating, but encourage them to stay in the room and even participate as observers or reflectors in the debrief conversation. As a group develops, the reticent participants will likely become more comfortable and see the safety in taking small risks. Rather than fearing failure, they learn to see failure as an opportunity for positive growth.

Early exercises include a basic name game to help participants become familiar with their learning group and to build comfort. Zip Zap Zop helps participants think about nonverbal connections through eye contact and gestures and gives them the opportunity to practice heightened attention to and presence with fellow players. When leading with Zip Zap Zop, often our participants express (usually nonverbally) reticence and concern about the applicability of the game. When we notice participants looking down and letting their attention and presence wane, we side-coach with: "Make strong, clear eye contact," "Make deliberate gestures," and "Remain ready to receive the pass." When we debrief and participants connect the affective response from the game to their work, they are moved to "buy in" to the improv method as a way to learn these skills. For example, participants discuss how the level of attention and clarity of eye contact in Zip Zap Zop is a valuable practice in their various communication contexts and with different communication partners.[2]

Participants also play Viola Spolin's (1963: 61–3) classic Mirror exercises to help them think about taking responsibility for their diverse audiences and giving up some control over their message in order to better attend to audience needs. For Spolin, "following the follower" is achieved when both mirror partners reflect one another without deliberately initiating. "Follow the follower" is essentially sharing control which requires a rejection of status and hierarchy. We invite participants to think about what they had to do in this exercise to help their partner be the best mirror they could be. We remind them that it isn't the partner's responsibility to keep up with fast or erratic motions; instead, it is the movement initiator's responsibility to slow down and make adaptations in order to help their partner succeed. Participants then connect "follow the follower" habit to the contexts of science outreach, patient interactions, and even classroom conversations. Even though they are experts in their field, the Mirror exercise reminds participants that they must continually work to create shared meaning with audiences, via perspective-taking and message adaptation.

The final activity in the workshop is Picture Story (Workbook 12.1). This activity provides a bridge between the concept of listening to, responding to, and connecting with an audience and the focus on storytelling in Workshop Two. It also provides an opportunity to help break the objectivity/subjectivity dichotomy that results from scientific training. Scientists are trained to objectively report facts and data from their work; therefore, the idea of introducing personal motivations for or fascinating stories about their work often seems counterintuitive to their communication objectives. Picture Story helps participants consider the importance of storytelling and emotion in helping audiences connect to information that is foreign to them.

The techniques we normally use for debriefing activities in a theatre setting require adaptation for this audience. Actors are trained to access emotions and the affective response to experiences. Conversely, scientists and physicians have been well-trained *not* to access their affective responses at work. Their training emphasizes the importance of objectivity. They attend to clear, concrete physical evidence and data, not vivid descriptions and stories. Thus, the strategies most effective for debriefing must involve making clear connections between behavior and emotion. Questions that focus on how a particular behavior elicits a particular emotional response help participants to change the way they work with one another and the public. We like to use the debriefing questions: "What? So, what? Now what?" This technique can help physicians and scientists to clearly connect the improv activities to their daily practice. For example, when debriefing the Mirror exercise, we might ask: "What just happened? Describe that experience." No participant's experience is "wrong"; it is important to Yes, And their experiences, even if some responses are not positive. After several participants share their experiences, we ask them to describe the takeaway lessons, the "so what?" We might inquire: "Applying this exercise to your communication with patients or someone who is not an expert in your field, why would you want to 'follow the follower' when explaining a complex concept from your research?" Finally, we guide the participants to name particular communication habits they might adopt that apply these takeaway lessons—the "now what?" For example: "How can you 'make your scene partner look good' when your partner is a journalist asking you about your work?" One participant explained in their post-evaluation survey, "Communication has many facets, and it's not simply 'message sent, message received'—there are many different aspects within it that can be intercepted and improved upon."

While the first workshop focuses primarily on audience-centered communication skills, we found that scientists and physicians also find value in discussing the connections between these games and their roles in collaborative teams such as lab teams or healthcare teams. One researcher found that many of the skills engendered by AI were important to building successful scientific research collaborations: "spending time together, practicing trust, discussing language differences, and engaging in team tasks" often encouraged a more productive team (Thompson 2009: 278). We found it valuable to share this type of research with participants as a way to expand the discussion into other professional applications.

Workshop Two: Distilling Your Message

Workshop Two introduces principles of clear communication and exercises which allow participants to practice defining their communication goals, identifying main points, explaining meaning and context, responding to questions, and using storytelling techniques to enliven messages (Figure 12.2). We coach participants to speak about their work effectively and responsively with multiple audiences, from peers and professors to family members and policymakers.

One of the core storytelling-based exercises in the second workshop is Half-Life (Workbook 12.2). Improvisers use this game to discover the beats in a scene and develop more efficient storytelling skills. With scientists and physicians, this activity helps them discover the core elements of their message that are most exciting and engaging for public audiences. Often scientists start with disciplinary background and experimental details that only experts would understand; they leave the engaging takeaway—the "so what?"—until the end of their talk. As a result, nontechnical audiences often lose interest from the get-go. Half-Life helps participants discover and foreground the "takeaway," that is, the central message in order to hook the audience quickly. It forces participants to condense

FIGURE 12.2 *Participants in the program.*

their message from two minutes, to one minute, and finally to thirty seconds which creates an opportunity for scientists and physicians to explore feelings associated with communicating in stressful situations. As mentioned earlier, this audience is not always adept at accessing emotional responses, so it is important to encourage participants to discuss their emotional experience after all activities. For example, we may ask participants to speculate on why their heart rates increased during Half-Life.

We also use the following example from the Alda Center to illustrate the importance of a succinct message with vivid, descriptive, and accessible language. First, we share the research summary statement with the participants: "I study *Didymosphenia geminate*, an invasive riverine species that impairs the recreational and ecological values of waterways." Participants readily recognize that this may be an accurate description, but it may not make clear to lay audiences what the researcher studies. In fact, even experts from other scientific fields might not immediately understand this statement. Then we share an alternative research summary: "I study rock snot, a kind of alga that forms brown, oozing masses that look like a sewage spill. These get so big that they block rivers and kill fish" ("Dealing with Complexity" 2013: 2). This vivid and humorous description both distills the central message and helps nonscientific audiences better connect to the ideas. Just as important, it has the potential to elicit laughter establishing a human connection and releasing tension in the room. "I study rock snot" also exchanges some of the expert's power and status for a shared interaction with the audience. The exercise allows us to revisit concepts like "follow the follower" from the Mirror exercise and the importance of vivid descriptions from Picture Story. One challenge we experience is that some participants think the first summary is stronger due to its scientific precision and accuracy. As facilitators, we welcome such challenges from the participants as they allow for a richer exploration of the meaning and application of these exercises. This objection allows us to further discuss communication as a shared process and that audiences must be oriented to complex ideas in accessible terms before layering in the complexity.

Another centerpiece of the second workshop is the Uncertain Dialogue (Workbook 12.3) activity from Coopman and Wood (2004). This activity helps participants to consider how much is conveyed through nonverbal communication. Often, when we hear our participants describe the process they use when practicing for a presentation, they focus almost exclusively on the verbal message. Uncertain Dialogue uncovers the importance of the nonverbal message in developing credibility and building a relationship with the audience. Further, Slepian and colleagues (2014) found that doctors who smiled, established eye contact, and were not angry when they discussed patient's choices were instrumental in helping their patients achieve positive health outcomes. Thus, immediate application of the importance of nonverbal communication is apparent for our participants.

The Uncertain Dialogue requires four participants to perform a short dialogue from a script. It is the only activity that feels more like a traditional "acting" activity; for that reason, it should not be used until later in the second workshop so that participants have time to become comfortable with each other and with AI as a training technique. Four volunteers (two pairs) perform identical dialogues, but each pair performs the dialogue with a different relationship, and the audience does not know that the dialogues are identical. After both pairs perform, encourage observers to identify that the dialogues were identical and only the nonverbal elements changed, and to guess the two different relationships and contexts for the scenes. After they have reached consensus about the two relationships, lead a discussion about the nonverbal clues that helped them infer the relationships. Ask the "actors" if they discussed how to act or if they intuitively knew how to perform their assigned relationship. This is a wonderful opportunity to remind your participants that the people who performed the scenes were not actors—they are regular people who knew how to "play" these roles using only nonverbal communication. You can encourage confidence by reminding participants that they already have the skills to use nonverbal communication to establish relationships, provided that they attend to it in their presentations. Then, direct the conversation toward nonverbal cues and contexts for communicating science and health information. Invite the participants to reflect on ways they can use nonverbal cues to complement their stories and create stronger relationships with their audiences. We have found this activity most effective when it is followed by opportunities to practice both verbal and nonverbal communication in a high-profile context like a public interview.

Workshop Three: Media Interview Training

Workshop Three allows participants to practice what they have learned in the first two workshops in a media interview scenario with a journalist in front of imagined audiences. The role-playing allows them to practice planning, developing, and delivering an engaging message about complex topics in an unscripted format. After each interview, invite all participants (as "audience members") to provide feedback about what stood out in the interview; what stories, descriptions, and metaphors were memorable; and what points remained unclear or relied too heavily on jargon. Workshop facilitators could give each participant a different imagined audience. For example, an interview could take place on a national morning show like *Good Morning America* or on a radio show like NPR's *Science Friday* or for a segment on a local high school's public television program where the target audience is middle school and high school students. We recommend that facilitators solicit help from a trained journalist for this portion of the workshop. While trained improvisers are certainly equipped to listen carefully and respond quickly with interview questions, it is valuable to simulate a real-life media interview as closely as possible. If you have access to a professional studio, consider taping the interviews and giving participants a copy of the interview for review and study.

While AI training has great potential for helping scientists and physicians practice communication skills, we must also be clear about the expectations and outcomes of such training. Behavior changes in communication take significant time and practice, particularly for communication practices that are deeply ingrained in professional norms and personal habits. Therefore, facilitators should not only expect some resistance to the idea of merging storytelling with scientific reporting but also recognize that a single workshop or workshop series will not be enough training to change habits. Workshop leaders should stress the importance of continued communication practice and development. We are clear with participants that we do not expect them to become the next Neil Degrasse Tyson, Bill Nye, Sanjay Gupta, or Atul Gawande. Rather, they should look for opportunities to practice presenting their research to small, safe audiences at campus colloquia or "Science on Tap" events. Consider sharing additional examples with workshop participants that they can use for further study. The three-minute thesis program by the University of Queensland, for example, offers excellent excerpts from researchers explaining technical concepts to the public. TED talks are also useful examples to consider.[3]

Scaffolding

At the beginning of the first workshop we explain to our participants that each activity builds on the previous game and exercise, and that each workshop builds directly on the previous workshop. We begin with lower risk activities (name games, icebreakers), building to higher risk, more complex ones (Half-Life, media interview). We invite participants to make connections between the games. For example, when we debrief the Half-Life activity, we ask them to apply the lessons they learned from the Mirror exercise and the Picture Story activity so that as they discover their central message, they are also thinking about attending to the needs of their particular audience and using vivid and emotional descriptions. We also begin each workshop with a review of the last one, reminding the participants of key takeaways. When we send email reminders for each of the workshops, we include a reflection prompt that we incorporate into the workshop conversation. Before the first workshop, for example, we send participants a video clip of comedian Stephen Colbert interviewing physicist Brian Greene on *The Colbert Report*. We ask participants to reflect on Greene's language choices and nonverbal communication as he explains the topic of string theory to Colbert and his audience. Colbert's training in improvisation also provides opportunities to highlight how he employs improvisational skills in the interview. All of these strategies are designed to help our participants connect the aims of the improv activities with their experiences in the lab, clinic, or classroom. Given that physicians and scientists are trained to be very linear, logical thinkers, they seem to react well to these scaffolding techniques because it helps them to clearly see immediate applications of these strategies.

Designing Your Program with the Audience in Mind

Following are a few additional considerations when bringing AI workshops to a higher education context. Institutes of higher education frequently resist change, many are steeped in tradition, and these long-standing practices are part of faculty members' socialization. This socialization also encourages faculty members to value, even revere, hierarchy and prestige. All of this seems in direct opposition to what improvisers value. Still, many academic programs see the importance of encouraging more team-based research and interdisciplinary collaboration (Rossing and Hoffmann-Longtin 2016). So be prepared to proffer clear connections between improvisation training and interdisciplinary, team-building efforts, as well as to debunk the widely held perception that improvisation is only about being funny and/or lacks structure or rigor.

You may want to consider the difference between voluntary versus involuntary participation in the workshop series. We had great success working with a group of faculty members and graduate students who self-selected into the program. The workshops were rated positively, and we have had a number of requests for a "master class" or additional training. Alternatively, we had a less successful outcome with a group of first-year PhD students in biomedical sciences. These students were required to participate in the program as a part of a first-year course. Students in this program were less likely than their voluntary counterparts to see the connections between the AI method and their need to present complex work to a variety of audiences. As you consider your training program, talk with your client about the advantages and disadvantages of requiring participation in the program. Be realistic about what you are able to accomplish with reticent participants, and ensure that you establish your credibility, early on, with your client requesting the workshop as well as with the participants in order to build value and trust.

One strategy we have found especially successful is to partner with an "insider" when developing the training. You can accomplish multiple goals by asking your client if there is a scientist or physician on the team who would be open to this type of training and willing to serve as your partner or "guide." First, the partnership helps you to gather information about pockets of resistance or concerns that you may need to address early on. Your partner can help you identify challenges and ways to mitigate them before the actual training occurs. The partnership strategy also helps you to "translate" some of the language of improvisation into the context of science, medicine, and/or higher education. By speaking the language of the context, you establish credibility and show a willingness to learn from and with your participants. Furthermore, you may find it valuable to become familiar with accrediting requirements and standards for science and professional health education programs in order to tie the outcomes and goals of AI workshops to the accreditation standards.

Finally, we suggest exploring alternative formats that have the potential to reach greater audiences in higher education settings. For example, in order to generate interest in the workshop series, we have offered two-hour teaser workshops that included four activities from the longer series. The experiential training in these shorter workshops still provides participants with the opportunity to learn, practice, and reflect on communication habits. They also provide opportunities for participants with extremely demanding workloads. Once again, be clear that these alternative formats simply offer a foundation for ongoing practice and development.

We have facilitated the "Making Sense of Science" workshop series five times. Participant feedback has been strong, with most citing an increase in confidence and in their ability to perspective-take with audience members. Within the network of AI practitioners, it will be important to continue exploring the benefits and limitations of training length, duration, and number of sessions. Gathering data and reaching informed conclusions about the effectiveness of this methodology is especially important to have when reaching out to the scientific community. To date, the majority of published data comes from medical improv training (e.g. Boesen et al. 2009; Watson 2011), which tends to focus predominantly on building interpersonal communication skills (such as empathy and listening) with patients or among healthcare teams. We are currently collecting data from our workshop series and collaborating with a number of Alda Center affiliates to coordinate data collection across multiple institutions.

Improvisation offers an opportunity for those working in the scientific and medical communities to move beyond traditional, skill-based public speaking or media training. The AI approach asks participants to consider their own identities as professionals and their commitment to public understanding of science and health. While still in the early stages of exploration, the three-part workshop series we employ at IUPUI and IUSM is an important step in helping scientists and physicians to grow in their ability to build relationships and collaboratively make meaning with their audiences. We encourage AI practitioners to reach out to institutes of higher education and to organizations designed to increase public engagement in science and health as a first step in closing the gap between physicians, scientists, and the public.

Notes

1 According to the National Science Foundation (NSF), 58 percent of doctoral scientists and engineers are working outside of four-year educational institutions. Furthermore, a 2012 survey of nearly 5,000 PhD students in the sciences indicated that, over the course of their PhD program, students' interest in traditional academic careers decreased, while their interest in work in private and government sectors increased (Sauermann and Roach 2012). On an anecdotal level, *Nature* has produced a popular blog series on a number of scientists who have pursued careers outside of the academy.
2 See Workbook 4.1 Whoosh Bang Pow which is similar to Zip Zap Zop.
3 Three Minute Thesis (3MT) was developed by the University of Queensland. The 3MT website features a showcase of past presentations (http://threeminutethesis. org/); the TED Talk website curated a list of "7 talks to make you love science" (https://www.ted.com/playlists/163/7_talks_to_make_you_love_scien) featuring talks by neuroscientist Suzana Herculano-Houzel, biologist Carin Bondar, physicist Brian Greene, and marine biologist Tierney Thys.

WORKBOOK

12.1 Picture Story

This full-group exercise allows participants to reflect on the impact of storytelling. It requires a moderate level of risk and disclosure. It is suited for any group that would benefit from the power of storytelling for developing a strong, personal connection with an audience.

At the end of this exercise, participants will ...

- have risked intimacy and exposure in sharing a personal story,
- have experienced the power of descriptive storytelling in influencing an audience,
- have identified additional opportunities to use stories to make an impact, and
- feel more intimately connected with the group of participants.

Running the Exercise

1. Hold up a blank sheet of paper and tell the participants that you have a picture to share with the group. Describe in detail the features of "the photograph," including the story behind it and any relationships between the people in it. The goal is to create a vivid and engaging story about the imaginary photograph—to make it real for the group.

2. After modeling the activity with this opening sheet of paper, ask the participants if they have a "photo" they would like to share with the group and pass the blank paper to anyone who wishes to tell the story of their picture. Specify if you would like the stories to be real or made up.

3. Continue until all participants (or as many as time allows) have had a chance to share a story. If it is a large group (more than sixteen), divide into smaller groups.

Debrief

Focus on elements that made these pictures and stories memorable and how they might incorporate similar elements in their communication.

- What made these pictures and their stories memorable? Why?
- How has your level of connection to your other participants changed during this exercise?
- What would happen if you started to "tell the story" about your work and why you do it, rather than just reiterating data?
- What stories can you tell about your work? (Perhaps prompt participants to think about their personal motivations for pursuing their work topic or an unlikely turn of events that led to a particular insight or discovery.)
- Share Story Spine and talk about storytelling structures. Invite participants to think about how their work projects may already follow a story structure or about how they can conceive of their work as a journey.

Suggestions

Participants are sharing personal stories so avoid side-coaching during the storytelling. Encourage volunteers by asking, "Who else has a story to share?" (rather than "… a picture to talk about") to emphasize the storytelling outcome. Be prepared with a story to get the group started, but not one that is *too* good. As the facilitator, the bar should not be so high that participants are intimidated. Ideally, all participants will have the opportunity to tell a story about their picture, but if some participants do not yet feel comfortable with this level of disclosure, allow them to participate by observing. This exercise could be combined with or followed up by Color/Advance (see Chapter 8).

Connections: For a particularly playful group that is willing to take risks, continue working on storytelling with the game Photo Album (Fotis and O'Hara 2016), also known as Slide Show (Hall 2014).

12.2 Half-Life

This exercise helps participants learn concise, powerful communication and discover the most critical elements of their story. It begins in pairs and ends with a full-group debrief. It is suited for anyone that could benefit from communicating in a more concise and targeted way.

At the end of this exercise, participants will have ...

- experienced delivering a specific and concise message;
- felt the impact of hearing a pointed, targeted message versus a rambling, vague message; and
- experienced the process of editing and refining.

Running the Exercise

Prior to the workshop, ask participants to come prepared to talk about a specific research project or ongoing work. With groups of eight or more this activity is best run in pairs. With smaller groups of three to six, it may be run as one group.

1. Ask the participants to form pairs. One partner is the Speaker, the other the Listener.
2. The Speaker has two minutes to describe their specific work. The Listener should neither ask questions nor interrupt the Speaker.
3. After two minutes, ask the Speakers to reflect on whether they successfully shared everything they hoped to share, then ask the Listeners to provide feedback to the Speakers (no more than two minutes) related to the following:
   - What was the main point?
   - What was still confusing or unclear?
   - What examples or descriptions were memorable?
4. Give the Speakers another opportunity to share this information, but shorten their time to one minute. Listeners remain silent.

5. The Speakers are asked again to reflect on what information they *really* want to share and what information they could omit. Again, the Listeners provide feedback to the Speakers, including:
   - What changes did the Speaker make that helped or hindered the story?
6. Give the Speakers one more opportunity to share this information, but shorten their time to thirty seconds.
7. After thirty seconds, ask Speakers to reflect on whether they successfully shared everything or if they left out critical information. Ask Listeners to provide feedback to the Speakers (no more than two minutes):
   - What changed over the three versions of the story?
   - What changes helped the story?
   - What changes hindered the story?
   - What was still confusing or unclear?
   - What examples or descriptions were memorable?
8. Switch roles and repeat Steps 2–7.

Debrief

- Speakers: Describe the difference between your first attempt (two minutes) and your final attempt (thirty seconds). What changed? What did you notice about your message as the time got shorter?
- Listeners: What changes did your partner make that improved the focus of the message?

Suggestions

Side-coaching examples: "Make eye contact"; "Find a way to connect"; "Introducing an idea a second or third time is called reincorporation and can strengthen comprehension"; "Trust your first impulses." During the one-minute and thirty-second version, remind the Speakers to:

- "Talk smarter, not faster"
- "Find the crux of the story"
- Ask "What does the audience *need* to know"

For further study, the "Three Minute Thesis" (3MT) program by the University of Queensland (2008) offers excellent examples of researchers explaining technical concepts to the public. TED Talks are also useful examples to consider.

Connections: For further exercises that help distill your message or create stories that are concise and persuasive, we suggest trying Color/Advance (see Chapter 8), Story Spine (see Chapter 7, endnote 4), and Spolin's (1963) Slow/Fast/Normal.

12.3 Uncertain Dialogue

This exercise requires four volunteers to read or perform a short, scripted dialogue. The exercise reveals the power of nonverbal communication cues.

At the end of this exercise, participants will have …

- knowledge of familiar and commonsense nonverbal cues,
- practiced communicating in nonverbal ways,
- awareness of how to communicate/build relationships with others through nonverbal means, and
- internalized the power of tone of voice, speed of speech, pauses, emotional undertones, body language, and body in physical relation to the other.

Running the Exercise

1. Give the following short scripted dialogue to four participants (two pairs of two). One pair is instructed to read the

dialogue as if they are a couple ending a long-term relationship. The other pair is instructed to read the dialogue as if they are about to rob a bank. The remaining participants ("the audience") have no prior knowledge of the dialogue or the characters each pair is playing.

Uncertain Dialogue

A: Hello.

B: Hello.

A: So, uh, how are you?

B: About the same. You?

A: Nothing new to report.

B: I thought maybe you might have something to tell me.

A: Has anything changed?

B: Not that I know of. Do you know of a change?

A: No.

B: So, what do you think we should do now?

A: I suppose we could go ahead and ...

B: Yeah, seems like it's a good plan.

A: Are you sure?

B: As sure as we ever can be in situations like this.

A: Want to reconsider? A lot is at stake.

B: No, I'm ready. Let's do it.

2. Give each pair only a few minutes to review their dialogue. Tell the group only that they will be seeing two dialogues. Do not tell them the scripts are the same.

3. After each pair performs their dialogue, ask participants to guess the relationship between the participants. Because the dialogues are identical, participants must rely on nonverbal cues (physical movements, tone of voice, etc.) to determine the relationship.

Debrief

- Same language, very different scenarios. What happened?
- How were the characters able to establish relationships with one another using no (or in this case, the same) words?
- How can we use these strategies when we are communicating with one another?
- How can we pay more attention to how we communicate, not just what we say?
- What message do you want to send with your tone of voice, speed of speech, space usage, and gestures? How can you achieve that?

Suggestions

The nature of both relationships will likely lead the two pairs to whisper or speak softly. Encourage them to use "stage whispers" so the rest of the group can hear them.

Avoid providing coaching or acting tips to the volunteers. Ask the participants to read through the dialogue a few times but do not have them "rehearse." Almost all participants will rely on experience and common knowledge to arrive at the best way to act; this strengthens the discussion of how we make meaning out of nonverbal communication cues.

Connections: The authors adapted this exercise from Coopman and Wood's *Everyday Encounters: An Instructor's Manual* (2004). Gibberish exercises are also wonderful tools for developing physical expression. For a group of scientists or physicians, we especially recommend Spolin's (1963) Gibberish Interpreter. You can adapt it by instructing one player to tell the group about something they do at work (e.g. in a lab or when prepping for surgery) but they can only speak in gibberish. Then, have a second player interpret/translate the gibberish for the group.

13

On the Notion of Emergence: A Conversation with Keith Sawyer and Neil Mullarkey

Facilitated by
Theresa Robbins Dudeck

Neil Mullarkey, along with Mike Myers, co-founded the improv troupe The Comedy Store Players in 1985. Neil still performs with them in London. His credits include *Whose Line Is It Anyway?* and two Austin Powers films. Since 1999, Neil has given keynote speeches and workshops on the applications of improvisational theatre to businesses in twenty-three different countries, which led him to write the book *Seven Steps to Improve Your People Skills* (2017).

Keith Sawyer is internationally known as a scientific expert on creativity, collaboration, and learning. He has published fourteen books, including *Group Genius: The Creative Power of Collaboration* (2007), and over eighty scientific articles. Keith is the Morgan Distinguished Professor in Educational Innovations at the University of North Carolina in Chapel Hill. He received his computer science degree from MIT and both his MA and PhD in psychology from the University of Chicago.

Theresa Robbins Dudeck is an impro and AI practitioner and scholar working in both academic and professional settings. She is considered one of the foremost teachers of Keith Johnstone's Impro System. Theresa is Johnstone's literary executor and author of *Keith Johnstone: A Critical Biography* (2013). She is also co-founder/co-director of the Global Improvisation Initiative (GII). Theresa received her PhD in theatre from the University of Oregon.

During one of our weekly phone check-ins, Caitlin and I were deep into a discussion about impro being an expression of theory when the idea—to facilitate a conversation between Keith Sawyer and Neil Mullarkey—emerged! We thought it would be exciting to get someone like Sawyer, an academic who writes prolifically about improvisational theory and practice but who is not an impro performer, to converse with someone like Mullarkey, a professional improviser who began to connect the theories to his practice only after years of performing with some of the greatest improvisers of his generation. What follows is the realization of that idea.

THERESA ROBBINS DUDECK: For this conversation, I'd like to look at two things you both talk about: (1) creativity, innovation, and collaboration; and (2) how theory informs your practice and vice versa. First, I want to start with a question about a theory that Daniel Pink proposed in *To Sell Is Human: The Surprising Truth about Moving Others* (2012). Pink's theory is that we are all in sales. We're all trying to sell something (ideas, skills, knowledge, etc.), whether we are educators or CEOs. And he believes "selling" today requires an improvisational skill set. Are we really all trying to *sell* something, and why is improvisation the preferred MO?

NEIL MULLARKEY: Perhaps we are selling something, which is, we want somebody to be influenced by what we say and do. It's interesting, when I do work with salespeople, I talk about the idea of an offer, and they know about the idea of a "value proposition." Maybe it isn't so far away anyway, but I'm not sure whether [Pink] is saying, in improv, are we kind of trying to hoodwink people, as in "selling you a pup."

To me, improv is that I try to stand next to you, for a moment, and we create something together which neither of us would have created on our own. Would that be a good sales pitch?

KEITH SAWYER: I agree with the core statement that everything about human social life is improvisation. In fact, everything about human cognition is improvisation. It's the nature of being responsive and interacting. Someone else who has creative agency. You don't know what that person's going to do. They don't know what you're going to do. That's typical of all social life. I primarily focus on creativity and the creative process, which in individuals has this characteristic of a wandering, zigzagging process.[1] A creative process, even for a solitary individual, is not linear. Ideas emerge from the process. In a way, it's an interaction with materials and with the world around you, and that interaction is improvisational. I can go into all sorts of psychological and social theories because I'm an academic, not an improv performer, but selling is not anywhere near the top ten things I would talk about improvisation being relevant to. I like Daniel Pink's first book the best, *A Whole New Mind: Why Right-Brainers Will Rule the Future.* That book is about creativity and adaptability, so that ties pretty closely into creative improvisation. But if it's sales, most people have this connotation of, like you said, hoodwinking somebody, but that's not the way I think about it.

If it's going to be improvisation, maybe a more positive, life-affirming notion [would be] sales as a negotiation. All negotiations are improvised. It's an improvisational interaction between the two negotiators, and then an effective sales encounter, both people gain value from the encounter. Neither person participates in a transaction unless they both get some value out of it. Certainly, they perceive that they've gained value or they wouldn't have participated in the exchange. But that negotiation, that process of finding the point at which they both get value, that's improvisational, sure.

NM: I had a thought that maybe in improv every moment I'm buying from you, I'm selling to you as well. I'm giving you something and you're giving something back. At some point, we forget who's selling and who's buying. That is the joy of Yes, And. I forgot whose idea started this, but it's our shared idea now.

By the way, Keith, you're a musician. In improvised song, the music and words emerge as you're giving me some of this and I've giving you some of that. We listen to one another and the "dialogue" is entirely mutual. The brilliance of improv is that I can be an individual completely, and completely part of the team. That's what I underline to people. You can be totally you while also being part of the team. Improv explicitly allows you to be both. That's why I think Keith and I feel a bit uneasy about the notion of selling, where one person is more passive than the other.

On the other hand, we have been selling and buying stuff, whether it's love, territory, food, for a long time. The transaction is more often about sharing, actually. That's why improv is such a beautiful thing, because it's fully recognizing your individuality and our need to belong.

At some point, the joy comes when I made a mistake and you celebrated my mistake or you made the mistake turn out not to be a mistake at all. That bum note I played became part of the new melody. That's what the joy of improv is, is that you'll buy whatever I give you, in a way. Holding the moment that may go that way or this, but we're going to go there together. I do teach salespeople but it's mostly about listening. From real listening, something will come to you and that's the zigzag. I take your offer, you take my offer, we zig and zag. If we go on straight to my idea, we wouldn't have perhaps gone to such a fruitful place.

TD: The idea of give and take. Keith, you talk about group flow in your book *Group Genius* (2007). It's that collective state of mind that is achieved when a group is improvising at the top of their abilities. Creativity driven by a "series of flashes" that often produces more surprising and imaginative outcomes than one person could produce on their own. My next question for you, Neil, has to do with group genius and group flow. I'm sure the Comedy Store Players achieves this. I'd like to hear how you bring that embodied knowledge of group flow to your clients? How do you translate that message, impart that set of skills?

NM: It's obvious when two (or six people as with the Comedy Store Players) are in flow. We do a half-hour narrated musical, and what's joyous is that something happens in one scene, perhaps somebody says something they didn't quite mean to say, which then becomes the spine of the story.

Last night, it was a western. There was a new sheriff in town (portrayed by my fellow player, Andy Smart). It turns out he was "the man with no name," but we did know his address. The town had written to the address saying, "Please, would you come be our sheriff?" Then later we doubt him. "Is he the right person?" A flash-back shows he was someone else living at the address, who picked up the envelope by mistake. He confesses, "Actually, I never was a sheriff. I was a magician's assistant and dancer." It came out almost before Andy could think. Yet somehow, that choice of job was the very thing that could defeat the James Gang. The group made the "mistake" the kernel of the denouement.

That, to me, was "flow." It was a throwaway where Andy perhaps couldn't think of a name immediately when asked. There wasn't just a moment, it was continuing moments which snow-balled into something beautiful. When you present that to peo-ple who are in organizations, they can see how that can work. They get frustrated because, in reality, many meetings don't work like that. It's six people pulling in different directions, or pairs of people pulling in three different directions. They have experienced group flow on occasion. When everyone's pitching in their idea, somebody's running with the ball, somebody passes the ball, and they get to a place which does feel like group genius. Certainly, it's a metaphor in sport and music and theatre. We totally understand. Whoever scored the goal, whoever played the solo was being sup-ported by the whole, and it wouldn't have been possible without the others.

People do see that in organizational life. It's harder to do, nine to five, day in, day out when there's territory to guard. The Comedy Store Players perform twice a week for two hours each. Maybe this week you're the one who gets to be the sheriff. But next week, I'll be the sheriff. It's sort of understood. We only have four hours to find the flow, whereas "regular" people have to do forty hours together, and you can't be in flow the whole time.

The challenge for applied improv is, "Okay, so what?" People love the show, and can see listening's good. Then they go back to work and have to deal with the politics, the blocks, the lack of Yes, And, and so forth. But I find so many people who say, "I can see Yes, And does help." Many have said the simple les-son of Yes, And has permanently changed the way they approach interactions.

TD: Keith, I think this also taps into what you talk about. The reason why it works well at the Comedy Store Players consistently, but maybe not always in the workplace. Once in a while, there's this hit of group flow. You talk about managers in group flow. If they want to participate, they have to participate as an equal, or that idea of granting autonomy and authority to the group's process.

KS: Everything I think of is based in this notion of improvisation, and almost more than that, the notion of emergence. The idea that the whole is greater than the sum of the parts. Based on research, everything that's new and creative emerges from the bottom-up, in an organizational setting especially. Innovation and creativity and new ideas, they emerge from the bottom-up. They do not come from a brilliant manager or leader coming up with the insight and then steering the entire organization in the direction of this brilliant insight. That's not the way innovation works, and it's not the way successful organizations work. If it's an organization that doesn't have to be creative, you can have success with a lot of structure and regimentation. But organizations today and the companies that hire Neil and me to do workshops and consulting, they realize that they need creativity and innovation to be successful. The core of everything I say is it's got to be emergent and bottom-up.

For creativity to emerge from the bottom-up, there has to be flexibility and freedom for individuals who perform creatively and generate new ideas. Then there has to be a culture of collaboration so that people can come together, and the interactions among people result in the emergence of even better ideas. It's the collective emergence of ideas from the group. But saying all that to organizations, that's not really enough.

There are certain things you need to *do* to make that more effective. I usually talk about five or six different categories, things like culture of the organization, incentives, norms and behaviors and practices, and the ways that leadership is executed and performed. There's a set of things that all have to be in alignment before you get effective emergent innovation from the bottom-up. The challenge of management, and this usually makes executives nod a little bit more, is that if all you have is unstructured improvisation and you have ideas bubbling up from the bottom everywhere in the organization, that's not the way to be successful either because it's too chaotic.

Every organization needs some sort of guidance, some sort of vision. The bubbling up, emergent improvisation has to be channeled in some way and something is going to be top-down, or top-down-ish, to provide that guiding structure. The challenge of managing innovation is to figure out what's exactly the right balance of providing freedom for the bottom-up emergence and providing guidance from the top-down. It's different for every company, it's different for every industry sector. Big banks are much more concerned about top-down regulations and policy than a software company might be. But I'll still argue that you're not going to be innovative, even at a bank, if you don't have some ability for this bottom-up, collaborative improvisational emergence to take place.

You could say the same thing about improvisation, that improvisation has guiding structures and practices and various principles that result in more effective improvisation. There's no such thing as completely free improvisation. At the minimum, the culture of the group or of the organization, that's always going to be there.

NM: I say, "hear, hear." I tell people we're trying to create an emergent structure, we want the story to continue, we want to take a minimal number of elements as they emerge and try to make sense of them in a story. Actually, when you see the Comedy Store Players, there's a lot of structure. As you say, there's a culture. The culture is Yes, And, a culture of trust between the performers.

There is formal structure where necessary. Every show starts and finishes on time; The Comedy Store, a separate organization, ensures the tickets have been sold. The food, the drink, the lights, the insurance are in place. We even do the same running order every show.

There's that repeating structure and then there's the emerging structure, which is what we say and do *that* night in *that* show.

This chimes with Ralph Stacey's work on leadership and "bounded instability."[2] Bill Critchley (formerly of Ashridge Executive Education) worked with Stacey.[3] He talked about "minimal structure, maximum autonomy." It's exactly what Keith was saying, which is you've got to have sufficient structure for it not to be chaos, but sufficient movement for there to be bottom-up creativity.

"Bounded instability" has echoes of Ronald Heifetz's "Adaptive Leadership."[4] Heifetz warns against a "technical fix" that can exacerbate the problem. In the example of the western above, some-body could have stepped in and given the new sheriff a name, to "fix" things. That would have denied us the beauty (and flow) of our unfolding story.

Improv can have applications in virtually any sphere. Certainly creativity, but even strategy, which is itself emergent. On the other hand, you don't just go, "Hey, let's do whatever today." I say to peo-ple, "Improv in your work doesn't mean turn up, go to any desk, go to any company, run amok."

Minimal structure, maximum autonomy means to create envi-ronments where people feel guided, and coached, and supported, and then they can be spontaneous or improvisatory. Don Sull says organizations should just have a few simple rules.[5] That's improv.

Our basic rules are listen and accept (Yes, And). Simple rules, but they're quite complicated, in a way. Which bit of what you said do I pick up? Because actually, I'm choosing which bit to "and," if you like. We continually are creating structure as we go while also being able to step outside it. We have guiding principles, structures, and culture.

TD: You both talk about achieving the right balance. A testimonial on your website, Neil, said that you get the right "balance of intel-lect, creativity, knowledge and fun to make the day effective." Keith, you wrote: "The key to innovation is always to manage a subtle balance of planning, structure, and improvisation" (2007: 29). You two are both aiming for a kind of balance to achieve improvised innovation. But culture is difficult to change in a big corporation. So, if you have a company that wants to work more from the bottom-up, how do you achieve the right balance between struc-ture and improvisation and take into consideration the importance of culture in an organization?

KS: I'm going to come back to your question. First, I'd like to talk about this notion of emergence, because Neil mentioned Stacey. I'm a jazz pianist. I would improvise as the pianist with several Chicago improv groups. While I was doing that, I would video-tape the performers, and then later I'd go back and transcribe the dialogue. Then I used various analytic schemes associated with conversation analysis to document and analyze what was going on. The academic details I have not been able to communicate, but I have written the higher-level, more business-y version of it in *Group Genius.*

In the process of doing all this analysis and writing a book called *Improvised Dialogues* (2003), I came across this theory of emergence. I [then] went into a detour in social theory and wrote several journal articles about the theory of emergence and the philosophy of science of emergence. That resulted in a book called *Social Emergence: Societies as Complex Systems* (2005). It was densely packed with social theory, the sort of thing that Stacey is doing.

I applied the notion of emergence directly to small groups and to social systems. I wasn't necessarily interested in neurons in the brain being a complex zone, or pieces of sand in a pile. But specifically, social groups as emerging. One thing it seemed to me that was unique about people when they're interacting is that they have a fairly complex communication language. Other complex systems that have been analyzed, their interaction mechanisms are very simple. Grains of sand in a sand pile, it's just sort of physical—momentum, pressure, or whatever. But the human language, the interaction is so complex that I argued it results in a totally different kind of emergence. That's what I call "collaborative emergence." Most complex systems have hundreds of thousands of units; but an improv group, like Neil's, because the nature of human language is so complex, my argument [was] that we could call that collaborative emergence even though it's only a small number of individuals. That's where I started to get very academic: What are the characteristics of human language that make it different from other kinds of communication systems?

Back to your question. You asked about the importance of culture. It's the hardest thing to get right. "Right" is maybe the wrong thing to say, but it's the hardest thing to get aligned with the types of innovation and creativity you want and need in your organization. You can't get the culture right without getting a lot of other things right too. I always say it's very hard to do this, or else everyone would be doing it, and every organization would be super innovative.

Most companies don't get there because so many things have to change. Managers aren't used to thinking about top-down. They're thinking about planning. They like to be able to make predictions and estimates about what's going to happen in the future. None of those things happen in improvisation. Big parts of the organization do not need to be innovative, and they probably shouldn't be innovative. Those parts of the organization make lots of money. I would never say 100 percent of the company's energy should be focused on improvisation and emergence. It's a difficult balance. Is it 80 percent that's boring and routine and generates ton of money, and 20 percent that's random and unpredictable? Or is it 90 percent and 10 percent? But it can't be the whole organization all the time. And there is the challenge of culture. What do you do about that? Eighty percent of the organization has one culture, which is all about efficiency and deadlines, and satisfying customers, [and] 20 percent of the time you got this other culture. That's not going to work, because then you have this huge culture clash. A lot of companies create a separate innovation lab. [They] put it in a different building, off in a different state or part of the country. Then the main part of the organization can keep being its efficient, boring self. All the creative people are off somewhere else. They develop radically different cultures, and then the innovation never gets into the organization.

TD: So, you're saying structure can't be separated from the innovation or the chaos?

NM: Ralph Stacey has this graph, with uncertainty versus disagreement. It recognizes that day to day, a leader has to make sure that things are efficient and produced on time, on budget, while also looking to tomorrow. The challenge of leadership is to try and hold the improvisational element alongside the so-called efficiency/predictable element.

KS: Yes, I agree.

NM: It's always interesting to me when, as you say, people put the innovation lab in a different space, somewhere "over there." John Cleese, in a lecture from 1991, talked about Open and Closed Modes. Open is "creative" and Closed is implementing an idea or plan. Can you be in both modes at the same time?

In "Agile" software development they have a "sprint" which may last only two weeks but it creates the right energy. It might be tough to be in "flow" forty hours a week. The leader has to create the space for flow within a structure that feels sufficiently stable. That's "culture" and it may simply be about the type of conversations that take place with colleagues, customers, and suppliers.

TD: Neil, how did you transition from being just an improviser to an improviser who deeply understood the theories underpinning your practice?

NM: Deeply? Or, all the stuff that I felt intuitively would apply to business, I have since found even more applicable. Fortunately, I have discovered plenty of clever research out there to add rigor to my instincts.

For instance, when I came across emergence and complexity, I thought, yes, that's improv! There are patterns. You can only really understand the scene, where it came from, once you've finished it, perhaps. Kierkegaard said we live our lives forward, but we understand them backward. You think the scene is going to be about a husband and a wife, then it turns out that they're both ghosts, or it's about the next-door neighbor. Those stumbling moments at the beginning are essential. That's another thing that my friends at Ashridge Business School say, "Say yes to the mess."

TD: I love that.

NM: Me too. It comes from Dr. Frank J. Barrett. In fact this is the title of his book, on jazz impro and leadership. Because for things to emerge, there's got to be a bit of a mess. If you try to impose a structure on an improv scene, too early, you could kill it. Error can be a source of innovation too. Like the cowboy who couldn't think of a name.

TD: For you, Keith, it seems improvisational theory came first. So, when did you first put the theory into practice? And do you feel it is important for your clients to grasp the theories underpinning the practice?

KS: In my research, I found that stage improvisation had very similar characteristics to everyday social life. And in particular, to effective teams. The theory is helpful to me, as a scientist, but I'm not sure that everyone in a group needs to be familiar with the theory. You can get better at collaboration from knowing how to engage in a set of practices. It's a way of being more than a way of knowing.

TD: At the end of my biography on Keith Johnstone, I asked this question to several impro teachers and performers, and it's a question I will continue to ask: What comes next? What academic and artistic disciplines and/or organizational structures might profit from improvisation? Moreover, what might the world look like if impro classes became a required discipline in schools everywhere?

NM: Improv should be taught in every classroom—junior school, high school, and most certainly business school. It is sometimes taught under "drama" at school and under creativity, collaboration, or leadership at business school. The simple fact is that improvisation sounds like making the best of limited resources, and that's certainly true. "Improv" or "impro" is even more. It is an artistic discipline (in art, theatre, music, and beyond) that includes finding overlooked resources and creating new resources—in others, in the world, and in ourselves.

If more people understood and could relax into the improv mode, they'd have more options. Business and organizational life would do better to be open to an improv mind-set, where structure emerges, where planning is a verb not an end in itself, and individuals can simultaneously shine yet be part of the team.

KS: There's a good body of research demonstrating how and when collaborating teams enhance learning. Learning teams can work in any subject, from the arts to the sciences. Improv theatre exercises can help students understand how to collaborate better. But I don't think that's the only way. I'd like for each teacher, in any subject area, to be able to foster effective collaboration among their students. And sometimes, that collaboration is most effective when it's more deeply embedded in that content area.

TD: I would like to close with my favorite Keith Johnstone (Johnstone 1979: 92) quotation: "Those who say 'Yes' are rewarded by the adventures they have, and those who say 'No' are rewarded by the safety they attain." Thank you, Neil and Keith, for saying "Yes" to this conversation and for your notable contributions to the impro community.

Notes

1 Sawyer's most recent book, *Zig Zag: The Surprising Path to Greater Creativity* (2013), further unpacks this idea.
2 Ralph Stacey has authored several books on strategic management including the popular textbook *Strategic Management and Organisational Dynamics: The Challenge of Complexity* (2011), now in its sixth edition. "Bounded instability" refers to a type of complex system that is "constantly poised at the edge between order and chaos." The term "edge of chaos," as mentioned in the introduction,

is the term most widely used to describe this type of system that never reaches a stable equilibrium allowing for optimal "creativity and growth" (Burnes 2004: 314–15).

3 Bill Critchley is an organization psychologist, consultant, executive coach, and author of numerous articles on organizational development and change.

4 See Heifetz et al. (2009).

5 Don Sull is a senior lecturer at MIT Sloan School of Management and author of *The Upside of Turbulence: Seizing Opportunity in an Uncertain World* (2009) and coauthor of *Simple Rules: How to Thrive in a Complex World* (2015).

APPENDIX A

Key Improvisation Tenets and Terms

Below are descriptions of key tenets and terms (in alphabetical order) commonly held by and part of the language of improvisers worldwide. We selected only those with most relevance to this set of case studies—many more exist and are beloved by improvisers. The specific wording for each differs from group to group and from place to place, evolving in response to the particular needs of those improvisers at that time. Our intention is not to strictly codify these terms, but rather to embrace the idea that they transform over time, like anything good in life.

Active or Responsive Listening, sometimes called "whole body listening," denotes a deeper listening, one that requires more than just hearing the words. Alan Alda (2017: 33) describes responsively listening to someone as "letting everything about them affect you; not just their words, but also their tone of voice, their body language, even subtle things like where they're standing in the room or how they occupy a chair."

Be Fit and Well, see Chapter 1, p. 22.

Be Obvious (not clever or funny) is a reminder to trust your impulses instead of trying to come up with an "original" idea. Good improvisers are focused on solving problems and on developing the story, and the best way to do that is to pay attention and respond authentically to the moment. "The improviser has to realize that the more obvious he is, the more original he appears," asserts Keith Johnstone (1979). "An artist who is inspired is being *obvious*" (87–8; emphasis in the original).

Be Willing to Be Changed, see Chapter 1, p. 22.

Circle of Probability is a structural storytelling concept developed by Keith Johnstone. As improvisers develop the plot onstage, audience members are anticipating what will happen next, creating their own shadow stories. When there's a close connection between the audience's amalgamation of shadow stories and the plot unfolding onstage, the audience is more likely to be dynamically engaged in the journey. Staying within the circle of probability does not mean pandering to the audience; it is simply a tool to train improvisers to move a story forward according to the logic of the imaginary world that has been established.

Commit asks you to give 100 percent to an exercise, regardless of how silly or challenging it is. Making that decision allows you to better pay attention to the offers around you, rather than worry about whether you are "in" or "out." Fully committing to an exercise is contagious, inspiring others to fully commit. Even when an exercise does not go as planned, committing helps develop self-confidence because you know your willingness to fail/succeed was never in doubt.

Give and Take refers to the principle of sharing control, that is, alternately giving/taking focus and giving/accepting offers. Give and take is crucial for any collaboration. It is about "diverting competitiveness to group endeavor" and "remembering that process comes before end-result" wrote Spolin (1963: 12). This tenet encourages those who typically give focus and accept others' offers to step up, take focus themselves, and give bold offers. The opposite is true for those who typically resist giving focus and make more offers than they accept—they are encouraged to give themselves over to the story or idea getting the most traction, rather than holding desperately to their own ideas.

Leap Before You Look invites you to act first then figure out what to do, rather than the opposite. Of course, many situations are better served by planning, but for the purpose of playing, this tenet reminds you to *discover* what comes next rather than try to control the future.

Make Your Partner Look Good asks you to focus on the other person and give them whatever they need in the moment. Another way to look at it is to be someone your partner enjoys working with. Find out what enthuses or inspires your partner. Delight them. Keith Johnstone (1979: 93) wrote: "The improviser has to understand that his first skill lies in releasing his partner's imagination." This all points to the benevolent nature of this tenet. Ultimately, when players are doing their best to make each other look good, all feel fully supported, and this creates a climate for collaborative creation and innovation. And if you are feeling self-conscious, having the objective to "make your partner look good" immediately takes the pressure off!

Offer/Block/Accept are three interlocking terms we use quite often in improvisation. An *offer* is anything a player says or does. A *block* is anything that prevents the action from developing, or that dismisses the reality created by your partner's offer. To *accept* moves the action forward by treating an offer as valid, by saying Yes (ideally Yes, And; see below) to it.

Right to Fail/Mistakes Are Gifts means it is possible to create with any offer, regardless of whether that offer was intentional, or even welcome. A judgment of bad/good or mistake/success is purely a framework we impose upon our actions. Learning to put aside that judgment and build with mistakes is one of the most powerful tenets of all. Failure is a part of the process of learning and, as any good improviser will tell you, some of the biggest mistakes turn into the best ideas. This is actually a "law of innovation" in collaborative organizations, according to Keith Sawyer (2007: 163–4): "Successes can't go up unless failures go up, too. And because we won't have the successes without the failures, we need to create organizational cultures that cherish failure." We suggest encouraging your students to fail good-naturedly or, as Johnstone advises, to "Screw up and stay happy!"

Side-Coaching is when a director off-stage gives directions to the improvisers on stage to help them stay focused on solving a problem and/or to moving a process forward in a positive direction. In Applied Improvisation, facilitators use side-coaching in the same way, usually minus the stage. It also gives facilitators an opportunity to offer immediate, in-the-moment feedback, which is a key attribute of improvisational practice.

Status is physical and verbal behavior that determines your placement in the social pecking order. Status is not what a person *is* (i.e. ascribed or fixed role) but what he *plays* (i.e. achieved status). Status exercises, games, and techniques are often used in Applied Improvisation facilitation and much of the methodology comes from the foundational work of Keith Johnstone. To learn more about status, we recommend visiting the chapter on "Status" in Johnstone's *Impro: Improvisation and the Theatre* (1979). Also, see Chapters 10 and 11 for discussions on power and status in conflict resolution work and in pedagogy.

Yes, And is the shorthand term widely used by improvisers to denote the fundamental principle of "accepting offers" (saying "Yes") and then building on those offers ("And") with new ideas to move the process forward. Yes, And keeps you from "blocking" your own and others' offers. The words themselves, "yes, and," are often used to help new improvisers develop the habit of accepting and building on offers. Unfortunately, Yes, And is often taught as a dogmatic rule in which students are told by their teachers they must always Yes, And every offer made. This advice ignores the complexity of the principle. For example, if saying "No" moves the premise, scene, or story forward, then it is considered an acceptance, not a block. And if an improviser makes an offer that demeans and/or compromises another improviser's personal safety, other improvisers—the one compromised and potential allies—learn to Yes, And their own reactions to the unwelcome offer, even if that means blocking the offer with a "No" or with something (a word or a gesture) other than "Yes." Whenever possible, use these situations as opportunities for debrief and reflection. This practice of constantly assessing what the character needs and wants in a scene and what you, as an improviser, need and want from your partner, alongside attuning yourself to your partner's needs (Make Your Partner Look Good), helps develop assertiveness and emotional intelligence. To help improvisers heighten their self-awareness and partnering skills, Keith Johnstone has recently added a cheerful "Nope" option to his impro training, encouraging students, in specific exercises, to voice a polite "Nope" if the offer made by their partner does not enthuse them or stay within the Circle of Probability (see above) being created. As mentioned earlier, improvisation rules must remain flexible and support, not hinder, the evolution of this work in transformative spaces.

APPENDIX B

About the Workbook and List of Workbook Exercises

We hope you will mix and match exercises from all case studies and try them yourself. While each set-up and debrief is written for that case study's target audience, we invite you to customize them to suit the needs of your unique set of participants. There are infinite variations and names for each exercise—the descriptions included here are not intended to be definitive. The debrief questions are intended to serve as starting points for discussion and can be used in any order, modified, or replaced altogether. While in theatrical improvisation these are commonly referred to as games, in this anthology we call each an "exercise," since this can denote an activity done to sustain or develop skills, to improve one's well-being, and/or to make something happen.

The following variables are not explicitly addressed, with the expectation that you will tailor them to suit your needs:

- Ways to divide a larger group into pairs or other smaller groups, then identify which person in each pair starts.
- Ways to adjust the exercise when the total number of participants does not distribute evenly (e.g. an odd number of participants will not divide equally into pairs).
- The number of participants; unless otherwise stated, exercises can be done with any number of participants.
- The size of the room.
- Time constraints.
- Whether participants are seated or standing.

About Connections

At the bottom of each exercise, we have included a section called "Connections." This space serves several purposes. The first is to credit the creator of the exercise, wherever possible. Several of the workbook exercises are original creations by the authors, others are adapted from existing exercises, many of which have been in circulation under various titles for years. Because it is imperative to honor the historical and theoretical foundations of our field, for exercises with no clear connection to an original source, this space is used to connect facilitators to foundational exercises by Spolin, Johnstone, and others that seem to share specific features and/or objectives with that particular exercise. We also use the "Connections" section to provide additional exercises and information intended to support and augment the objectives outlined.

List of Workbook Exercises

BIBLIOGRAPHY

Alan Alda Center for Communicating Science. 2016. "About Us."
Accessed June 24, 2017. http://www.aldakavlilearningcenter.org/get-
started/about-us.

Alan Alda Center for Communicating Science. 2016. "Dealing with
Complexity." Accessed June 24, 2017. http://aldacentersbustg.prod.
acquia sites.com/sites/default/files//2016/3.%20 Learn/Workshops/
WORKSHOP%20PREP/Dealiing-with-Complexity.pdf.

Alda, Alan. 2017. *If I Understood You, Would I Have This Look on My
Face?* New York: Random House.

Applied Improvisation Network. Accessed June 22, 2017. http://
appliedimprovisation.network/.

Baker Miller, Jean. 1995. "Domination and Subordination." In *Race,
Class & Gender in the United States: An Integrated Study*, edited by
Paula S. Rothenberg, 57–64. New York: St. Martin's Press.

Berryman, Mere, Therese Ford, Ann Nevin, and Suzanne Soohoo. 2015.
"Culturally Responsive Contexts: Establishing Relationships for
Inclusion." *International Journal of Special Education* 30 (3): 39–51.

Boal, Augusto. 1992. *Games for Actors and Non-actors.*
London: Routledge.

Boesen, Kevin P., Richard N. Herrier, David A. Apgar, and Rebekah M.
Jackowski. 2009. "Improvisational Exercises to Improve Pharmacy
Students' Professional Communication Skills." *American Journal of
Pharmaceutical Education* 73 (2): 35.

Boushey, Heather, and Sarah Jane Glynn. 2012. "There Are Significant
Business Costs to Replacing Employees." Center for American
Progress. November 16. https://www.americanprogress.org/issues/
economy/reports/2012/11/16/44464/there-are-significant-business-
costs-to-replacing-employees/.

Bowles, Norma, and Daniel-Raymond Nadon, eds. 2013. *Staging Social
Justice: Collaborating to Create Activist Theatre.* Carbondale: Southern
Illinois University Press.

Box, George E. P. 1979. "Robustness in the Strategy of Scientific Model
Building." In *Robustness in Statistics*, edited by R. L. Launer and G. N.
Wilkinson, 201–36. New York: Academic Press.

Boyd, Drew, and Jacob Goldenberg. 2014. *Inside the Box: A Proven System of Creativity for Breakthrough Results*. New York: Simon & Schuster.

Boyd, Neva L. [1945] 1975. *Handbook of Recreational Games*. New York: Dover Publications.

Brown, Shona L., and Kathleen M. Eisenhardt. 1998. *Competing on the Edge: Strategy as Structured Chaos*. Boston: Harvard Business School Press.

Brownell, Sarah E., Jordan V. Price, and Lawrence Steinman. 2013. "Science Communication to the General Public: Why We Need to Teach Undergraduate and Graduate Students this Skill as Part of Their Formal Scientific Training." *Journal of Undergraduate Neuroscience Education* 12 (1): E6–10.

Burnes, Bernard. 2004. "Kurt Lewin and Complexity Theories: Back to the Future?" *Journal of Change Management* 4 (4): 309–25.

Bush, Robert A. Baruch, and Joseph P. Folger. 2005. *The Promise of Mediation: The Transformative Approach to Conflict*. San Francisco: John Wiley.

Caines, Rebecca, and Ajay Heble. 2015. *The Improvisation Studies Reader: Spontaneous Acts*. London; New York: Routledge.

Caplan, Kerri. 2006. "Drama Therapy: A Possible Intervention for Children with Autism." MA thesis, Concordia University, Montreal (oai:spectrum.library.concordia.ca:9267).

Cassady, Jennifer M. 2011. "Teachers' Attitudes toward the Inclusion of Students with Autism and Emotional Behavioral Disorder." *Electronic Journal for Inclusive Education* 2 (7). http://corescholar.libraries. wright.edu/ejie/vol2/iss7/5/.

Chishti, Muzaffar, and Fay Hipsman. 2014. "Unaccompanied Minors Crisis Has Receded from Headlines but Major Issues Remain." *Migration Information Source*. September 25. http://www. migrationpolicy.org/article/unaccompanied-minors-crisis-has-receded-headlines-major-issues-remain.

Coleman, Peter T., Morton Deutsch, and Eric C. Marcus. 2000. "Power and Conflict." In *Handbook of Conflict Resolution: Theory and Practice*, 108–30. San Francisco: Jossey Bass.

Coopman, S. J., and J. T. Wood. 2004. *Everyday Encounters: An Instructor's Manual*. Boston, MA: Cengage Learning.

Courtney, Richard. 1968. *Play, Drama & Thought: The Intellectual Background to Dramatic Education*. London: Cassell.

CRLT Players. 2016. "About the Players." Center for Research on Learning and Teaching. Accessed June 22, 2017. http://www.crlt. umich.edu/crltplayers/about-players.

D'Amico, Miranda, Corinne Lalonde, and Stephen Snow. 2015. "Evaluating the Efficacy of Drama Therapy in Teaching Social Skills to

Children with Autism Spectrum Disorders." *Drama Therapy Review* 1 (1): 21–39.

Davis, Jocelyn R., Henry M. Frechette, Jr., and Edwin H. Boswell. 2010. "Leaders Manage Climate." In *Strategic Speed: Mobilize People, Accelerate Execution*, 107–30. Boston: Harvard Business Review Press.

Drath, Wilfred H., Cynthia D. McCauley, Charles J. Palus, Ellen Van Velsor, Patricia M. G. O'Connor, and John B. McGuire. 2008. "Direction, Alignment, Commitment: Toward a More Integrative Ontology of Leadership." *The Leadership Quarterly* 19 (6): 635–53.

Derald Wing Sue et al. 2007. "Racial Microaggressions in Everyday Life: Implications for Clinical Practice." *American Psychologist* 62 (4): 271–86.

Dudeck, Theresa Robbins. 2013. *Keith Johnstone: A Critical Biography*. London: Bloomsbury.

Fine, Gary Alan, and Michaela DeSoucey. 2005. "Joking Cultures: Humor Themes as Social Regulation in Group Life." *Humor: International Journal of Humor Research* 18 (1): 1–22.

Fisher, Roger, and Daniel Shapiro. 2006. *Beyond Reason: Using Emotions as You Negotiate*. New York: Penguin Books.

Fisher, Roger, William L. Ury, and Bruce Patton. 2011. *Getting to Yes: Negotiating Agreement Without Giving In*. Updated revised edition. New York: Penguin Books.

Fotis, Matt, and Siobhan O'Hara. 2016. *The Comedy Improv Handbook: A Comprehensive Guide to University Improvisational Comedy in Theatre and Performance*. New York: Focal Press.

Freire, Paulo. (1968) 2000. *Pedagogy of the Oppressed*. New York: Continuum.

Frost, Anthony, and Ralph Yarrow. 2007. *Improvisation in Drama*. New York: Palgrave Macmillan.

Frost, Anthony, and Ralph Yarrow. 2016. *Improvisation in Drama, Theatre and Performance: History, Practice, Theory*. London: Palgrave Macmillan.

Funk, Cary, and Lee Rainie. 2015. "Public and Scientists' Views on Science and Society." *Pew Research Center: Internet, Science & Tech*. January 29. http://www.pewinternet.org /2015/01/29/public-and-scientists-views-on-science-and-society/.

Garff, Chris [ChrisGarff1's channel]. 2011. "Utah Heroes Save Motorcyclist from Burning Wreckage." YouTube video. 14:08. Posted September 15. https://www.youtube.com/watch?v= GV3hz2PEZNs.

Garschagen, Matthias et al. 2016. *World Risk Report 2016*. Berlin: Bündnis Entwicklung Hilft and UNU-EHS.

Gee, Val, and Sarah Gee. 2011. *Business Improv: Experiential Learning Exercises to Train Employees to Handle Every Situation with Success.* New York: McGraw-Hill.

Giroux, Henry. 2017. "Higher Education and Neoliberal Temptation: A Conversation with Henry Giroux," by Almantas Samalavicius. *Eurozine,* January 11. Accessed January 14, 2017. http://www.eurozine.com/higher-education-and-neoliberal-temptation/.

Gladwell, Malcolm. 2005. *Blink: The Power of Thinking without Thinking.* New York: Back Bay Books.

Glass, Ronald David. 2001. "On Paulo Freire's Philosophy of Praxis and the Foundations of Liberation Education." *Educational Researcher* 30 (2): 15–25.

Goleman, Daniel. 1995. *Emotional Intelligence.* New York: Bantam Books.

Hall, William. 2014. *The Playbook: Improv Games for Performers.* San Francisco: Fratelli Bologna.

Halpern, Belle Linda, and Kathy Lubar. 2003. *Leadership Presence: Dramatic Techniques to Reach Out, Motivate, and Inspire.* New York: Gotham Books.

Halpern, Charna, Del Close, and Kim Johnson. 1994. *Truth in Comedy: The Manual of Improvisation.* First ed. Colorado Springs: Meriwether Publishing.

Harper, Shaun R., ed. 2008. *Creating Inclusive Campus Environments: For Cross-Cultural Learning and Student Engagement.* Washington, DC: NASPA.

Heathcote, Dorothy, Liz Johnson, and Cecily O'Neill. 1984. *Dorothy Heathcote: Collected Writings on Education and Drama.* London: Hutchinson.

Heddon, Deirdre, and Jane Milling. 2006. *Devising Performance: A Critical History (Theatre and Performance Practices).* Basingstoke [England]; New York: Palgrave Macmillan.

Heifetz, Ronald A., Alexander Grashow, and Martin Linsky. 2009. *The Practice of Adaptive Leadership: Tools and Tactics for Changing Your Organization and the World.* Boston: Harvard Business Press.

Hocker, Joyce, and William Wilmot. 2014. *Interpersonal Conflict.* New York: McGraw Hill.

Huffaker, Julie S. 2017. "Me to We: How an Organization Developed Collaborative Leadership Culture." PhD dissertation, Fielding University, Ann Arbor. ProQuest/UMI (10258071).

Improv Encyclopedia. Accessed June 22, 2017. http://improvencyclopedia.org/.

Innes, Christopher. 1993. *Avant Garde Theatre, 1892–1992.* New York: Routledge.

Jackson, Paul Z. 2003. *58 ½ Ways to Improvise in Training*. Wales, UK: Crown House Publishing.

Johnstone, Keith. (1979) 1987. *Impro: Improvisation and the Theatre*. New York: Routledge.

Johnstone, Keith. 1999. *Impro for Storytellers*. New York: Routledge.

Joyce, Bruce, and Beverley Showers. 2002. "Student Achievement through Professional Development." In *Designing Training and Peer Coaching: Our Need for Learning*, edited by Bruce Joyce and Beverley Showers. Alexandria, VA: ASCD.

Kegan, Daniel L. 1971. "Organizational Development: Description, Issues, and Some Research Results." *Academy of Management Journal* 14 (4): 453–64. doi:10.2307/255060.

Kegan, Robert, and Lisa Laskow Lahey. 2016. *An Everyone Culture: Becoming a Deliberately Developmental Organization*. Boston: Harvard Business School Press.

Kempe, Andy, and Cathy Tissot. 2012. "The Use of Drama to Teach Social Skills in a Special School Setting for Students with Autism." *Support for Learning* 27 (3): 97–102.

Kolb, David A. 1984. *Experiential Learning: Experience as the Source of Learning and Development, Vol. 1*. Englewood Cliffs, NJ: Prentice-Hall.

Koppett, Kat. 2013. *Training to Imagine: Practical Improvisational Theatre Techniques for Trainers and Managers to Enhance Creativity, Teamwork, Leadership, and Learning*. Sterling, VA: Stylus Publishing.

Kriesberg, Louise, and Bruce W. Dayton. 2017. *Constructive Conflicts: From Escalation to Resolution*. Lanham, MD: Rowman & Littlefield.

Kulhan, Bob, and Chuck Crisafulli. 2017. *Getting to "Yes And": The Art of Business Improv*. Stanford, CA: Stanford Business Books.

Laloux, Frederic. 2014. *Reinventing Organizations*. Brussels: Nelson Parker.

Lange, Catherine de. 2013. "Careers for Scientists Away from the Bench." *Naturejobs Blog*. May 21. http://blogs.nature.com/naturejobs/2013/05/21/careers-for-scientists-away-from-the-bench/.

LeBaron, Michelle, and Venashri Pillay. 2006. *Conflict across Cultures: A Unique Experience of Bridging Difference*. Boston: Intercultural Press.

Lederach, John Paul. 2003. *The Little Book of Conflict Transformation*. Intercourse, PA: Good Books.

Lederach, John Paul. 2005. *The Moral Imagination: The Art and Soul of Building Peace*. New York: Oxford University Press.

Leonard, Kelly, and Tom Yorton. 2015. *Yes, And: How Improvisation Reverses "No, But" Thinking and Improves Creativity and Collaboration*. New York: Harper Business.

Lichtenstein, Benyamin B. 2014. *Generative Emergence: A New Discipline of Organizational, Entrepreneurial, and Social Innovation.* Oxford: Oxford University Press.

Lipmanowicz, Henri, and Keith McCandless. 2013. *The Surprising Power of Liberating Structures: Simple Rules to Unleash a Culture of Innovation.* Seattle: Liberating Structures Press.

Lubkemann, Stephen. 2002. "Where to Be an Ancestor? Reconstituting Socio-spiritual Worlds and Post-conflict Settlement Decision-Making among Displaced Mozambicans." *Journal of Refugee Studies* 15 (2): 189–212.

Madson, Patricia R. 2005. *Improv Wisdom: Don't Prepare, Just Show Up.* New York: Bell Tower.

McCauley, Cynthia D., Charles J. Palus, Wilfred H. Drath, Richard L. Hughes, John B. McGuire, Patricia M. G. O'Connor, and Ellen Van Velsor. 2008. *Interdependent Leadership in Organizations: Evidence from Six Case Studies.* Greensboro: Center for Creative Leadership.

McWaters, Viv, and Johnnie Moore. 2012. *Creative Facilitation.* Victoria, Australia: Beyond the Edge.

Medical Improv. 2016. "About." Accessed June 22, 2017. http://www.medicalimprov.org/.

Mithen, Steven. 1996. *The Prehistory of the Mind: The Cognitive Origins of Art, Religion, and Science.* London: Thames & Hudson.

Monzó, Lilia D., and Suzanne Soohoo. 2014. "Translating the Academy: Learning the Racialized Languages of Academia." *Journal of Diversity in Higher Education* 7 (3): 147–65.

Nair, Nisha. 2008. "Towards Understanding the Role of Emotions in Conflict: A Review and Future Directions." *International Journal of Conflict Management* 19 (4): 359–81.

Patel, Leigh. 2016. *Decolonizing Educational Research: From Ownership to Answerability.* New York: Routledge.

Peteet, Julie M. 1995. "Transforming Trust: Dispossession and Empowerment among Palestinian Refugees." In *Mistrusting Refugees,* edited by E. Valentine Daniel and John Chr. Knudsen, 168–86. Berkeley: University of California Press.

Pink, Daniel H. 2012. *To Sell Is Human: The Surprising Truth about Moving Others.* New York: Riverhead Books.

Poynton, Robert. 2008. *Everything's an Offer: How to Do More with Less.* Portland, OR: On Your Feet.

Robertson, Brian J. 2015. *Holacracy: The New Management System for a Rapidly Changing World.* New York: Henry Holt and Company.

Rogoff, Barbara. 2003. *The Cultural Nature of Human Development.* New York: Oxford University Press.

Rossing, Jonathan P., and Krista Hoffmann-Longtin. 2016. "Improv(ing) the Academy: Applied Improvisation as a Strategy for Educational

Development." *To Improve the Academy* 35 (2): 303–25. doi:10.1002/tia2.20044.

Rothman, Jay. 1997. *Resolving Identity Based Conflicts*. San Francisco: Jossey Bass.

Rouhana, Nadim N., and Korper, Susan H. 1996. "Dealing with the Dilemmas Posed by Power Asymmetry in Intergroup Conflict." *Negotiation Journal* 12 (4): 315–28.

Salit, Cathy Rose. 2016. *Performance Breakthrough: A Radical Approach to Success at Work*. New York: Hachette Books.

Sauermann, Henry, and Michael Roach. 2012. "Science PhD Career Preferences: Levels, Changes, and Advisor Encouragement." *PloS One* 7 (5): e36307. doi:10.1371/journal.pone.0036307.

Saunders, Harold H. 1999. *A Public Peace Process: Sustained Dialogue to Transform Racial and Ethnic Conflicts*. New York: Palgrave.

Sawyer, Keith. 2007. *Group Genius: The Creative Power of Collaboration*. New York: Basic Books.

Sawyer, Keith. 2003. *Improvised Dialogues: Emergence and Creativity in Conversation*. Westport, CT: Ablex Publishing.

Sawyer, Keith. 2005. *Social Emergence: Societies as Complex Systems*. Cambridge: Cambridge University Press.

Sawyer, Keith. 2013. *Zig Zag: The Surprising Path to Greater Creativity*. San Francisco: Jossey-Bass.

Schuler, Adriana L. 2003. "Beyond Echoplaylia: Promoting Language in Children with Autism." *Autism* 7 (4): 455–69.

Slade, Peter. 1954. *Child Drama*. London: University of London Press.

Slepian, Michael L., Kathleen R. Bogart, and Nalini Ambady. 2014. "Thin-Slice Judgments in the Clinical Context." *Annual Review of Clinical Psychology* 10: 131–53.

Smith, Linda Tuhiwai. 1999. *Decolonizing Methodologies: Research and Indigenous Peoples*. London: Zed.

Sommers, Marc. 2001. *Fear in Bongoland: Burundi Refugees in Urban Tanzania*. New York: Berghahn Books.

Spolin, Viola. (1963) 1999. *Improvisation for the Theater: A Handbook of Teaching and Directing Techniques*. Third edition. Evanston, IL: Northwestern University Press.

Stacey, Ralph D. 2011. *Strategic Management and Organisational Dynamics: The Challenge of Complexity*. Sixth ed. Harlow, UK: Pearson Education Ltd.

Sull, Don. 2009. *The Upside of Turbulence: Seizing Opportunity in an Uncertain World*. New York: Harper Business.

Sull, Don, and Kathleen M. Eisenhardt. 2015. *Simple Rules: How to Thrive in a Complex World*. Boston: Houghton Mifflin Harcourt.

TheThiagiGroup. Accessed June 22, 2017. http://www.thiagi.com/.

Thompson, Jessica Leigh. 2009. "Building Collective Communication Competence in Interdisciplinary Research Teams." *Journal of Applied Communication Research* 37 (3): 278–97.

Ting-Toomey, Stella, and John G. Oetzel. 2001. *Managing Intercultural Conflict Effectively*. Thousand Oaks, CA: Sage Publications.

Tint, Barbara S., Viv McWaters, and Raymond van Driel. 2015. "Applied Improvisation Training for Disaster Readiness and Response: Preparing Humanitarian Workers and Communities for the Unexpected." *Journal on Humanitarian Logistics and Supply Chain Management: Special Edition on Humanitarian Games* 5 (1): 73–94.

Trujillo, Mary Adams, S. Y. Bowland, Linda James Myers, Phillip M. Richards, and Beth Roy, eds. 2008. *Re-centering: Culture and Knowledge in Conflict Resolution Practice*. New York: Syracuse University Press.

University of Queensland. 2008. "Three Minute Thesis: About 3MT." Accessed June 22, 2017. http://threeminutethesis.org/index. html?page=191537&pid=193447.

Vera, Dusya, and Mary Crossan. 2005. "Improvisation and Innovative Performance in Teams." *Organization Science* 16 (3): 203–24. http://www.jstor.org/stable/25145963.

Voutira, Eftihia, and Barbara E. Harrell-Bond. 1995. "In Search of the Locus of Trust: The Social World of the Refugee Camp." In *Mistrusting Refugees*, edited by E. Valentine Daniel and John Chr. Knudsen, 207–24. Berkeley: University of California Press.

Watson, Katie. 2011. "Perspective: Serious Play: Teaching Medical Skills with Improvisational Theater Techniques." *Academic Medicine* 86 (10): 1260–5. doi:10.1097/ACM.0b013e31822cf858.

Way, Brian. 1967. *Development through Drama*. London: Longmans.

Wheeler, Michael. 2013. *The Art of Negotiation: How to Improvise Agreement in a Chaotic World*. New York: Simon and Schuster.

INDEX

Lightning Source UK Ltd.
Milton Keynes UK
UKHW021839030821
388225UK00010B/236